THE·COMPLETE
DOLLMAKER

Alice D. Weiner

Illustrated by Evelyn D. Guzinski

 Sterling Publishing Co., Inc.   New York

*This book is dedicated to all doll artists but especially to my friends
who are members of the Peninsula Doll Artists Club of San Mateo,
California. They will see the extension of many of their ideas
in the pages that follow.*

EDITED BY KATHERINE BALCH

Library of Congress Cataloging in Publication Data

Weiner, Alice D.
   The complete dollmaker.

   Bibliography: p.
   Includes index.
   1. Dollmaking. I. Title.
TT175.W44 1985   745.592'21   85–10010
ISBN 0-8069-5590-2
ISBN 0-8069-6224-0 (pbk.)

Cover Illus. (Clockwise from upper left) *Flower
Girl (hinged, cloth body), Santa Claus (a block
"person"), Sailor Boy (soft-sculptured head with
wrapped-armature body), 19th-Century Girl (porcelain). See pp. 34, 176, 72, and 85, respectively.*

Contents

METRIC EQUIVALENCY CHART

MM—MILLIMETRES   CM—CENTIMETRES

INCHES TO MILLIMETRES AND CENTIMETRES

INCHES	MM	CM	INCHES	CM	INCHES	CM
⅛	3	0.3	9	22.9	30	76.2
¼	6	0.6	10	25.4	31	78.7
⅜	10	1.0	11	27.9	32	81.3
½	13	1.3	12	30.5	33	83.8
⅝	16	1.6	13	33.0	34	86.4
¾	19	1.9	14	35.6	35	88.9
⅞	22	2.2	15	38.1	36	91.4
1	25	2.5	16	40.6	37	94.0
1¼	32	3.2	17	43.2	38	96.5
1½	38	3.8	18	45.7	39	99.1
1¾	44	4.4	19	48.3	40	101.6
2	51	5.1	20	50.8	41	104.1
2½	64	6.4	21	53.3	42	106.7
3	76	7.6	22	55.9	43	109.2
3½	89	8.9	23	58.4	44	111.8
4	102	10.2	24	61.0	45	114.3
4½	114	11.4	25	63.5	46	116.8
5	127	12.7	26	66.0	47	119.4
6	152	15.2	27	68.6	48	121.9
7	178	17.8	28	71.1	49	124.5
8	203	20.3	29	73.7	50	127.0

YARDS TO METRES

YARDS	METRES	YARDS	METRES	YARDS	METRES	YARDS	METRES	YARDS	METRES
⅛	0.11	2⅛	1.94	4⅛	3.77	6⅛	5.60	8⅛	7.43
¼	0.23	2¼	2.06	4¼	3.89	6¼	5.72	8¼	7.54
⅜	0.34	2⅜	2.17	4⅜	4.00	6⅜	5.83	8⅜	7.66
½	0.46	2½	2.29	4½	4.11	6½	5.94	8½	7.77
⅝	0.57	2⅝	2.40	4⅝	4.23	6⅝	6.06	8⅝	7.89
¾	0.69	2¾	2.51	4¾	4.34	6¾	6.17	8¾	8.00
⅞	0.80	2⅞	2.63	4⅞	4.46	6⅞	6.29	8⅞	8.12
1	0.91	3	2.74	5	4.57	7	6.40	9	8.23
1⅛	1.03	3⅛	2.86	5⅛	4.69	7⅛	6.52	9⅛	8.34
1¼	1.14	3¼	2.97	5¼	4.80	7¼	6.63	9¼	8.46
1⅜	1.26	3⅜	3.09	5⅜	4.91	7⅜	6.74	9⅜	8.57
1½	1.37	3½	3.20	5½	5.03	7½	6.86	9½	8.69
1⅝	1.49	3⅝	3.31	5⅝	5.14	7⅝	6.97	9⅝	8.80
1¾	1.60	3¾	3.43	5¾	5.26	7¾	7.09	9¾	8.92
1⅞	1.71	3⅞	3.54	5⅞	5.37	7⅞	7.20	9⅞	9.03
2	1.83	4	3.66	6	5.49	8	7.32	10	9.14

To change degrees Fahrenheit to degrees Celsius, use this equation:
$(°F - 32) \times 5/9 = °C$

12 inches = 1 foot
3 feet = 1 yard

2 pints = 1 quart = 0.95 litre
4 quarts = 1 gallon = 3.8 litres

To change fluid ounces to millilitres, multiply by 29.573.

To change dry ounces to grams, multiply by 28.349.

To change pounds to kilograms, multiply by 0.454.

AMERICAN TERM	BRITISH TERM
C-clamp	G cramp
Styrofoam	expanded polystyrene
Dacron	Terylene

Introduction

Imagination is not a talent of some men
but is the health of every man.—RALPH WALDO EMERSON

People from the Nile to the St. Lawrence rivers have been making dolls since the dawn of civilization. These lifelike images have served as sources of pleasure and also of religious inspiration. Some dolls now even qualify as pillows or soft sculpture.

Of course, modern dolls and stuffed animals are usually for children, but recently they have gained equal popularity among collectors. This redirection has affected the way dolls are made: those for children must be durable, cleanable, and safe, whereas those for adults can be delicately painted, sequined, buttoned and wired, and some can even be sewn into their clothing. In addition, these dolls for adults can be articulated or stationary, placed in appropriate settings, made with delicate and fragile materials, and finished with exquisite detail. In this book are instructions on how to make dolls for both adults and children.

The explosion of interest in making dolls has been simultaneous with the availability of a wide variety of craft materials and equipment, all of which can be used in a home studio. For specialty items, be sure to consult the *Doll Reader* (Hobby House Press, Cumberland, Md.). Distributors and manufacturers for all types of doll materials, excluding leather and sculpture, advertise here. The sculpting materials of the artist, the porcelain of the ceramist, the wax compounds of the candlemaker, excellent new adhesives, and the availability of small and relatively inexpensive kilns, to mention only a few innovations, all contribute to the craft.

Many books, magazine articles, and pamphlets have been written to instruct in dollmaking. Most of the current books, however, have one theme in common: they present attractive projects and explain in detail how the projects are duplicated. But once the dollmaker has completed the projects and wishes to attempt more complex original ideas, it becomes abundantly clear that the necessary information is hopelessly fragmented and scattered.

The intent of this book is multifaceted: (1) to provide in one book a complete source for materials, techniques, patterns, and also thorough how-to instructions; (2) to emphasize that dollmaking is not a paint-by-number activity but a truly creative art; when you have mastered the techniques and understood the materials then you can let your imagination soar; (3) to show repeatedly how dollmaking is built on a foundation of artists' principles, methods, and approaches; (4) to demonstrate that the craft borrows skills and materials from a wide range of artisans and adapts those skills to making dolls; (5) to show that ideas are not so much revolutionary as evolutionary, and that every observation contains the seed for a different expression. What the book does not seek to do is to duplicate the format of other publications, which give only step-by-step instructions for a specific project.

Because much of the subject matter overlaps, information for making a particular doll has been placed in several places. For example, those who wish to make a cloth doll with a hardened mask will find body patterns in chapter 1, mask-purchasing information in chapter 2, making masks from existing dolls in chapter 4, and painting the mask in chapter 6.

In addition to the special tools required for each technique, you will need the following items: a well-stocked sewing box and a versatile sewing machine; a modest tool box containing a small electric drill, a vise, a needle-nose plier, a wirecutter, a tiny saw, sandpaper, and a variety of craft glue; rulers, pens, and tracing paper; a magpie's collection of fabric scraps, lace, fur, ribbon, buttons, beads, feathers, wigs, yarn, and embroidery thread; wire of several gauges, metal washers, cotter pins, and some wooden dowels; bags of stuffing; a simple palette of acrylic paints and good quality brushes as well as ordinary brush-on cosmetics.

Most avid dollmakers quickly acquire an overflow of their work. There is a ready market for these handmade and original dolls when they are neatly and tastefully presented. Many boutiques buy attractive dolls or will take them on consignment for sale. Craft fairs and doll shows are excellent outlets for overproduction. This is not to imply that an artist is immediately reimbursed for time and material. Realistic pricing usually precludes adequate payment for actual time spent. Some accomplished and experienced artists, however, do command premium prices. This success is not quickly, easily, or universally achieved. In any event, selling one's excess production provides a reason for creating more dolls.

I am an enthusiastic doll crafter, having begun about nine years ago with published patterns for cloth dolls. It soon became evident that a single source of information on materials and techniques for the intermediate worker was nonexistent. An abundant file of published material, participation in dollmaking seminars and some private instruction, but most important, untold hours of experimentation and development have provided the basis for this book. The dolls shown in the photographs are derived from my original designs. I would like to give a special word of gratitude to the artist, Evelyn D. Guzinski, my sister, without whom the book would not have been possible.

I hope that this book will serve as a handy guide for all dollmakers—present and future—and that they will find in these pages inspiration, a new perspective, and information that they did not have before.

Part I
THE DOLL

1 The Doll's Shape

PROPORTIONS OF THE HUMAN FIGURE

Dolls do not have to be realistic in proportion, and the makers of antique dolls that we now treasure did not strive to present the human form in any realistic way. You may not desire to do so, either. A knowledge of proportion, however, can be useful in at least three separate situations:

1. In using patterns, you sometimes cannot discern if the arms will be too short or too long, or, for example, if the torso is out of proportion to the legs. When the doll is completed, you notice that it does not look right. But the correction would require more time than it is worth. By applying guidelines in advance, you will bypass this common error.
2. People of specific ages can be portrayed.
3. Since you, as the dollmaker usually begin with a sculpture of the head, the most puzzling question is: "What size must I make the body, the arms, and the legs to match this head?" Of course, intuition and observation will easily answer that question, but for those who require more direct guidelines, see Table 1 and the charts that follow (Illus. 1–7).

The proportions of the human body change at each age from birth to maturity, and they differ for male and female. At birth a child's head is approximately one fourth of his entire length, but the head of an adult female is about one seventh of her mature height, and an adult male head is about one eighth of his entire height. As the body matures the relationship of the length of the head to the length of the body changes as does the relationship of the arms and legs to the balance of the figure.

Guide to Body Proportions

The charts that follow (Illus. 1–7) describe the physical characteristics of a one-year-old, two-year-old, four-year-old, and six- and eight-year-old as well as an adult male and female. This is done in terms of the artist's rules of proportion, which relate various measurements to the length of the head. For the dollmaker the critical measurements are:

- head—from top to chin
- torso—from chin to crotch
- leg—from crotch to foot
    —from hip to foot
- arm—from shoulder to wrist
- foot
- hand

The charts convert each of these measurements into inches so that the principles of proportion can be applied in making the doll. For each age given, the charts show the correct length of the torso and the limbs given a doll's head of 1 inch, 1½ inches, and 2 inches in length. The actual measurement is shown as a horizontal bar on the chart. (It is also given in numbers in the table that follows the charts.) Sizes larger than those shown can be calculated by adding equivalents. For example, the information supplied for a 4-inch head would be twice that shown for the 2-inch head. If adding fractions seems too unwieldy, use the "lay-on" measurement technique. Place a ruler on the first bar to be measured and mark with your finger that length on the ruler. Then place this point on the ruler against the second surface and add its length. Repeat the process until you have measured the entire surface. Now that the parts have been added, you can obtain the total length, which is the final reading on the ruler. The method does not yield strictly accurate results, but it does avoid tedious detail and, for many purposes, is adequate.

In the drawings in Illus. 1–7, you can see the following: the length of the arms in relation to the rest of the body, the location of the elbows, the location of the knees, and the width of the

(Continued, p. 20)

TABLE 1
GUIDE TO STANDARD PROPORTIONS

Doll Represents a One-Year-Old	Measurements in Inches		
Head	1	1½	2
Torso—Chin to Crotch	1¾	2⅝	3½
Leg—Crotch to Foot	1¼	1⅞	2½
—Hip to Foot	1⅝	2½	3¼
Arm—Shoulder to Wrist	1¼	1⅞	2½
Foot★	<½	<¾	<1
Hand★	<½	<¾	<1
Total Length	4	6	8

Two-Year-Old

Head	1	1½	2
Torso—Chin to Crotch	2	3	4
Leg—Crotch to Foot	1½	2¼	3
—Hip to Foot	1⅞	2¾	3¾
Arm—Shoulder to Wrist	1½	2¼	3
Foot★	½	<¾	<1
Hand★	½	<¾	<1
Total Length	4½	6¾	9

Four-Year-Old

Head	1	1½	2
Torso—Chin to Crotch	2⅛	3³⁄₁₆	4¼
Leg—Crotch to Foot	2⅛	3³⁄₁₆	4¼
—Hip to Foot	2½	3¾	5
Arm—Shoulder to Wrist	1¾	2⅝	3½
Foot★	>½	>¾	1
Hand★	>½	>¾	1
Total Length	5¼	7⅝	10½

Six-Year-Old

Head	1	1½	2
Torso—Chin to Crotch	2¼	3⅜	4½
Leg—Crotch to Foot	2¼	3⅜	4½
—Hip to Foot	2½	3¾	5
Arm—Shoulder to Wrist	1⅝	2½	3½
Foot★	½	¾	1
Hand★	>½	>¾	>1
Total Length	5½	8¼	11

Eight-Year-Old

Head	1	1½	2
Torso—Chin to Crotch	2¼	3⅜	4½
Leg—Crotch to Foot	3	4½	6
—Hip to Foot	3¼	4⅞	6½
Arm—Shoulder to Wrist	2	3	4
Foot★	¾	1	1½
Hand★	¾	>¾	>1
Total Length	6¼	9⅜	12½

Adult Female

Head	1	1½	2
Torso—Chin to Crotch	3	4½	6
Leg—Crotch to Foot	3½	5¼	7
—Hip to Foot	4	6	8
Arm—Shoulder to Wrist	2½	3¾	5
Foot★	<¾	<1	<1½
Hand★	>¾	>1	>1
Total Length	7½	11¼	15

Adult Male

Head	1	1½	2
Torso—Chin to Crotch	3¼	4⅞	6½
Leg—Crotch to Foot	3¾	5⅝	7½
—Hip to Foot	4¼	6⅜	8½
Arm—Shoulder to Wrist	2⅞	4¼	5¾
Foot★	1	1½	2
Hand★	1	1¼	1½
Total Length	8	12	16

★Hands and feet are somewhat smaller than actual size.
   Note: Measurements are approximate; they should be used only as a guide. If larger sizes are required, add equivalents.

Illus. 1. Proportions for making realistic dolls: one-year-old.

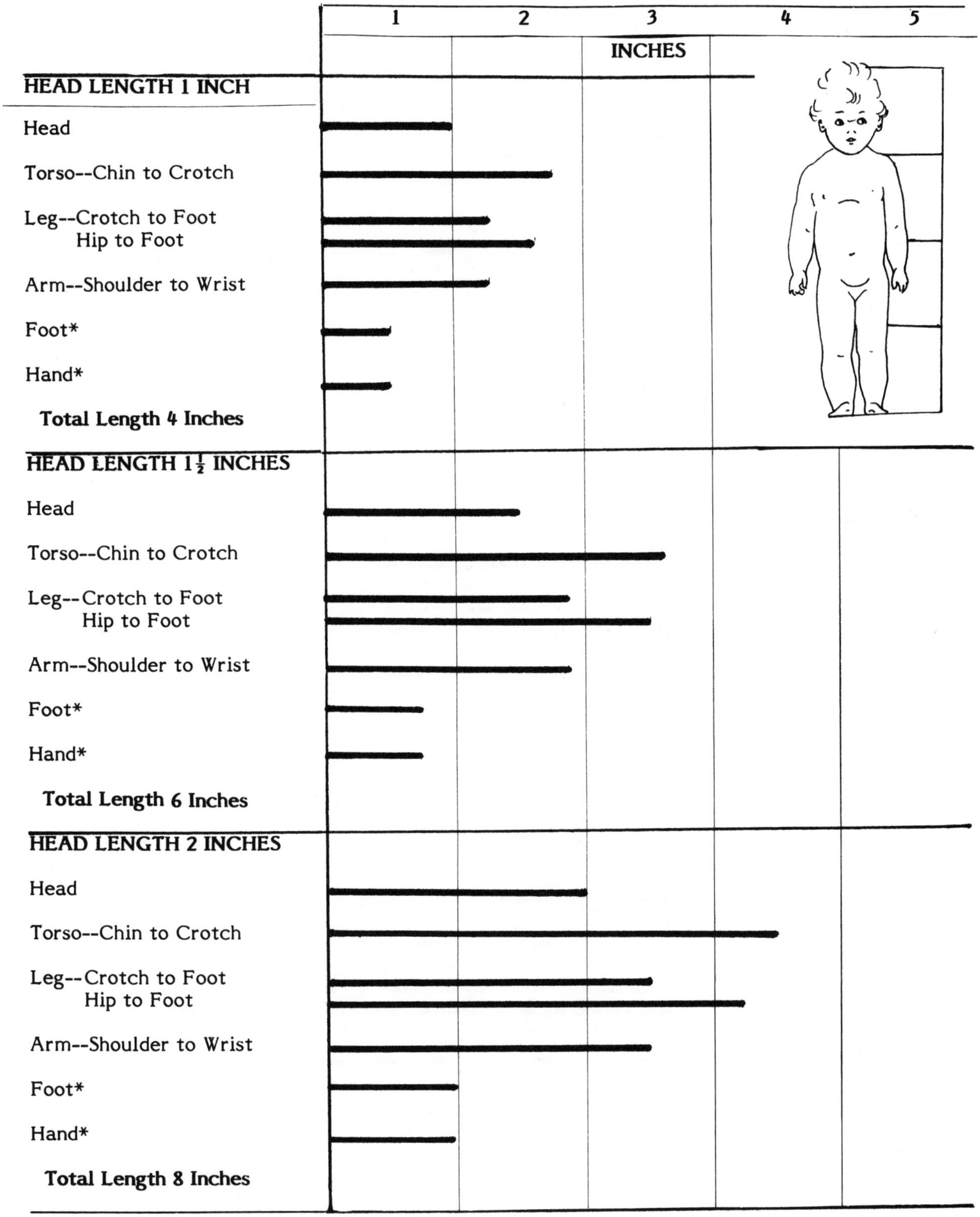

	1	2	3	4	5
			INCHES		

HEAD LENGTH 1 INCH

Head

Torso--Chin to Crotch

Leg--Crotch to Foot
Hip to Foot

Arm--Shoulder to Wrist

Foot*

Hand*

Total Length 4 Inches

HEAD LENGTH 1½ INCHES

Head

Torso--Chin to Crotch

Leg--Crotch to Foot
Hip to Foot

Arm--Shoulder to Wrist

Foot*

Hand*

Total Length 6 Inches

HEAD LENGTH 2 INCHES

Head

Torso--Chin to Crotch

Leg--Crotch to Foot
Hip to Foot

Arm--Shoulder to Wrist

Foot*

Hand*

Total Length 8 Inches

* Somewhat smaller than human proportions

Note: Measurements are approximate; they should be used only as a guide.
        Larger sizes are derived by adding equivalents.

Illus. 2. Proportions for making realistic dolls: two-year-old.

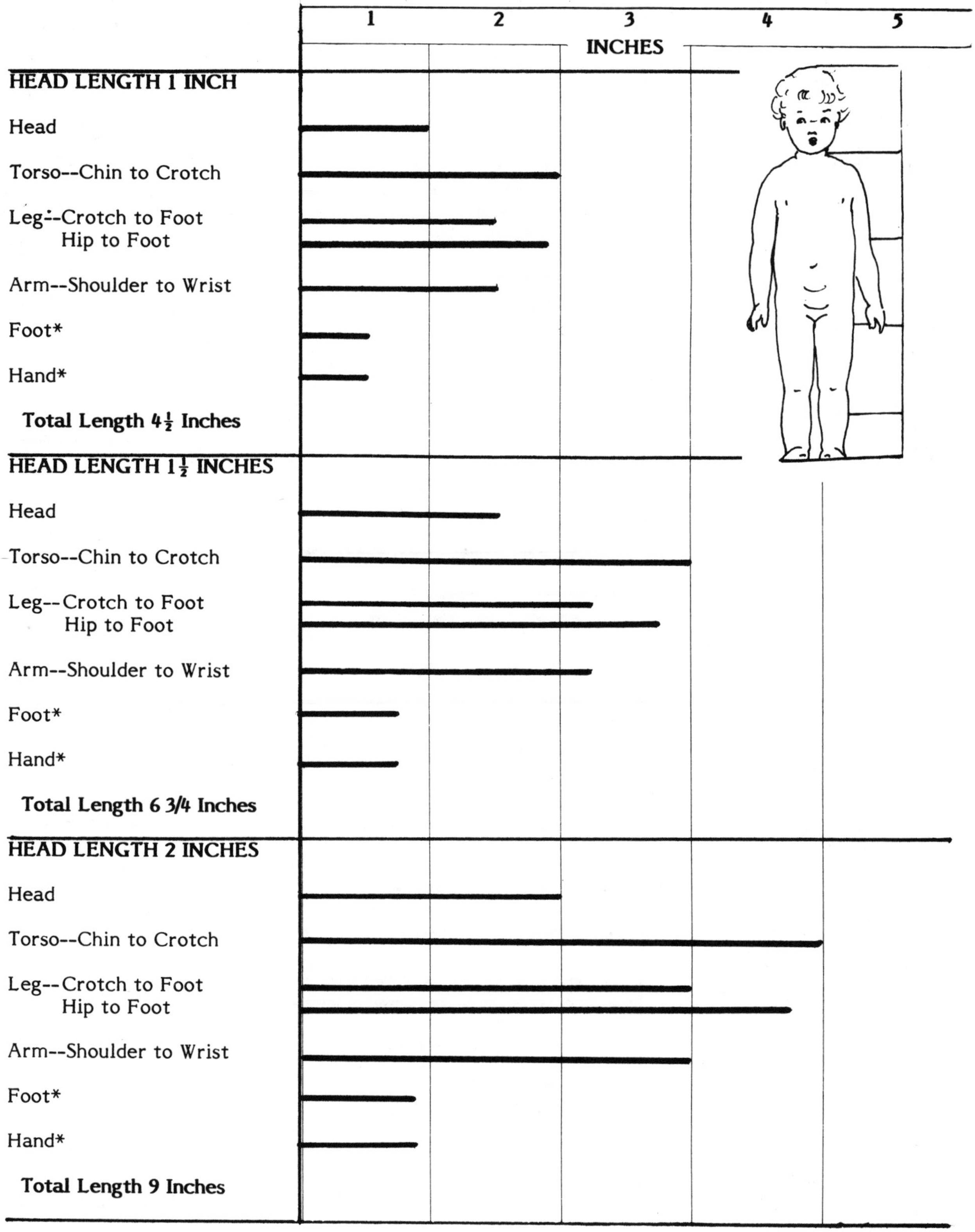

	1	2	3	4	5
			INCHES		

HEAD LENGTH 1 INCH

Head

Torso--Chin to Crotch

Leg--Crotch to Foot
     Hip to Foot

Arm--Shoulder to Wrist

Foot*

Hand*

Total Length 4½ Inches

HEAD LENGTH 1½ INCHES

Head

Torso--Chin to Crotch

Leg--Crotch to Foot
     Hip to Foot

Arm--Shoulder to Wrist

Foot*

Hand*

Total Length 6 3/4 Inches

HEAD LENGTH 2 INCHES

Head

Torso--Chin to Crotch

Leg--Crotch to Foot
     Hip to Foot

Arm--Shoulder to Wrist

Foot*

Hand*

Total Length 9 Inches

* Somewhat smaller than human proportions

Note: Measurements are approximate; they should be used only as a guide.
     Larger sizes are derived by adding equivalents.

Illus. 3. Proportions for making realistic dolls: four-year-old.

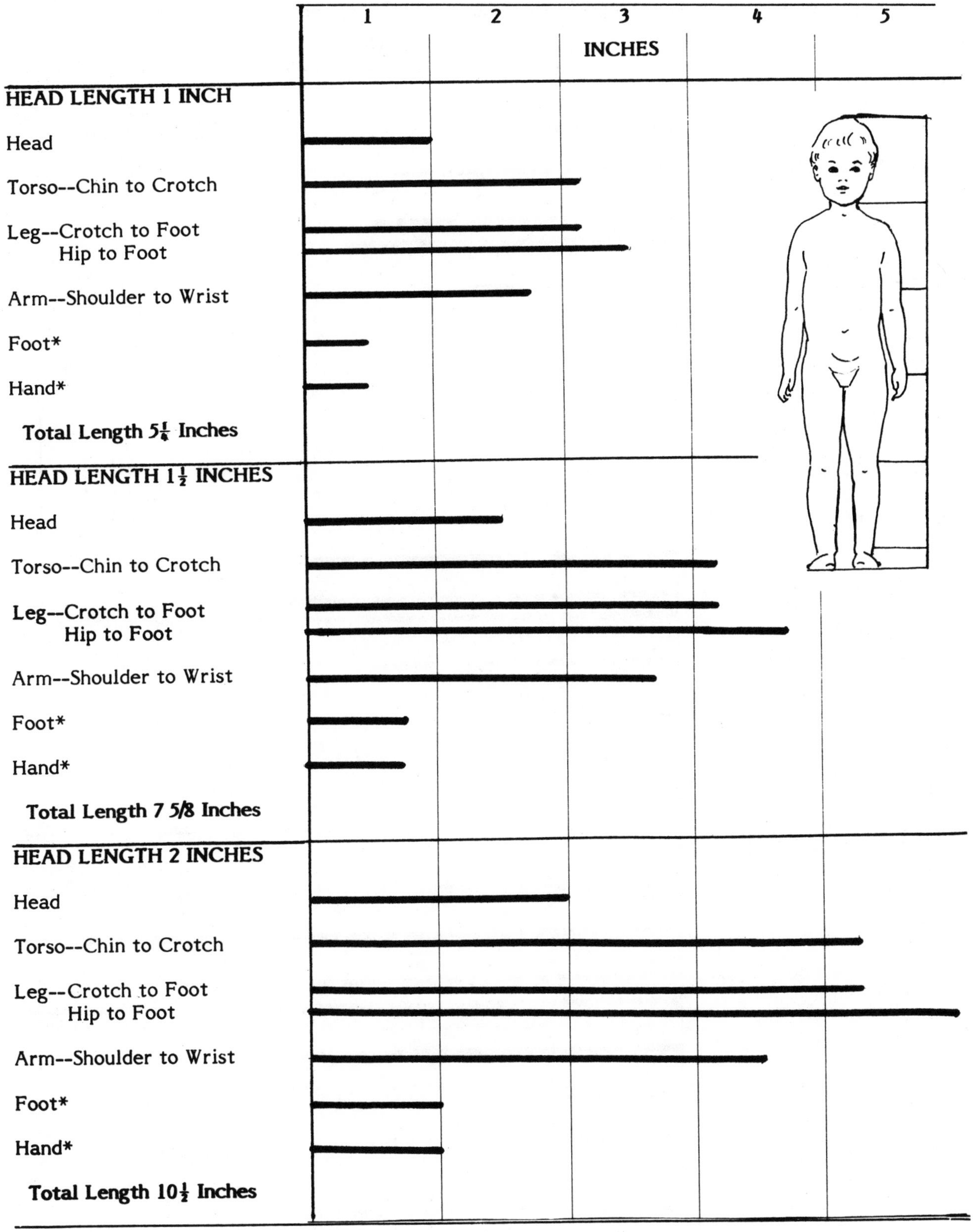

INCHES

HEAD LENGTH 1 INCH

Head

Torso--Chin to Crotch

Leg--Crotch to Foot
   Hip to Foot

Arm--Shoulder to Wrist

Foot*

Hand*

Total Length 5¼ Inches

HEAD LENGTH 1½ INCHES

Head

Torso--Chin to Crotch

Leg--Crotch to Foot
   Hip to Foot

Arm--Shoulder to Wrist

Foot*

Hand*

Total Length 7 5/8 Inches

HEAD LENGTH 2 INCHES

Head

Torso--Chin to Crotch

Leg--Crotch to Foot
   Hip to Foot

Arm--Shoulder to Wrist

Foot*

Hand*

Total Length 10½ Inches

* Somewhat smaller than human proportions

Note: Measurements are approximate; they should be used only as a guide.
Larger sizes are derived by adding equivalents.

Illus. 4. Proportions for making realistic dolls: six-year-old.

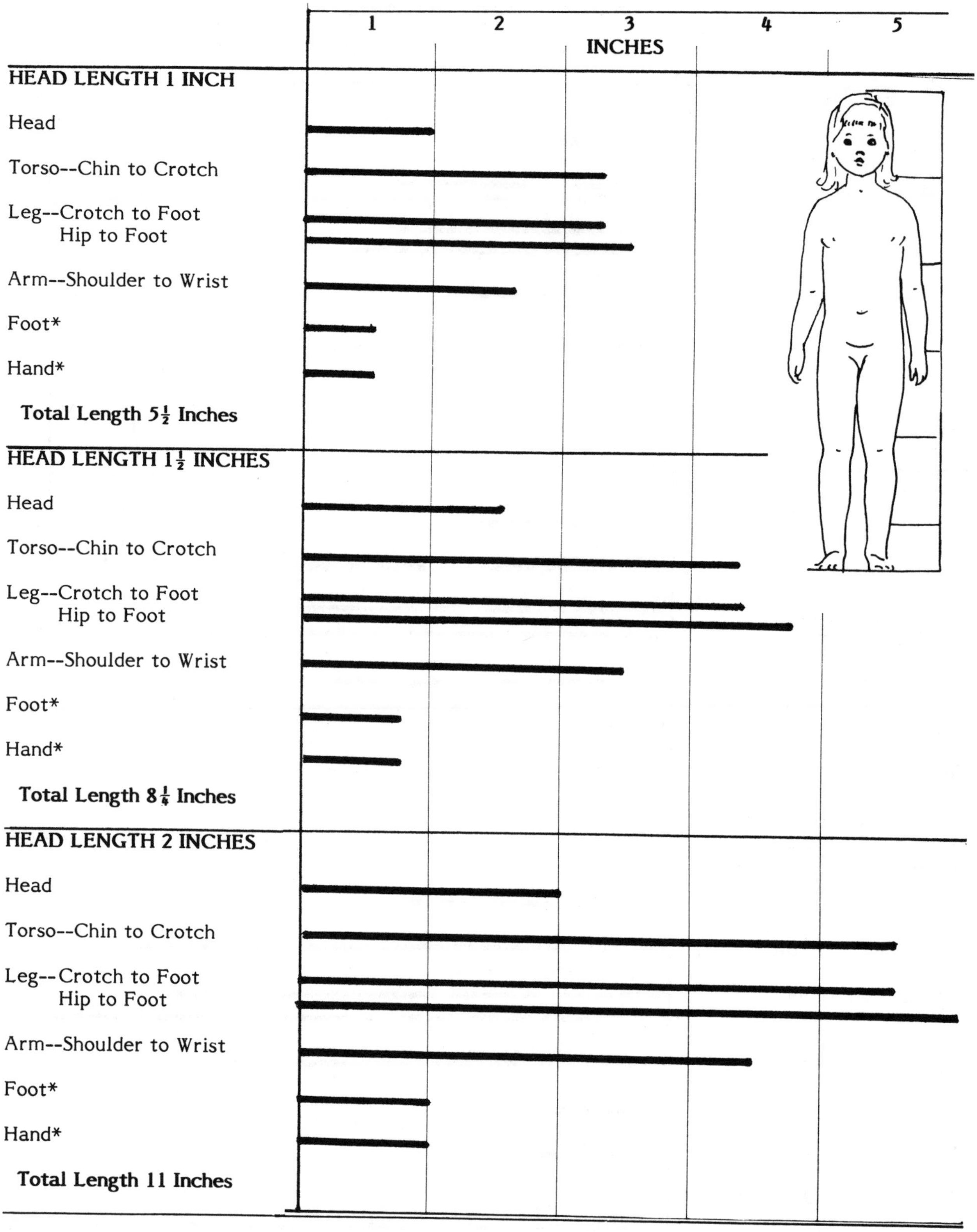

INCHES: 1 2 3 4 5

HEAD LENGTH 1 INCH

Head

Torso--Chin to Crotch

Leg--Crotch to Foot
Hip to Foot

Arm--Shoulder to Wrist

Foot*

Hand*

Total Length 5½ Inches

HEAD LENGTH 1½ INCHES

Head

Torso--Chin to Crotch

Leg--Crotch to Foot
Hip to Foot

Arm--Shoulder to Wrist

Foot*

Hand*

Total Length 8¼ Inches

HEAD LENGTH 2 INCHES

Head

Torso--Chin to Crotch

Leg--Crotch to Foot
Hip to Foot

Arm--Shoulder to Wrist

Foot*

Hand*

Total Length 11 Inches

* Somewhat smaller than human proportions

Note: Measurements are approximate; they should be used only as a guide.
Larger sizes are derived by adding equivalents.

Illus. 5. Proportions for making realistic dolls: eight-year-old.

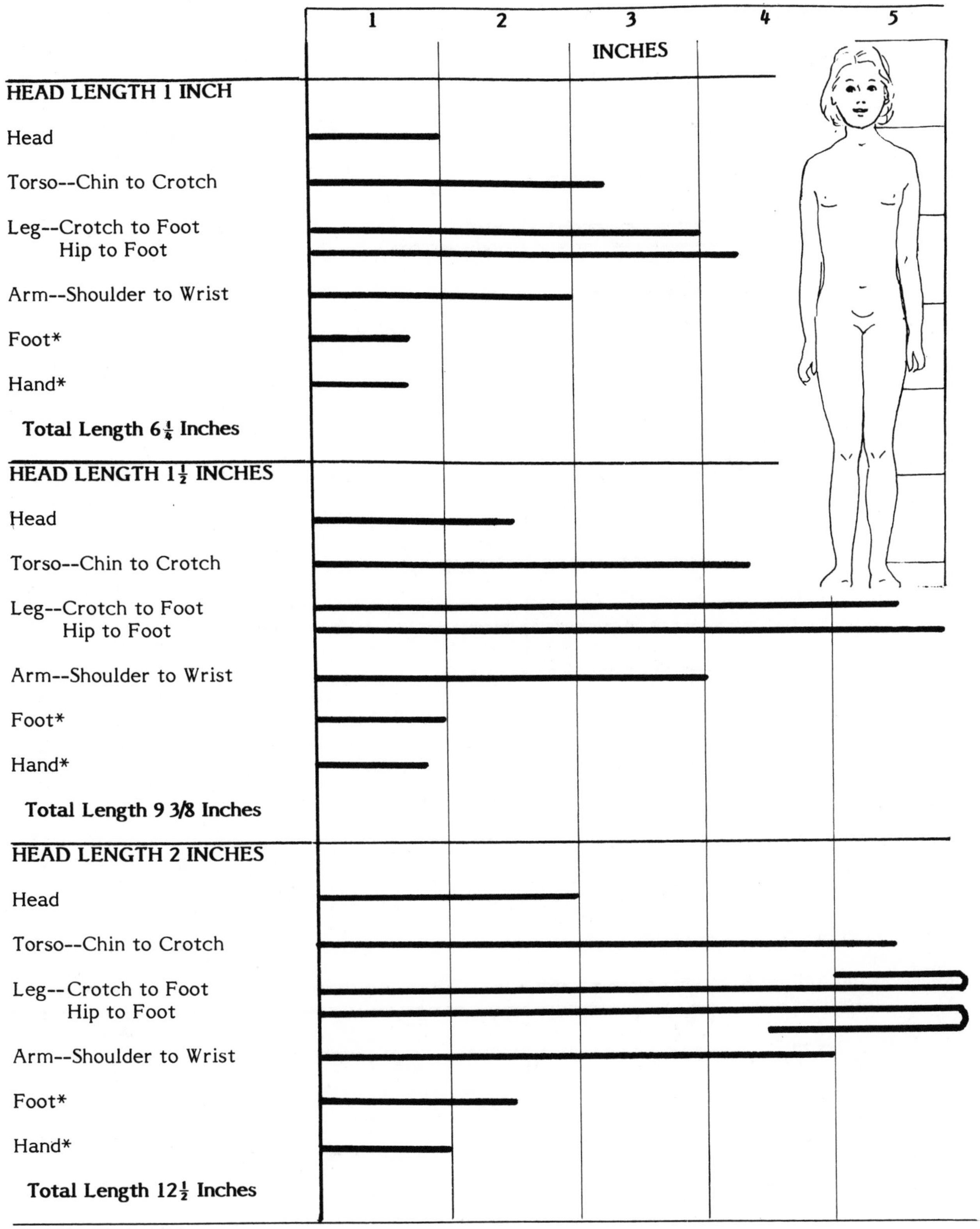

INCHES

1   2   3   4   5

HEAD LENGTH 1 INCH

Head

Torso--Chin to Crotch

Leg--Crotch to Foot
      Hip to Foot

Arm--Shoulder to Wrist

Foot*

Hand*

Total Length 6¼ Inches

HEAD LENGTH 1½ INCHES

Head

Torso--Chin to Crotch

Leg--Crotch to Foot
      Hip to Foot

Arm--Shoulder to Wrist

Foot*

Hand*

Total Length 9 3/8 Inches

HEAD LENGTH 2 INCHES

Head

Torso--Chin to Crotch

Leg--Crotch to Foot
      Hip to Foot

Arm--Shoulder to Wrist

Foot*

Hand*

Total Length 12½ Inches

* Somewhat smaller than human proportions

Note: Measurements are approximate; they should be used only as a guide.
      Larger sizes are derived by adding equivalents.

Illus. 6. Proportions for making realistic dolls: adult female.

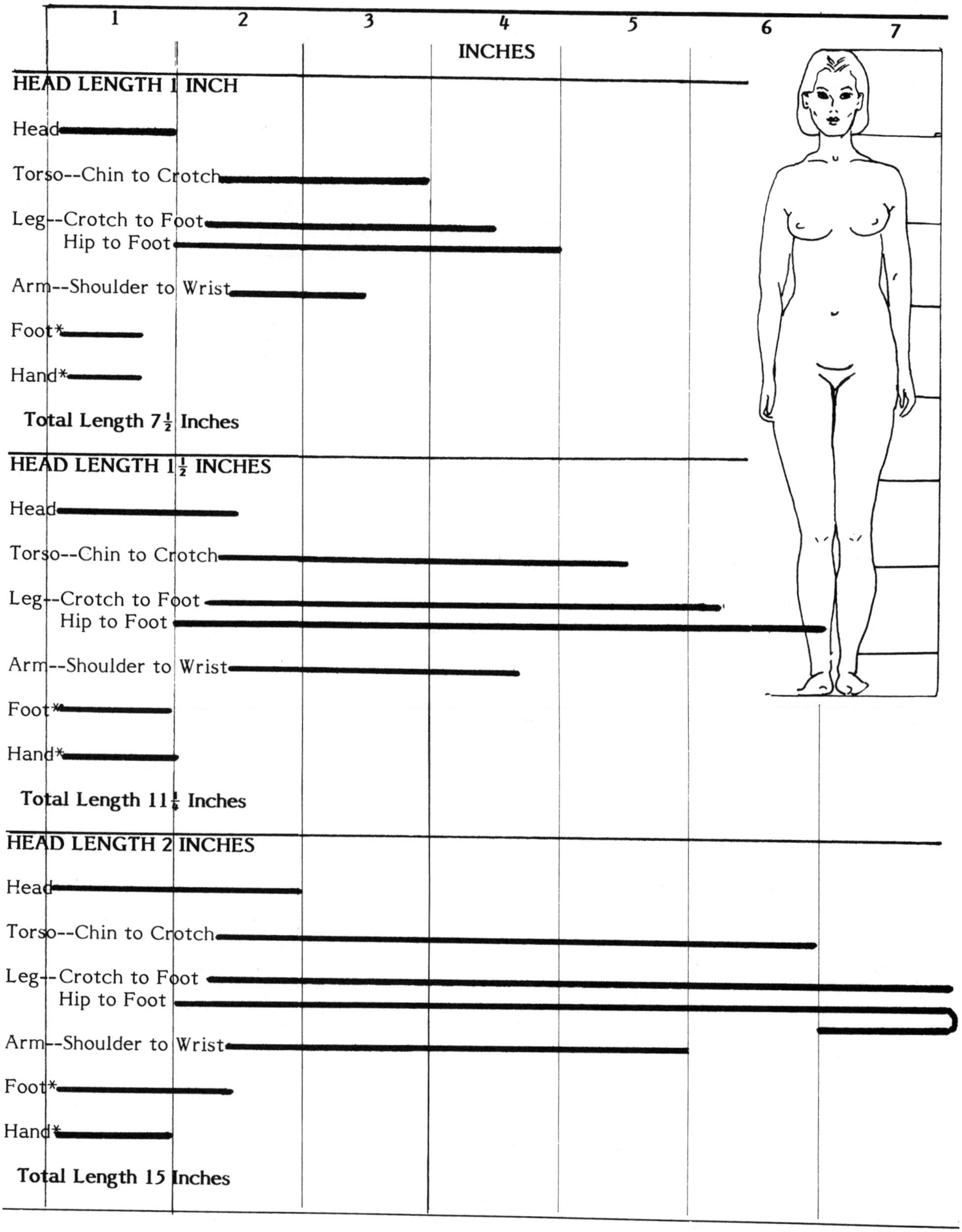

INCHES

HEAD LENGTH 1 INCH

Head

Torso--Chin to Crotch

Leg--Crotch to Foot
    Hip to Foot

Arm--Shoulder to Wrist

Foot*

Hand*

Total Length 7½ Inches

HEAD LENGTH 1½ INCHES

Head

Torso--Chin to Crotch

Leg--Crotch to Foot
    Hip to Foot

Arm--Shoulder to Wrist

Foot*

Hand*

Total Length 11¼ Inches

HEAD LENGTH 2 INCHES

Head

Torso--Chin to Crotch

Leg--Crotch to Foot
    Hip to Foot

Arm--Shoulder to Wrist

Foot*

Hand*

Total Length 15 Inches

* Somewhat smaller than human proportions

Note: Measurements are approximate; they should be used only as a guide.
      Larger sizes are derived by adding equivalents.

Illus. 7. Proportions for making realistic dolls: adult male.

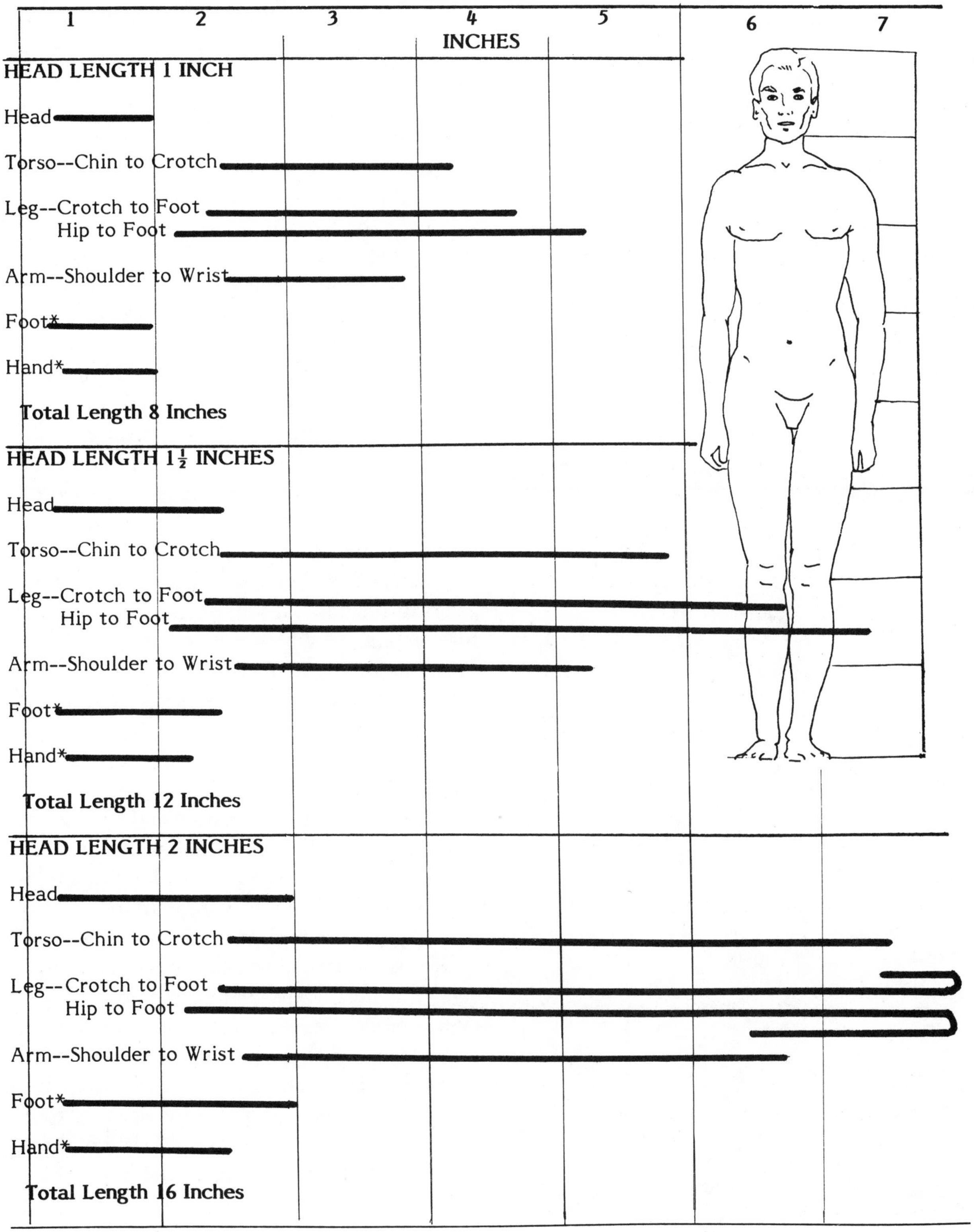

	1	2	3	4	5	6	7

INCHES

HEAD LENGTH 1 INCH

Head

Torso--Chin to Crotch

Leg--Crotch to Foot
    Hip to Foot

Arm--Shoulder to Wrist

Foot*

Hand*

Total Length 8 Inches

HEAD LENGTH 1½ INCHES

Head

Torso--Chin to Crotch

Leg--Crotch to Foot
    Hip to Foot

Arm--Shoulder to Wrist

Foot*

Hand*

Total Length 12 Inches

HEAD LENGTH 2 INCHES

Head

Torso--Chin to Crotch

Leg--Crotch to Foot
    Hip to Foot

Arm--Shoulder to Wrist

Foot*

Hand*

Total Length 16 Inches

* Somewhat smaller than human proportions

Note: Measurements are approximate; they should be used only as a guide.
       Larger sizes are derived by adding equivalents.

body in relation to the width of the head. (Be sure to make appropriate adjustments if you want to depict the arms and legs in a fixed, bent position.) The hands and feet on dolls seem awkward if they are correct in proportion. Making them small, unless exaggeration is desired, seems to make them fit better.

Of course people come in all proportions, and the charts and data given are only generalities. A petite woman might measure only six or six and one-half heads, and a female fashion model might be eight heads high. Use the charts to draw a full-size sketch of the proposed doll so that the parts, when complete, will be in proportion to each other. A working diagram, as shown in Illus. 8, is used to coordinate the parts of the doll in progress.

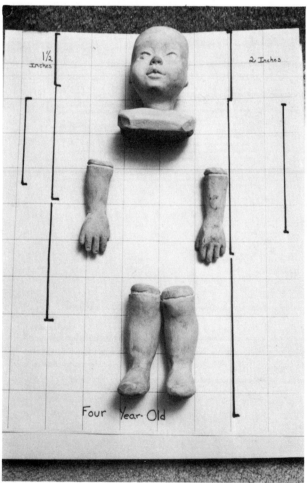

Illus. 8. Working diagram of doll in progress.

PROPORTIONS OF THE HEAD
Faces come in all shapes and sizes—round, square, narrow, and wide, with long and short noses, square jaws, and narrow chins, eyes that are wide-set or close. The combination and variation of these and other features make a face unique. There are, however, standard proportions that serve as a guide when drawing and sculpting the human head.

Just as the proportions of the body are different for the male and female adult doll as contrasted to the proportions of the infant's and child's body, so do the proportions of the head differ. As the artist in drawing the head, you are attempting to depict a three-dimensional object on a two-dimensional canvas. Like a sculptor you must envision a dimensional head. No depiction of the human head can be effective if we forget that beneath the skin there is a bony skull, a system of muscles, and pads of flesh.

Observe the proportions of the face in order to locate the features correctly no matter what medium you use. Following the standard proportions as given in Illus. 9–14 will yield beautiful faces. Be sure to study the differences from the standards shown if you want to depict characters or portraits. If you want to use any sculpture technique, whether it be needle modelling or shaping any other material, you should consider the head a three-dimensional mass in order to make it lifelike.

Adult Male
The adult male face is broader and squarer than the female face. The angles and planes are accentuated, and the muscles are visible. Pleasant proportions indicate that the length of the face from the hairline is approximately the same as the width of the face at the temples, including the ears. The head is divided exactly in half by the eyes. The eyes are spaced approximately as wide as the nose at the nostrils. Viewed in profile (Illus. 9), the head is divided in thirds from hairline to chin, and the nose projects to the second third. The ear follows the slant of the jaw and extends from the eye to the length of the nose.

Adult Female
The female doll's head is narrower and more oval than the male head. The planes of the face are softened and the muscles are less visible. The brows are slightly higher; the eyes are larger and farther apart. The lips are smaller but fuller.

Pleasing proportions for the female face indicate equal distances between the width of the face at the temples, not including the ears, and the length of the face from brow to chin. A beautiful woman can be depicted by placing the eyes and mouth precisely and shaping the nostrils proportionately. The head is divided exactly in half by the eyes. There is some variation between the male and female face in the location of the lips in the lower face. As viewed in profile (Illus. 10), the female head is somewhat flatter than the male head.

Infant and Child

The bone structure of an infant's head is not yet developed, and the jawbone, cheekbones, and bridge of the nose are small in proportion to the entire face. The nose is up-turned, and the bridge, which is little defined, is concave. The nostrils are round. The upper lip appears full and protrudes. The chin, which is little developed, recedes. The eyes are almost adult size, and because the iris is fully developed, the eye displays less white than does the adult eye. The eyes are wide open and slightly farther apart than they

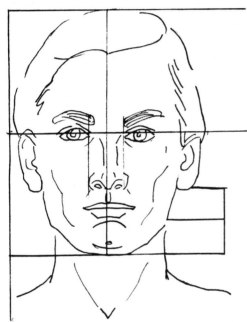

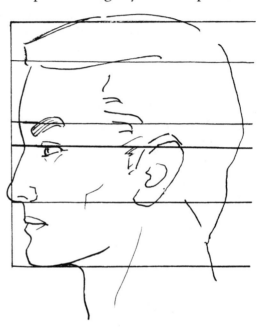

Illus. 9. Standard proportions of adult male head.

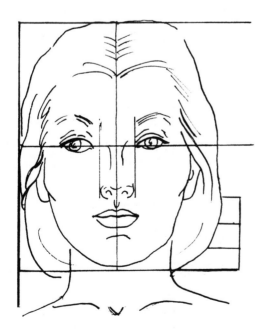

Illus. 10. Standard proportions of adult female head.

are wide. The face is smooth and the chin is plump. The cheeks are full, round, and fleshy. The ears vary greatly in size by individuals. The eyebrows are light and transparent, and the eyelashes are long. And the neck is short and plump.

As the child develops, the eyes appear to be smaller, the chin elongates, and the nose becomes more prominent. The boy's face begins to assume a more angular appearance. The neck elongates, and while still round, it appears to be thin in proportion to the head.

As the child approaches adolescence the face begins to take on more of an adult appearance. The eyes are finally at the half-way mark, as is the case of the adult. The mouth loses its baby look, and the jaw develops. The girl retains more of a smooth, rounded appearance.

Infant—first year. The facial proportions of an infant (Illus. 11) differ markedly from those of the adult, and failure to place them accurately will result in the depiction of little old men instead of babies. The face is small in relation to the size of the head, occupying only the lower half of the head. The eyes are more widespread than a single eye-width. The lips are full, and the center of the upper lip is accentuated. The width of the face at the temples, excluding the ears, is wider than the length of the face as measured from the hairline. Viewed in profile the head is completely round. The ear is somewhat farther back than the midline.

Child—second through fourth year. The second phase of the development of the child's face is demonstrated by the elongation of the jaw and the shifted location of the eye (Illus. 12). The

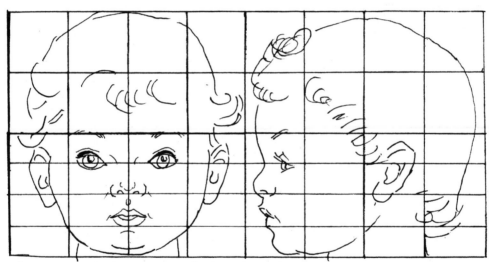

Illus. 11. Standard proportions of infant's head, first year.

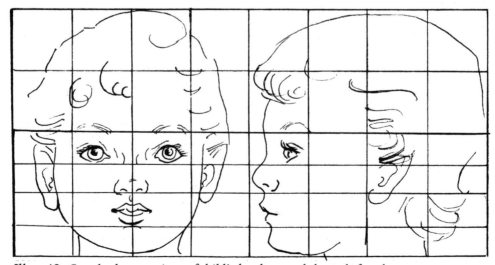

Illus. 12. Standard proportions of child's head, second through fourth year.

length of the face, as measured from the hairline, is now about the width of the temples, including the ears. The brows mark the midpoint of the head. Viewed in profile, ear position and size remain virtually the same as the infant's. The head is still round in shape. The upper lip protrudes; the nose is somewhat up-turned and the chin is beginning to have more definition.

Child—fifth through tenth year. The development of the child's face during this period begins to show differentiation between the boy and the girl (Illus. 13). The boy's face assumes more angularity, and the girl's face maintains its roundness. The girl's forehead is slightly higher than the boy's forehead. For both, the nose is still short and up-turned. The lips are full; the upper lip is long and protruding. Though the eyes have changed little, they are less wide open and appear to be smaller in relationship to the face.

Adolescent. From the beginning of adolescence, the child's face begins to assume adult characteristics (Illus. 14). The chin has elongated, but the eyes have not yet reached the midmark of the head, as is the case with the adult head. The cheeks are rounder, and the features are somewhat less developed. The rate at which the features begin to suggest an adult face varies greatly among children.

Illus. 13. Standard proportions of child's head, fifth through tenth year.

Illus. 14. Standard proportions of adolescent head.

AGING FACE

The most popular subject for dollmakers is the infant or child, and who can deny that the most attractive results spring from depicting plump cherubs. The second most popular subject is probably the character or aging figure. It is in the lines of aging that many stories can be written. To depict the aging face accurately, you must do more than draw wrinkles. The aging face is most successfully captured in those materials that permit maximum shaping, such as porcelain, wax, and needle sculpture. The aging process affects the individual face in widely different ways, but in general there are certain changes. The proportions of the face do not alter, but the flesh of the cheeks, especially around the eyes and mouth, begins to sag. Pouches form under the eyes. Lines form at the corner of the eyes and mouth and at the sides of the cheeks. The lips become thinner. The eyelids droop, and the brows seem to drop closer to the bridge of the nose. The hairline recedes. The cheekbones, corners of the jaw, and cartilage of the nose become more prominent. Extreme old age accentuates all of these characteristics, and the eye sockets and cheekbones become more evident. The nose becomes bulbous.

PROPORTIONS OF THE HANDS AND FEET

The details of the anatomy of a doll's torso are expressed only infrequently since the doll is always dressed. The hands, however, are always visible and merit careful rendering. The feet, generally shod, are less important. A major problem is that the size of the hand and foot in relation to the entire size of the doll appears to be awkward when realistic proportions are used. Generally, somewhat smaller hands and feet will look more appropriate unless exaggeration is desired.

The feet can be bare if consistent with the doll's characterization but are generally shown without much anatomical detail. The feet of a cloth doll can be shown wearing shoes or boots by including footwear in the construction of the leg. In a mouldable surface, the shoes might be painted on feet that have been modelled in a shoe shape. If more realism is desired on a modelled foot, glue leather or plastic on the foot to simulate a separate shoe. Attach a separate sole.

Hands are expressed in a variety of ways, from the simple stuffed mitten shape (with only a thumb delineated) to finely detailed hands (Illus. 15). Mechanical problems, skill, and the medium used dictate the amount of detail that can be rendered.

Direct observation is probably the best instructor. The shape of a hand is defined by the middle finger, which is longest. The index finger and the third finger are about equal. The little finger reaches just to the top knuckle of the third finger. The tendons, muscles, and pads of the hands are more obvious in a male hand. In old age the joints become enlarged. A female hand is smaller and more delicate than a male hand. A more graceful, delicate hand can be depicted by lengthening and pointing the fingers. Babies' hands differ greatly from adults' hands in that the palms are thicker and the fingers are short and pudgy. The knuckles are obscured by flesh and are marked only with dimples. The wrist bears a bracelet of creases. The fingers of a child's hands are in about the same proportion as an adult's, but the hand is generally much smaller, plumper, and the knuckles are somewhere between a dimple and a definition of bone.

FACIAL EXPRESSIONS

Dolls most frequently have neutral or pleasant, smiling expressions displaying nothing but sunny dispositions. You may, however, want a doll to permanently demonstrate another emotion: sadness, thoughtfulness, anger, coyness, or any other human feeling.

If you choose a medium, such as flat cloth, the facial expression is limited to the position of the eyebrows, the shape of the eye and direction of the gaze, and the shape of the lips. If, however, you choose needle sculpture, porcelain, or wax, the detail can be more finely established, and the masses of the face, as defined by the play of muscles, must also be delineated in order to capture the desired expression. For example, if you want the face to express happiness, turn the mouth corners up, make the cheeks rounded and raised, the eyes narrow and arched, and the brows lifted.

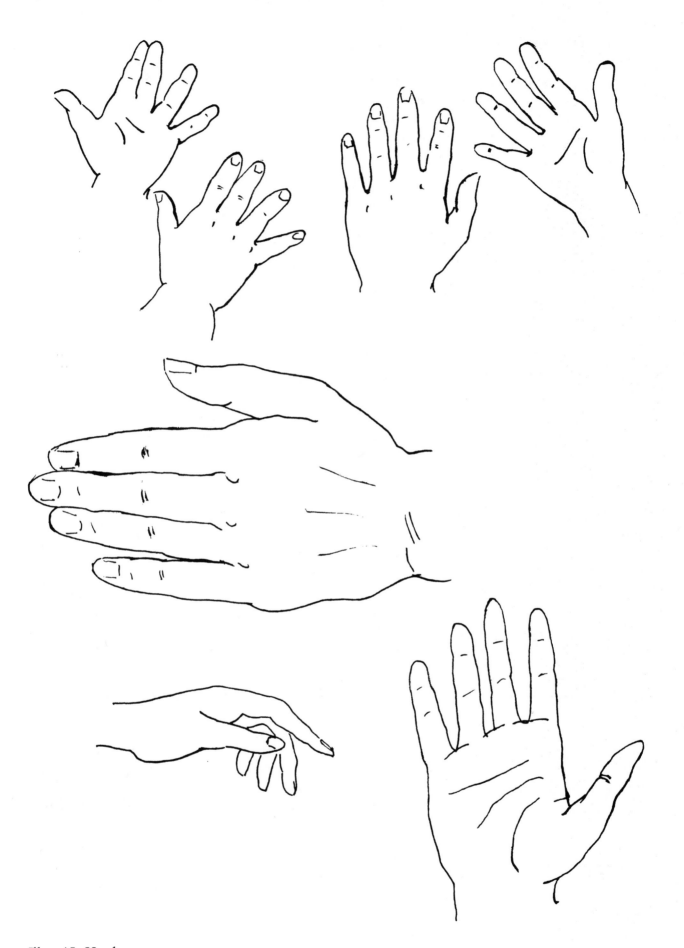

Illus. 15. Hands.

Some of the possible facial expressions drawn as a cartoonist might present them are shown in Illus. 16. Just as an artist relies on a model to depict emotion, so should the dollmaker find examples to use as a guide. A file of photographs clipped from magazines for this express purpose serves well. If all else fails, use your own face as reflected in a mirror. It takes some genius and a lot of practice to transfer expressive faces from the imagination without the help of direct observation.

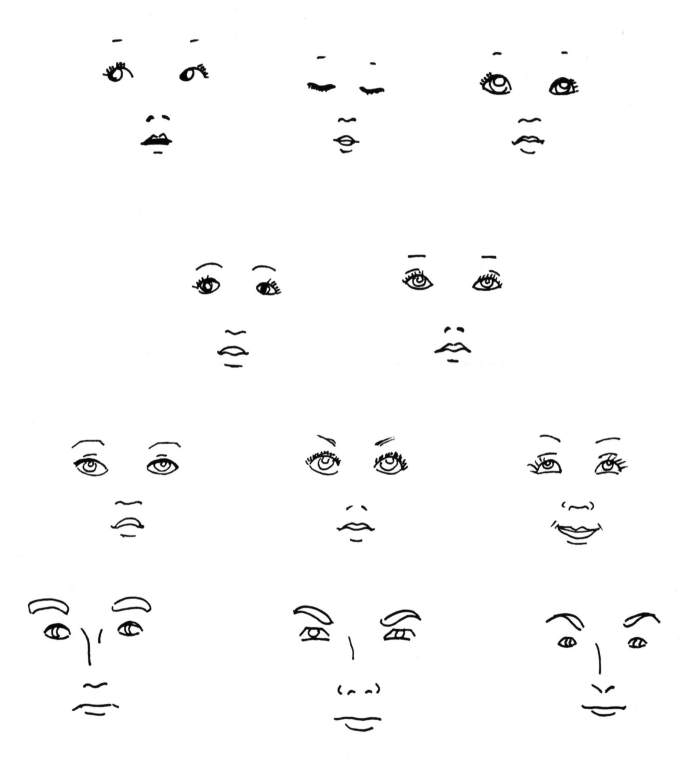

Illus. 16. Facial expressions.

BODY EXPRESSIONS

To achieve lifelike poses, use wire armatures. A cloth body fashioned on an armature can demonstrate a wide variety of poses: a bent head, a cocked head, standing with weight shifted to one leg, a seated figure, or an outstretched and bent arm, to suggest only a few of the possibilities. A child's stance with toes pointed inward and an arched back could lend startling realism. Even the slightest variation from a straightforward pose and direct glance suggests emotion and activity and gives life to a doll. Frequently, adding motion makes an extraordinary doll out of an ordinary one. Observation of motion is the greatest teacher of the artist as well as the dollmaker.

In addition to adding motion to the doll in the above manner, you can place dolls in a setting that tells a story. They can hold an object, be accompanied by an animal, or be occupied with a specific activity. Body expression not only implies action but it suggests that the doll's body expresses the same human condition as does the head. An old person is depicted with an appropriate body—with stooped shoulders and sagging contour.

2 Pattern Designs for the Stuffed Doll

A doll made entirely of cloth is a good beginning project. The requirements—a pattern and some appropriate fabric, stuffing, and an idea—permit entry into the craft without the acquisition of a wide variety of tools. A cloth doll can be as simple as a pillow person or as sophisticated and complicated as a historically costumed mannequin. It can be a realistic or cartoon character. Cloth dolls are not necessarily the province of the novice; there are many fine original doll artists who use cloth exclusively because of its inherent qualities. Frequently, only the body is made of cloth, while the head and limbs consist of other materials.

The basic principle involved in the fabrication of cloth dolls is the conversion of two-dimensional cloth into a three-dimensional shape by sewing. This is accomplished by the use of contoured patterns, darts, gathers, creative stuffing, reinforced wire, and needle shaping. Your choice of fabric also has an important effect on the ultimate results. The only factor that dictates the construction of the doll is its ultimate owner. Dolls for children must be cleanable, durable, and safe.

CONSTRUCTION BASICS

It is assumed that the reader has had some experience in fabricating cloth dolls. But first I will give some basic general information and introduce you to some new techniques. Whatever methods you elect, try to visualize the process before beginning the assembly so that you can outline a construction strategy. How the doll is to be assembled depends upon the pattern and the chosen mechanical design. But to know beforehand what seams are best left open for attaching limbs and a head, whether attachments will be made on a sewing machine or by hand, or how other details are to be executed gives some indication of the order in which you should proceed.

Preparing the Pattern

It is an unusual pattern that can be successfully used without careful examination and adjustment. Regardless of the source, if you plan to be a thrifty dollmaker, you should examine the pattern before cutting. The first questions to be answered are: (1) Are the physical proportions accurate and aesthetically pleasing? (2) Are both sides of the pattern identical (fold and match)? (3) How will the final result be affected by the fabric I chose? (4) What changes can I make to better express my idea?

Next, determine whether the pattern includes a seam allowance and, if so, its width. Frequently, instructions state that the seam allowance is to be added to the pattern piece as it is cut. You can either use a pattern that does not include seam allowance and add it in the cutting process or change the pattern so it does include seam allowance. Consistency is important. The 1-inch full-size patterns at the end of this chapter already include a ⅛-inch seam allowance so you can trace the piece directly onto the cloth. This will make the cutting and sewing easier when constructing complicated shapes. The narrowest possible seam allowance as determined by the firmness of the fabric is the easiest to work with. It requires less clipping and trimming.

Reproducing the Pattern

The simplest method for reproducing a full-size pattern as it is given is to trace it on a piece of paper. If the pattern will be used repeatedly, mount the sheet of tracing paper on cardboard and cut out the pieces, taking care to mark each with all of the appropriate designations for matching, a description, and indications where clipping is required. Semirigid plastic purchased in sheets or rolls or salvaged from gift boxes and the like can also be used. Mark the plastic with a soft-tipped marker. By mounting the pattern pieces on cardboard or using plastic, you can then trace the pieces directly onto the fabric.

Because only a minute variation in a small pattern produces a large variation in proportion to the whole, it is essential to cut accurately. Sometimes only half of a pattern piece is given, and the instructions indicate that the edge of the pattern is to be placed on the fold of the material in order to cut the entire piece. A more accurate cutting can be obtained by placing the pattern half on a fold of paper and cutting it out. You can then use the entire paper pattern for cutting the material. Patterns stored in separate envelopes that are clearly marked will prove to be an invaluable source of information.

All too often some interesting patterns are larger or smaller than desired. An easy and inexpensive solution is to have them reduced or enlarged on a copy machine in a print shop.

Enlarging the Pattern by Squares

Often a desirable pattern is published as a small drawing on a tiny grid and must be enlarged to be used. Although it may seem confusing at first, here are some suggestions to facilitate the effort. The small drawing always indicates the scale for which it is designed; usually each square represents one square inch. By visualizing how the pattern pieces will fit together and by counting the appropriate squares, you can approximate the finished dimensions. If you want to vary the size somewhat, elect a slightly different scale. Remember, though, that to double the scale is to quadruple the size; to halve the scale is to reduce the size by three fourths. Therefore, make small incremental variations.

Some drafting supply shops carry sheets of paper that are ruled into inch squares. Or you can rule-off a master-grid pattern and duplicate it in a print shop to provide extra copies. A simple method for transferring a small pattern to large grid paper is as follows:
- Count the number of squares in the length and in the width of the original pattern piece and draw the boundaries on the larger grid.
- If the drawing is complicated, number the squares on the original and then number the corresponding squares on the larger grid.
- Mark each grid line with a dot at the precise point where the original pattern line crosses the grid line.
- Finally, draw the contour line by connecting the dots, while at the same time consulting and comparing it to the original pattern.

Don't overlook the possibility of using the tiny original pattern to make miniature animals, Teddy bears, and dolls.

Transferring and Cutting the Pattern

Always consider grain lines, or direction, of the fabric weave when cutting, even if there is no obvious texture, since minute differences in drape, stretch, and color are the result of inconsistencies. Use any napped fabric, including fur fabric, with the nap running in either direction for specific effects, which must be determined beforehand. Whatever the decision, it is essential that you reverse the pieces when using napped fabric in order to cut a right and left side. To forget to reverse is to make an error correctable only by cutting another piece that is reversed.

Fabric can be saved and pieces more accurately cut if you cut each of the pattern pieces separately and lay them flat rather than relying on fold placement. If it is more convenient to cut several layers of fabric at one time, be sure to reexamine each cut piece and retrim for accuracy. The slightest degree of slippage results in considerable variation in size. Cut fur fabric with the point of the shears close to the backing in order to avoid cutting the individual hairs. Cut leather and fur on the back with a razor blade or craft knife. Sharp shears are essential.

For simple shapes pin the pattern on the cloth as you would for any sewing project. For more complicated shapes with intricate detail, however, or when using fur fabric, it is easier to trace the pattern on the wrong side of the cloth. Marking on the cloth should be done lightly so that it will not smear or smudge through the surface. Whatever the method, it is essential to try the marker first on a scrap of the fabric. A good technique is to trace the pattern on the fabric with a soft pencil, tipping the pencil point so that the marking is just outside the pattern edge. This line forms the cutting line, and thus the marking can be eliminated completely. Of course this can be done only if the seam allowance has already been added.

Stitching

Sewing is done by hand or by machine, or more usually, by a combination of both. But either method must result in neat, accurate, and secure seams. The narrowest possible seam allowance eliminates the need to trim seams and makes turning possible without clipping. The sewing method depends largely on the fabric selected. Fabrics that don't fray, such as felt, fur fabrics, and velour, can best be sewn on a sewing machine with a small and narrow zigzag stitch placed over the cut edge. While the stitching does show when the piece is stretched by the stuffing, it is even and does not detract from the appearance.

Some woven fabrics tend to fray and make stitching difficult. On problem fabrics it is sometimes best to trace the pattern on the fabric and make both a zigzag and a straight-stitch seam before cutting. A tight back stitch is preferable when sewing by hand.

When accurate stitching on the sewing machine is difficult, baste the pieces or simply pin them. Place the pins perpendicular to the seam, with the heads of the pins at the raw edge. Withdraw them in front of the machine needle. It is sometimes easier to sew small pieces by hand than to attempt machine stitching. For instance, detail's for a doll's fingers are more easily executed by hand, though the seams of an arm can be sewn by machine. After the seams are sewn, examine them carefully to make sure that the sewing is accurate and that no portion of the seam has been missed. If the doll is to be tightly stuffed and there is any hint of ravelling, stitch a second time for reinforcement.

Turning

Use a blunt chopstick or small dowel to complete the turning. The handle end of a crochet hook facilitates turning of the fingers. A pair of medical forceps is a useful tool. Forceps come in a variety of lengths and shapes and are available from any medical supply house. With the forceps, grasp the inside of the sewn portion, lock the handles, and turn the fabric. They can also be used to pull needles through resistant seams and to place small bits of stuffing into narrow places. Whatever the tool used, take special care to avoid piercing the cloth. A difficult turn can be facilitated by folding the bottom of the piece to the inside, starting the turn at the fold (instead of the bottom), and working until the entire piece is inside out.

Stuffing Materials

Dacron (Terylene) or polyester fibres are excellent stuffing materials. Both are available in bulk or in batting form. Each has its special use. The bulk material is used for stuffing, and the batting is best in needle sculpture and in padding. It is also possible to purchase bags of polyester or Dacron trimmings that result from the custom-quilting process. The scraps are sold by the pound at somewhat lower prices. A search through the Yellow Pages telephone directory will yield the name of several custom quilters.

Because it is heavy, kiln-dried sawdust is a good stuffing material when porcelain or low-fired ceramic heads are affixed to cloth bodies. Since sawdust scatters and is difficult to use, try the following method:

• Hold the unstuffed body inside a large grocery

bag so that the spilled sawdust can be recaptured.

- Insert a broad-stemmed funnel or improvised cardboard cone into the body and coax the sawdust into the funnel to direct it.
- Press the sawdust hard to make it compact.

A combination of polyester and sawdust makes a hard stuffing if it is tightly compressed. Whatever the material, a doll is not properly stuffed unless it is as firm as it can be without the seams bursting. Most stuffed dolls benefit from the insertion of a dowel or wire in the neck area to maintain the position of the head.

To achieve some interesting effects, fill bodies of soft sculptures with sand. When confined in a closely woven, tightly sewn material, they make comic beanbags heavy enough to sit firmly. Horticultural-grade sand is usually used because it is coarse and free of dust. Birdseed is sometimes used as an alternative.

Weighting

Polyester and Dacron stuffing is light in weight, and dolls so filled tend to topple if the head is disproportionately heavy. A lead fishing weight or lead drapery weight wrapped in stuffing and inserted into the base of the body provides balance and results in a more substantial feel. For tiny Teddy bears or small animals, ball bearings can also be used. A heavy pebble in the absence of anything else will do the trick just as well.

Fabric Selection

Any tightly woven material that will not ravel excessively can be used to make a doll. The weight and color are the critical qualities. An opaque fabric is desirable to hide the stuffing's unevenness. But if the right color is available and the fabric is too thin, it can be used in two identical thicknesses.

Knit fabrics of limited stretch as well as felt are most useful. Felt should be as close to 100 percent wool and as heavy in weight as possible. The felt sold for craft use, which is less than 30 percent wool, will not withstand the stretching required in the stuffing process. If none else can be found, craft felt can be used with a lightweight woven underlining for reinforcement.

A wide variety of knit fabrics is available. Stockinettes are sold in doll supply shops, but the best one I have found is available by mail order from West Germany (Gustav Adolf Dietz, Postfach 434, Fabricstrasse 15, 7800 Freiburg im Breisgau, West Germany). Velours with limited stretch are good substitutes and can be used on either the napped or knitted side. Since velour is a napped fabric, cut it with care, reversing pieces for a left and right side. The degree of stretch of the knit fabric will result in an undetermined variation from the dimensions of the original pattern. The direction of the stretch—horizontal or vertical—and the direction in which the pattern is laid out will also affect the outcome. When used on the horizontal grain the result is additional width; when used on the vertical grain it will add length.

A simple stretch test will indicate beforehand how much residual relaxation exists in the fabric and will enable you to make the appropriate adjustment in the pattern before cutting. The first step is to determine whether the stretch is in the horizontal or vertical grain of the material. Material that stretches in both directions is best left for needle sculpture and would not be suitable for a stuffed doll. When the direction of stretch has been established, grasp the fabric firmly with both thumbs placed exactly 4 inches apart as measured against a ruler. Pull the fabric as hard as possible and again measure at its maximum stretch. If the fabric then measures about 5 inches (the usual increase for velour), it has stretched 1 inch in 4 inches, or 25 percent. When the stretch is a scant 25 percent, or less, no adjustment in the pattern is necessary although some variation from the pattern dimensions are to be expected.

If the stretch is somewhat more than this amount, however, adjust it as necessary in the following way. Make the pattern narrower on each of the raw edges so that the sum of the amount taken off equals the number of inches that must be removed. The amount taken off must be equal on each of the raw edges in order to preserve symmetry. For example, a doll that is to have an 8-inch waistline is to be made in a

(Opposite page) 1A. Ballerina (cookie-cutter body), Lenci-style doll, Infant and Toddler dolls (shoulder-plate attachment). See pp. 37, 54, and 46, respectively.

A

1B. Polyform figures of Santa Claus and Mother Goose. Bodies are made of cloth over wire armature (p. 66).

2B. Dolls made with purchased masks (p. 76).

3B. Dolls made with masks that were formed from the original ceramic mould (p. 77).

(Opposite page) 1C. (Left) *This doll was made from a cookie-cutter pattern and then needle-sculptured;* (right) *a plastic doll was used as a model to make the complete porcelain body of this doll (pp. 69 and 71).*

B

C

1D. *Costumed cookie-cutter dolls (p. 37).*

2D. *Dimensional-neck dolls: (left) neck is part of the head; (right) neck is part of the torso (p. 46).*

3D. *Shoulder-plate mannequins in Victorian costume (p. 46).*

4D. *Porcelain figures with cloth and wire-armature bodies in 1776 costume (pp. 71 and 85).*

(Opposite page) *1E. Soft-sculptured figures (p. 69).*

D

1F. Jointed clothespin people (p. 175).

2F. Three examples of block people. The simple clown provided inspiration for the needle-sculptured pair (p. 176).

(Opposite page) 1G. Oval-body dolls completed (p. 38).

F

G

H

knit fabric that stretches an ample 25 percent. The additional stretch of 2 inches (0.25 × 8 = 2) would give the finished doll a waist measuring 10 inches (8 + 2 = 10). If there are only two pieces in the construction, each of the four raw edges would have to be reduced ½ inch (4 × ½ = 2) so that the total would be reduced 2 inches. A body made in four segments would have eight raw edges, and each edge would have to be reduced ¼ inch (8 × ¼ = 2) to achieve a reduction of 2 inches in total.

To eliminate stretch, knits can be used as an outer layer and be lined with a woven fabric. Wherever double layers of cloth make foot and hand detailing difficult, simply cut off the lining at the wrist and ankle to avoid bulk. In this application as in the use of an underlayer with felt, place the two layers of material accurately together, retrim to match precisely, and use as a single fabric.

Choosing a Fabric Color

Pale colors are usually selected and vivid shades generally avoided. Pinks and browns are best for babies and young children; ivory, tan, peachy colors, and brown shades are suitable for older children and adults. But to be innovative, you might use green for a mermaid. Color is modified by overdyeing with commercial dyes: add minute amounts of tan to darken a light shade or add a little blue to tone down a bright color. Since many fabrics are a mixture of synthetic fibres, however, the results are not always predictable. Dyeing may be the only way to achieve the right color in seasons in which the fashion world does not dictate usable shades.

Creative Stuffing

The recommended stuffing materials are polyester, Dacron (Terylene), and kiln-dried sawdust, used alone or together. Insert the soft material in small pieces and force as tightly as possible into the cavity. Stuff the small recesses, the fingers and toes, first and continue to the larger areas. While stuffing a larger cavity, push the filling to the outside as you hollow and refill the center. Polyester does have a tendency to

(Opposite page) 1H. Little sock doll with flowers, and the animated Crissy Creeper (pp. 176 and 180).

settle and even when tightly packed will in time loosen. Leave the seams open for a few days so the stuffing will settle; then augment it.

The creative aspect of stuffing requires that the word *stuffing* be deleted and the word *sculpture* be substituted. To significantly alter cloth shapes, sculpture with small wads of filling material: round the contours, make the baby's wrist plump, delineate the sharpness of the knees, curve the outer portion of the thighs, locate the elbows, exaggerate the nose and chin, and suggest cheekbones. It is not the process of stuffing that we are concerned with but rather the defining of the doll's flesh under the skin. It makes a difference. To ensure symmetry, be sure to examine the work critically as the sculpture process continues. It is possible to move small amounts of filling by judiciously employing a large needle pushed through the skin to prod the stuffing into a better position. Place a little white glue on the polyester to dry it to stiffness. This is useful in shaping the nose but must be done with care to avoid staining the outer cloth cover.

Wire Reinforcement

Wire reinforcement for the purpose of retaining the rigidity of the arms and legs of the all-cloth doll is a simple technique. Cut an appropriate length of 14- or 16-gauge wire and wrap it with stuffing to be inserted into the limb or torso. It is important to coil or tape the end so that it will not pierce the cloth. Copper wire is easy to bend. Brass and galvanized wires are more rigid. A very rigid wire can be cut from a coat hanger to use in large dolls. Wire the fingers by using pipe cleaners either bent or taped and inserted into the stitched areas. A more complicated method, in which an armature of wire is built to be wrapped and sculptured, is described in chapter 3 (page 61).

Needle Shaping

Needle shaping is a simple technique in which carefully placed and tightened stitches add contour to stuffed dolls and animals. A tiny overcast stitch anchors the thread, which is drawn through the stuffing to the opposite side where the tension of the thread is adjusted and anchored with another overcast. This is repeated until the tension is firm. In this way dimples can be pulled through the hand, the knee can be shaped by anchoring the side seams, the eyes can be indented by pulling through the head, the neck is shaped, and the elbow can be better indicated. Needle shaping is one technique that differentiates a handmade doll from the ordinary commercial doll and puts it into a special classification. Needle sculpture, a more advanced technique, carries these methods to their ultimate in making soft sculptures. Needle sculpture is explained in chapter 3 (page 61).

Occasionally, careful inspection of the finished doll indicates that an additional tuck or dart needs to be taken. The doll will never disclose your secret.

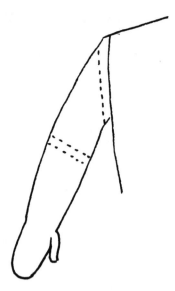

Illus. 17. Place stitching as shown to make hinges.

Joints

The patterns given in this chapter are for all-cloth dolls, and the variations can be finished by simply sewing the heads and limbs directly on the torso. But it is also possible to add more mobility to a doll by creating joints.

Hinge. Make a hinge by leaving a small portion of the limb unstuffed and placing a row of stitching through that portion. This enables the limb to bend at the elbow (Illus. 17), knee, or hip.

Shank. Make a shank with several loops of extra strong thread for sewing on buttons and for carpets. Stitched through the torso and fixed to the limb, this shank of threads is left loose between the two attachments. Reinforce the shank by wrapping with thread to secure (Illus. 18). The shank enables marionette movement and is used most frequently to attach the arms of an upside-down doll. The arms will then flip up and down when the doll is reversed.

Illus. 18. Stitch several loops between torso and limb. Then wrap with thread to secure.

Sewing through. To enable the limbs on small animals and dolls to move, sew them to the body with a heavy, waxed thread. Complete the arms and legs with rounded tops. Make the attachment by sewing through the first limb, extending through the torso and then through the second limb (Illus. 19). Repeat the stitching until the attachment is firm. This is most effective on a small doll where there is not more than just a few inches of stuffing to penetrate.

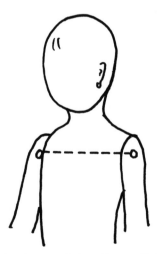

Illus. 19. Make arm joints for small dolls by sewing through first limb, extending through torso, and then through second limb.

Button joints. Large flat buttons can be used as joints. Buttons serve as the anchors and can be placed on the outside of the limbs when using the sew-through method just described. Hide buttons by placing them under the doll's skin of the inner side of the limb and under the skin of the torso so that they work against each other. It is usually easier to attach the arms and legs before the limb is completely stuffed and closed. If the doll will be manipulated enough to wear through the cloth, glue leather or plastic under the button to protect the cloth from abrasion. The pulling-through in a large doll can be a formidable task. Sew several strong threads through the torso before it is completely stuffed and leave the ends on the outside for later attachment of the limbs. For enormous dolls insert a length of PVC (polyvinyl chloride) rigid plastic pipe, a plumbing product, into the torso between the limbs and pull the connecting cord, or better yet, run elastic through the pipe. The ends can be secured with buttons.

Mechanical disc joints. The principle of mechanical jointing is based on fastening two flat discs so that they rotate against each other and provide mobility. Place them, like the button joint, under the doll's skin but fasten the discs together with a cotter pin rather than by sewing. Fibreboard (hardboard) discs are available from some doll-parts suppliers, and plastic discs are available in some craft stores. But any disc that is readily available can be substituted. Any circle of rigid material that has a center hole or can be pierced with a center hole is adaptable: buttons, plastic caps from prescription bottles, plumbing washers, electrical washers, metal fender washers, or even the plastic-circle insert from a popular push-up frozen dessert can be used. With a bit more effort, you can cut thin circles from an appropriate size wooden dowel and drill the center hole. A trip to a hardware or automotive supply shop will produce appropriate discs. A cotter pin is available in many lengths and gauges from the same retail outlets. Fabric benefits from some reinforcement to prevent excessive wear from the hard discs. This can be provided by gluing circles of leather or plastic fabric to the disc or to the fabric. The hole in the disc must be sufficiently small so that the cotter-pin

head does not slip through. Use a smaller washer as an adapter or widen the cotter-pin head by spreading with a needle-nose plier (Illus. 20).

Where mechanical jointing is to be used, sew, turn, and partially stuff the limbs. Attach them by inserting the joint under the skin of both parts, restuffing and closing seams with invisible stitches. This joint is also used to attach the head to the torso of the all-time favorite Teddy bear. When the head is to be attached, stuff it hard and gather to close with only the cotter pin protruding. Also gather the neck to close. The jointing is facilitated by leaving open the back seam of the torso until the head is securely fastened.

Make a tight mechanical joint as follows:
- Assemble the first portion of the joint by inserting and adjusting the cotter pin so that the head of the pin will not slip through the hole. Use a smaller washer as an adapter if the hole is too large. Or spread the head of the cotter pin.
- Push the cotter pin through the skin of the limb and then through the skin of the torso in the desired location.
- Place the second disc of the joint on the cotter pin, which is now on the inside of the torso.
- Then bend the cotter pin into a "foot" using a needle-nose plier.
- Bend the two portions of the cotter pin into the rounded crown shape.
- Press the discs tightly together and force the foot tightly to the second disc to form a tight closure.

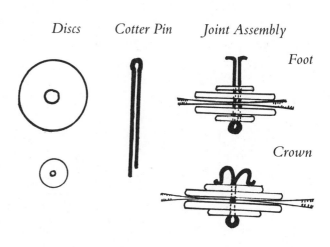

Illus. 20. Mechanical disc joints.

Wire as an arm joint. A cloth doll can be given mobility or posed in the suggestion of action by using wire. Insert the wire into the first arm, push it through the body and incorporate it into the opposite arm. It is easier to leave the final closure of the arm till last, enabling a firm connection of the wire. For easy bending use 14- or 16-gauge copper wire. Secure the wire in the stuffing with dabs of white glue.

Wooden dowel as a neck joint. For an unusual effect a cloth head can be constructed separately from the torso. Place the head on a dowel of appropriate length and diameter and glue it in place. When the body pattern is adjusted, the neck is slightly elongated. Reinforce the cloth neck edge by sewing it over an appropriate size bone ring (found in shops with other crochet supplies). Insert the dowel with the head attached into the reinforced neck so the doll's head can rotate. If the doll is to be enjoyed by curious children, the attachment will need to be more secure. This can be accomplished by inserting the dowel into the completed neck before you stuff the body. The dowel portion inside the torso is wrapped with a heavy yarn so that when it is glued it forms an obstruction, which will not permit the dowel to be pulled through the neck ring.

Finishing the Cloth Doll

Cloth dolls are most often finished by embroidering the faces; however, there are many alternatives: painting with acrylic paints, gluing on felt eyes and mouth, judicious use of soft-tipped pens and colored pencils to draw the features, and the use of fabric paints. Painting techniques are discussed in detail in chapter 6 (page 91). The degree of realism depends solely upon the artist. Eyes can be buttons, felt circles, or constructed of layers of felt to indicate the iris and pupil. The nose can be totally absent, be represented by an embroidered shape, or be stuffed and appliquéd in place. The ears can be absent, be represented by a comic half-circle, or be a coil sewn in place. Eyelashes may be omitted or be represented by an embroidered fringe. Mustaches are embroidered or glued into position.

The face is best applied after the doll is finished to ensure correct placement of the features.

Some preliminary planning should be done because mistakes leave smudges. Consult any source that will assist you in designing the desired face. Don't hesitate to trace a face that you like and adapt it to your project. Simplicity is the keynote. If the proportions of the face are visualized correctly and the eyes properly placed, the rest of the face will be successfully executed.

Whatever the method of presenting the face, apply dry blush, which is available in any cosmetics department, to bring the face to life. Dust it on the cheeks; on the nose and chin of a comic character; and on the knees, hands, feet, and elbows of a baby or child. While it does rub off in time, it can be easily renewed and enhances the presentation of the doll. Also apply dry eye makeup in shades of blue, green, or brown to shade the eyes. A darker shade than the skin can be dusted lightly on the sides of the nose and under the chin to give the illusion of contour. Scotchgard stain repeller sprayed on the doll will preserve the surface.

The hair may be a carefully fabricated wig or be as simple as glued-on yarn. Wig material for cloth dolls ranges from embroidery thread to human hair—with yarn, theatrical crepe hair, ravelled macramé cord, and fur in between. The possibilities are endless.

PATTERNS CLASSIFIED

There are many patterns available for making a stuffed cloth doll. Close inspection of patterns, however, reveals that only a few basic construction concepts exist, and many of the patterns are just variations on these basic ideas. This chapter presents full-size patterns for five specific constructions, together with suggestions for their modification and variation. The intent is to demonstrate that almost any cloth doll can be made by using these patterns with modifications and adaptations. The patterns used as presented are shown in the photographs, and even without change they will make some attractive dolls. Additionally, most of the body patterns can be used with sculptured heads. A pattern for a body without a head—Lenci style—is included and can be used with any head desired. Dollmaking, like all other creative activities, is largely a trial-and-error process. The first attempt might best be considered the "work-out," and subsequent repetitions might be used to perfect the idea.

Here are descriptions of the patterns:

• "Cookie cutter": This is the simplest pattern and is frequently used. The entire doll is made of only two pieces—a front and a back. Sometimes both pieces are identical; other times they are different in order to introduce more dimensionality. The pattern can be used to make upside-down dolls, in which the top half is placed end to end. Made in stretch materials, needle-shaped, and wired, they are entirely different from a flat doll made in a woven fabric. Patterns, including optional legs, are given for a woman and a child. A baby pattern is included, but it is not exactly to the same scale. Of all the constructions the cookie cutter is the most easily recognized.

• Oval body: This construction is most often used for infant and toddler dolls. It consists of a four-part body with attached or jointed arms and legs. The front panel face is most appropriate to the child or toddler doll, while the center-seam profile head is best for the older-child or the adult doll. The body can be adapted to a sculptured head, and the legs finished with sewn-on shoes for a comic effect. While at first the results appear to be dissimilar, the dolls shown are closely related in construction.

• Dimensional neck: The patterns given are two variations on a Japanese theme. In both, the head is affixed separately to the body by a shaped neck. In one variation the neck is part of the body and pierces the head, and in the second variation the neck is part of the head and is inserted into the body. The body is a good basic pattern with many applications. The shaped head can also be used as the armature for needle sculpture.

• Dimensional head with shoulder-plate attachment: Two variations of this construction are presented, and at first glance, they appear not to relate to each other. However, both utilize intricate seaming for dimension and feature a head pattern that extends to the chest and shoulder area. The head is attached to the torso by this shoulder plate. The first variation is a toddler or infant altered by the use of differentiated arms and legs. The second variation is a pair of mannequins to be wired for posing.

• Body without a head—Lenci style: No collection of basic patterns is complete without this one. Lenci, the felt doll made for over 60 years in Italy, is a collector's prize. This body pattern is usable with separate heads made of any hard material or can be used with a cloth head augmented with a stiffened mask.

METHODS FOR MODIFYING PATTERNS

Here are some suggestions for modifying the patterns.

• The size of the pattern can be changed by enlarging or reducing.
• The body proportions can be changed by lengthening or shortening the torsos, the legs, and the arms to designate reality or caricature.
• Curves can be accentuated or straightened.
• Seams may be altered to make slimmer or stouter dolls.
• Hands and feet can be given more detail by stitching and inserting wire. The hands can be posed in an upward or downward position by using darts. Patterns can be redrafted by slashing and folding to bend or straighten arms and legs.
• Joints can be incorporated.
• Ears can be added.
• Some of the patterns can be wired.
• Body patterns can be used with sculptured heads instead of cloth heads.
• "Seats" may be inserted for more dimensionality.
• Soles can be added to the feet to add shape.
• The dolls can be finished and wigged in a wide variety of ways, painted and costumed with any idea in mind.

Feel free to alter the basic patterns in whatever way you wish. These suggestions are offered to inspire innovative and creative interpretations of some basic ideas.

FULL-SIZE PATTERNS

"Cookie Cutter"

The "cookie cutter" pattern uses only the simplest of all the constructon methods. Its dimensionality depends upon creative stuffing, darts, and in this instance slashing and gathering at the neck (Illus. 21 and Color Illus. 1D).

Baby. This pattern makes a doll about 8 inches long but can be easily enlarged (Illus. 22).
  Suggestions for assembly:
- The back of the pattern is longer than the front. Fold the excess in the back upwards at the end of the torso and stitch it into the side seam to form the seat.
- Gather and fit the slash made at the neck so that the dots marked *A* match. This forms a rounded chin.
- The doll can be hinged or wired. The body resembles the frog-shape body of the antique doll and can be used with a porcelain head.
- Ears can be applied to the cloth doll to finish it more realistically.

Woman and child. Patterns for the woman and child differ somewhat in scale from the preceding baby pattern but are essentially the same in concept (Illus. 23–24). The dimensionality relies on creative stuffing, darts, and slashes and gathers of the face to give fullness to the cheeks. The pattern for the front and the back of the head are different. The front of the head is larger, and it is slashed and gathered. Optional front-

seam legs are given for each doll. Cut them out separately and attach them to the torso where appropriate after they are stuffed.
  Suggestions for assembly:
- Gather and fit the slash in the neck so that the circles marked *A* match.
- Place a chopstick or skewer into the neck and torso to keep them rigid.
- These dolls can be wired with 14- or 16-gauge copper wire.
- While simple in concept, these dolls can be elaborately finished and costumed.
- To ensure accuracy of doll's shape, stitch all of the seams and then make a small opening in the center of the back in order to stuff the doll. When project is finished, the closing will not show.

Oval Body

At first glance the patterns that follow may appear to be unrelated, but they are based on the same construction concept (Illus. 25 and Color Illus. 1G).

Infant and toddler. This pattern with variations in size and presentation is probably the most frequently seen (Illus. 26). It portrays an infant and child with a panel face. The seaming gives dimension to the head and produces realistic baby shapes. There are two optional head patterns, and the limbs are shown either bent or straight. The bent limbs might depict the infant; the straight legs better describe the toddler.
  Suggestions for assembly:
- Construct the body and the head separately and attach before completing the stuffing.
- Attach the gathered, stuffed, and appliquéd nose (best sewn invisibly) before you close the head.
  Optional treatment:
- The doll can be button jointed.
- For more detail, stitch fingers and toes.
- Turn the arms in an upward position instead of downward attachment to show the baby sleeping. Represent closed eyes by a fringe of eyelashes.
- Finishing of the doll can be whimsical or realistic. It is an excellent doll for children since it can be almost completely machine sewn. For variety, make the arms and legs more plump.

Illus. 21. Cookie-cutter pattern dolls.

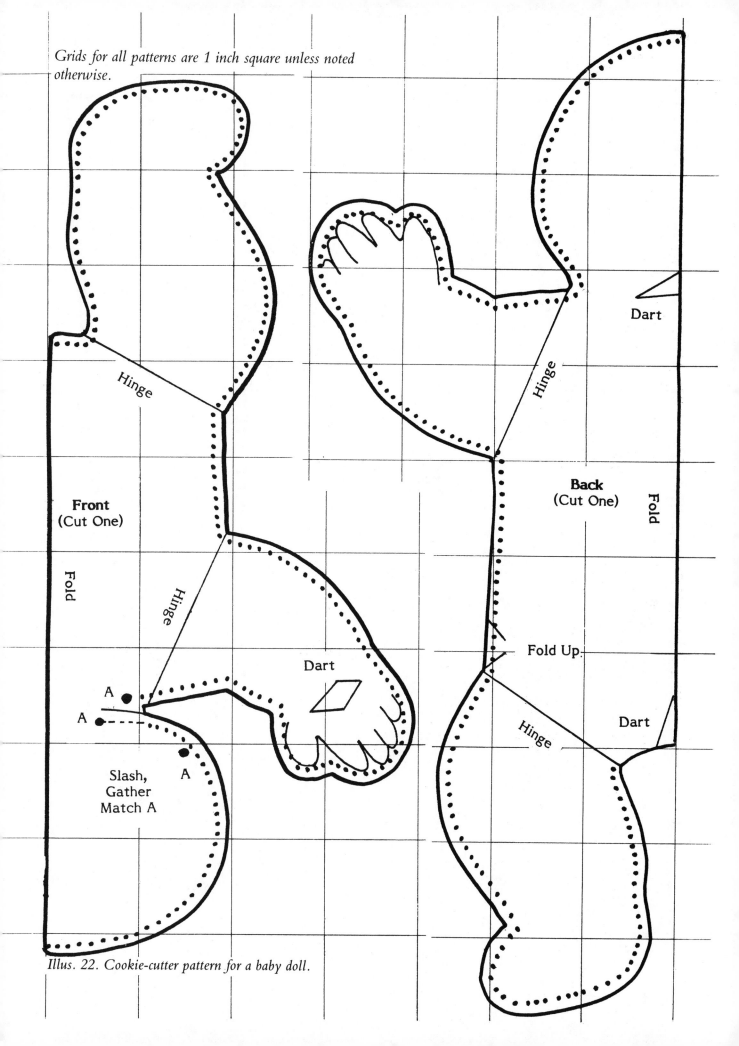

Grids for all patterns are 1 inch square unless noted otherwise.

Dart

Hinge

Hinge

Back
(Cut One)

Fold

Front
(Cut One)

Fold

Hinge

Fold Up

Dart

Hinge

Dart

A

A

A

Slash,
Gather
Match A

Illus. 22. Cookie-cutter pattern for a baby doll.

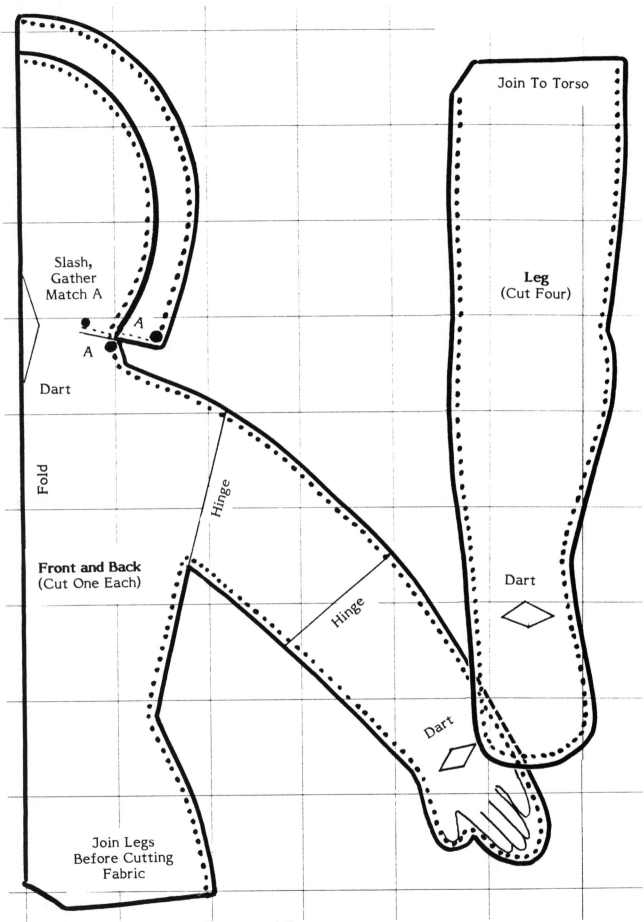

Illus. 23. Cookie-cutter pattern for a woman doll.

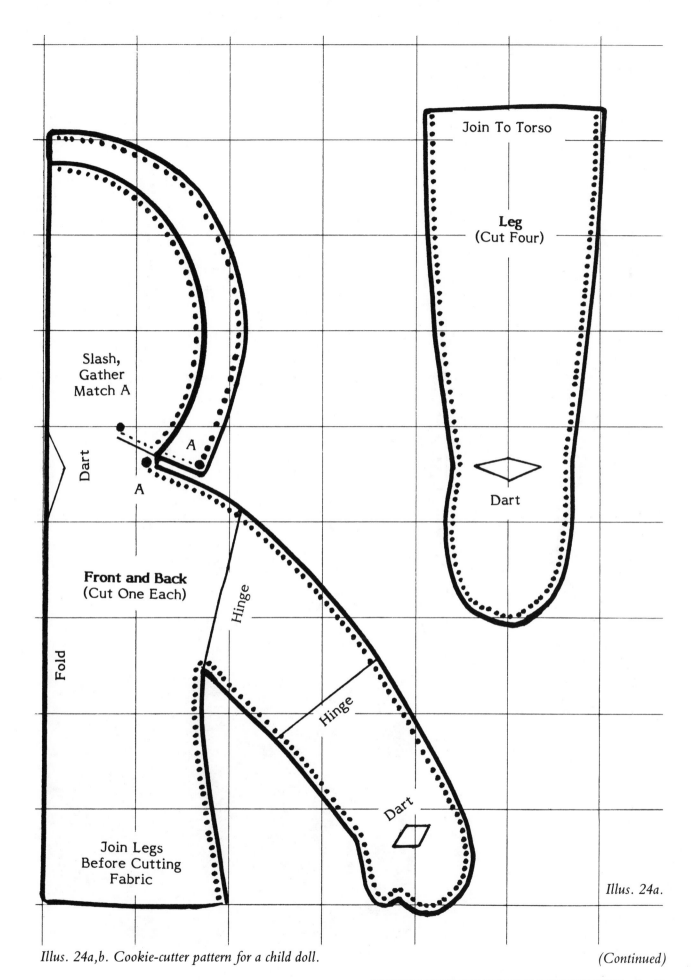

Slash,
Gather
Match A

Dart

A

A

Front and Back
(Cut One Each)

Fold

Hinge

Hinge

Dart

Join Legs
Before Cutting
Fabric

Join To Torso

Leg
(Cut Four)

Dart

Illus. 24a.

Illus. 24a,b. Cookie-cutter pattern for a child doll.

(Continued)

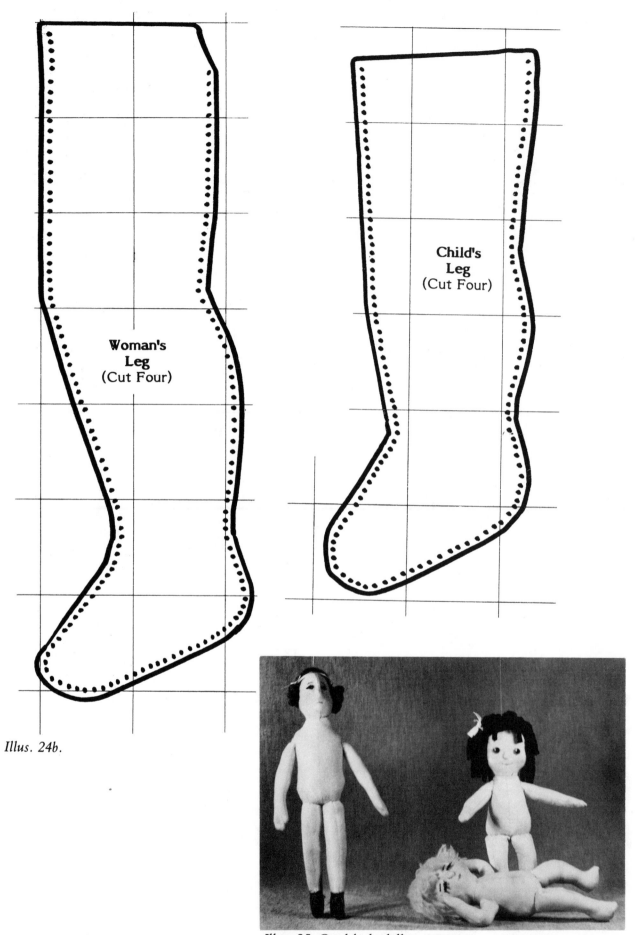

**Woman's
Leg**
(Cut Four)

**Child's
Leg**
(Cut Four)

Illus. 24b.

Illus. 25. Oval-body dolls.

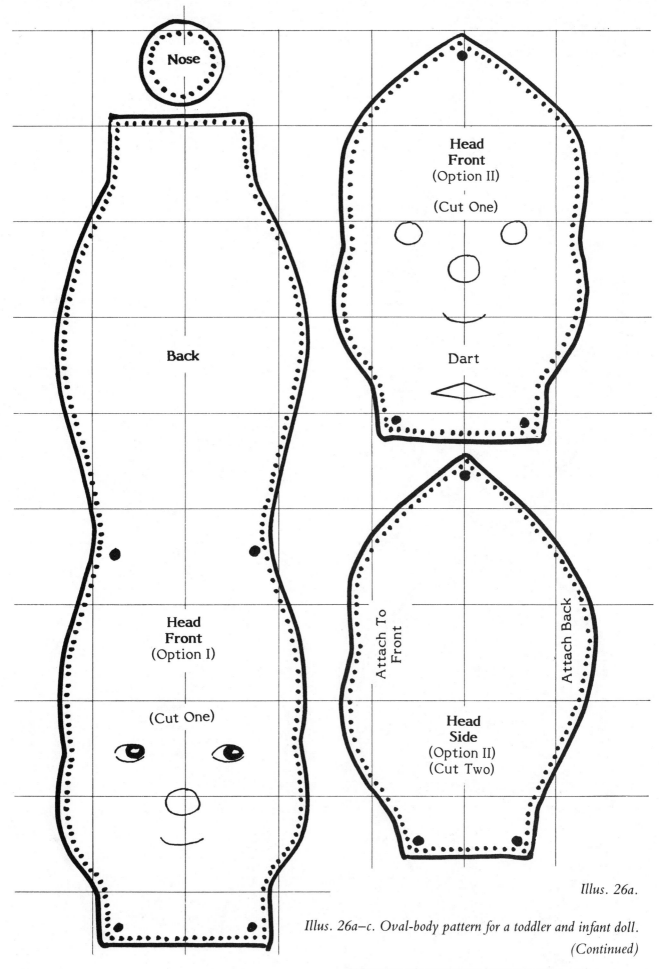

Nose

Back

Head Front (Option I)

(Cut One)

Head Front (Option II)

(Cut One)

Dart

Attach To Front

Attach Back

Head Side (Option II) (Cut Two)

Illus. 26a.

Illus. 26a–c. Oval-body pattern for a toddler and infant doll.

(Continued)

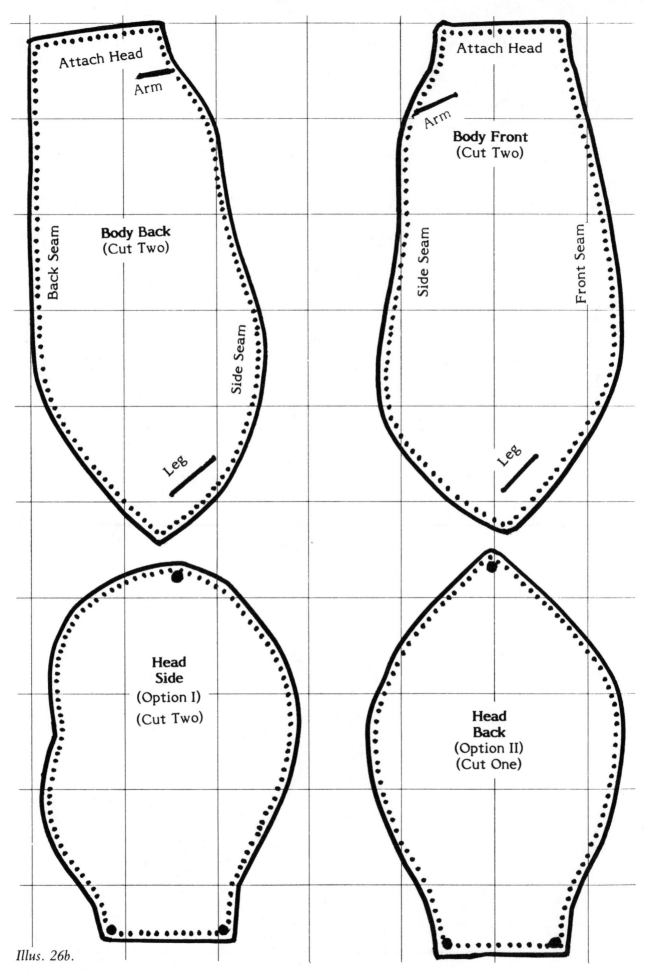

Attach Head

Arm

Body Back
(Cut Two)

Back Seam

Side Seam

Leg

Attach Head

Arm

Body Front
(Cut Two)

Side Seam

Front Seam

Leg

**Head
Side**
(Option I)
(Cut Two)

**Head
Back**
(Option II)
(Cut One)

Illus. 26b.

44 ◆ PATTERN DESIGNS FOR THE STUFFED DOLL

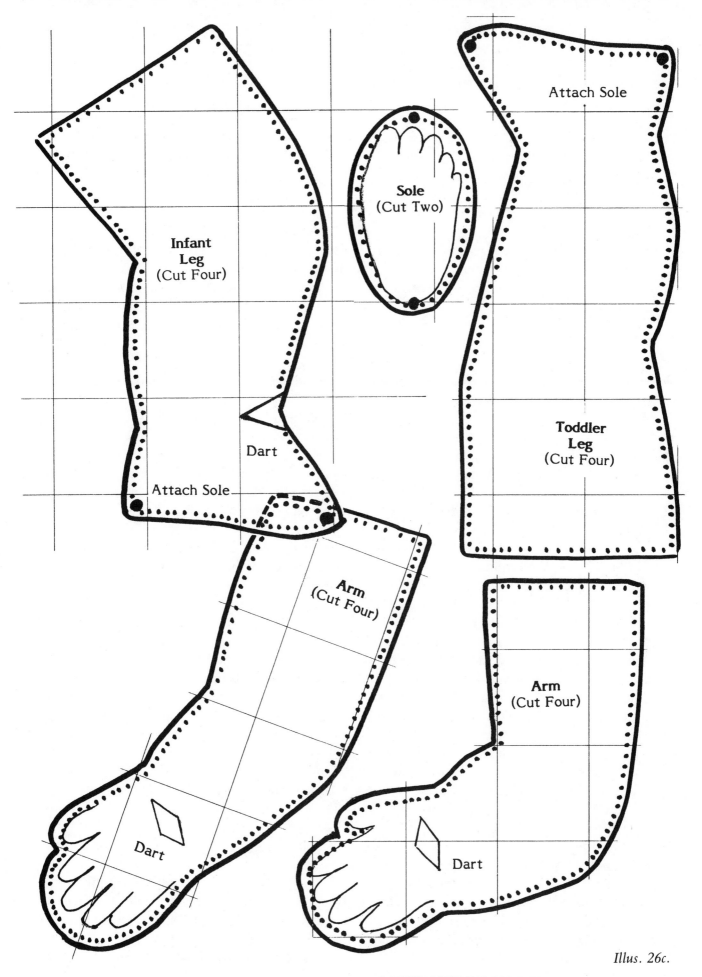

Infant Leg (Cut Four)

Sole (Cut Two)

Attach Sole

Toddler Leg (Cut Four)

Dart

Attach Sole

Arm (Cut Four)

Dart

Arm (Cut Four)

Dart

Illus. 26c.

Woman. The adult pattern, while based on the oval body construction, substitutes a profile head in which the shaping is accomplished by a center front seam (Illus. 27). The head can also be made with a gusset, much as animal heads are made, to give dimension. Two leg patterns are given, one of which provides a comic shoe.

Suggestions for assembly:
• Make the head and body separately and then attach them. Complete the stuffing after attachment.
• Designate separate shoes by cutting the leg and shoe each of different material, remembering to leave appropriate seam allowances for joining.

Optional treatment:
• By altering the profile, you can change the doll's facial expression in whatever way you choose.
• For additional detail, place the head on a dowel.
• The doll can be jointed in a variety of ways.
• Finishing and costuming can be done in the widest possible interpretations.

Dimensional Neck, Separate Head—Two Variations

These dimensional-neck-with-separate-head dolls (Illus. 28 and Color Illus. 2D) are elaborations on a Japanese theme. The blonde doll (left) features a head with an elongated neck that pierces the torso. The brunette (right) in contrast, features a torso with an elongated neck that pierces the head. To transform the flat faces, pad and use the heads as foundations for needle sculpture. Either variation has many options. See Illus. 29–30 for the two body patterns and three alternative arm patterns (*B* is superimposed on *A*), one of which is a comic arm with an extended thumb. The bodies, heads, arms, and legs are interchangeable for a variety of different effects.

Suggestions for assembly:
• To stiffen the body insert a dowel or chopstick.
• Attach head to the body before either is completely stuffed. Stuff around the attachment.
• As in assembling most machine-sewn cloth dolls, attach the stitched, turned, and stuffed arms and legs to the body before sewing up or stuffing the body.

Optional treatment:
• Proportions can be changed. To represent a child, shorten arms and legs. To make comic characters, greatly elongate the arms and legs.
• The body, with neck removed, is a standard body shape and is usable with any other head.
• Sew hinges at elbow or knee for a flexible doll.

Shoulder-Plate Attachment

Dolls made from shoulder-plate patterns (Illus. 31, 33 and Color Illus. 1A, 3D) are more complicated in concept and are somewhat realistic cloth dolls. The first set of patterns (Illus. 32) is for the infant and toddler. The second set (Illus. 34–35) is for making adult mannequins. Fashion them in knit fabrics and stuff them creatively. Wire the adult dolls.

Infant and Toddler. The completed toddler doll is about 11 inches long. Bent and straight arm and leg alternatives are given. The pattern (Illus. 32) includes a set-in seat that can be added to any body pattern and that significantly changes the contour of the body. The soles of the feet are also set in to provide dimensionality. Instructions for assembling the head are included in the pattern.

Suggestions for assembly:
• Seam the front and lower part of the legs and insert the sole before completely closing the back seam.
• Complete and stuff the arms and legs and sew into the seams of the torso as the torso is constructed. The legs and front of the seat can be sewn to the body in the same operation.
• Weight the bottom of the body to offset the heaviness of the head.
• Attach the head by pulling the chest portion over the torso. After positioning it correctly, sew it firmly in place.

Optional treatment:
• To add realism, appliqué a nose and apply ears.
• For a different effect, appliqué a hard mask to the face.
• Needle shaping is a good finishing technique.

Man and Woman. The completed adult dolls (Illus. 33) are about 14 inches tall. The man is slightly larger than the woman. They are excellent figures for period costuming and can be finished elaborately with styled wigs. They are

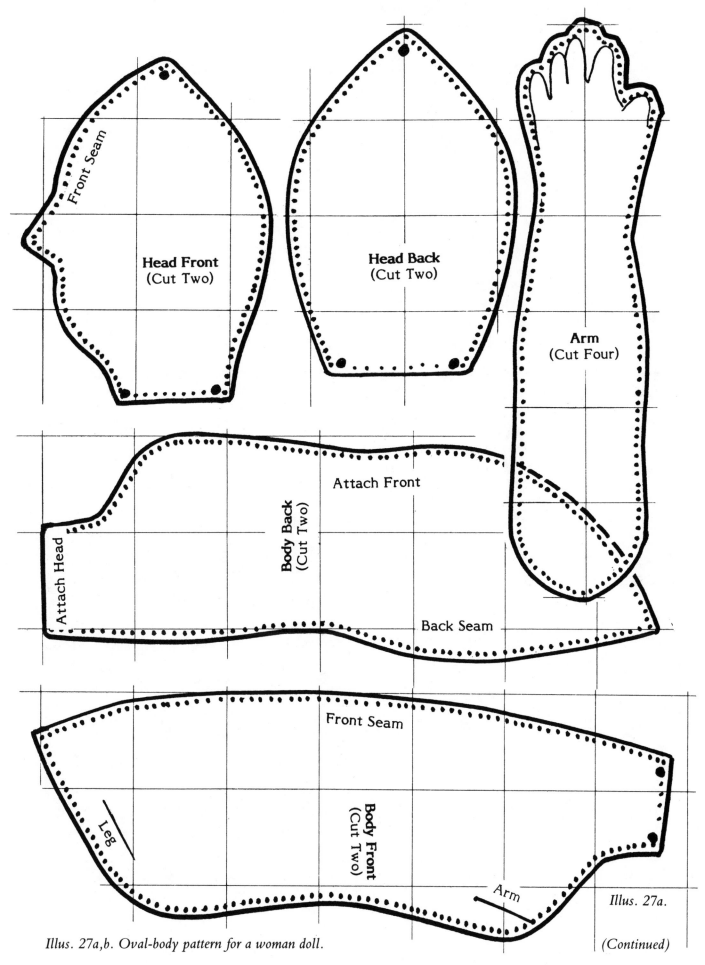

Head Front
(Cut Two)

Front Seam

Head Back
(Cut Two)

Arm
(Cut Four)

Attach Front

Attach Head

Body Back
(Cut Two)

Back Seam

Front Seam

Leg

Body Front
(Cut Two)

Arm

Illus. 27a.

Illus. 27a,b. Oval-body pattern for a woman doll.

(Continued)

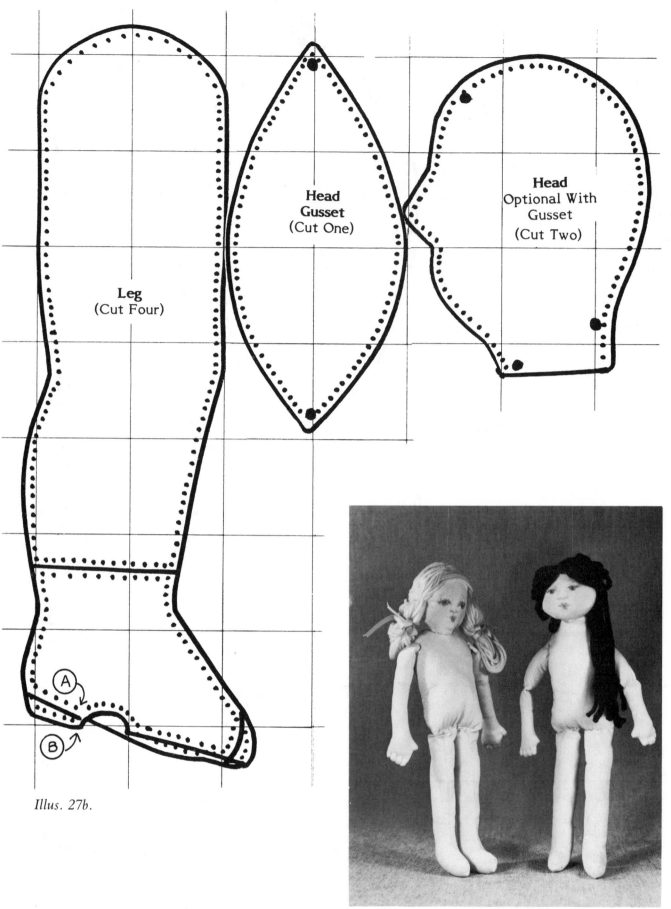

Leg
(Cut Four)

Head Gusset
(Cut One)

Head
Optional With Gusset
(Cut Two)

Ⓐ

Ⓑ

Illus. 27b.

*Illus. 28. Two variations of dimensional-neck dolls:
(left)* elongated neck, *(right)* elongated torso.

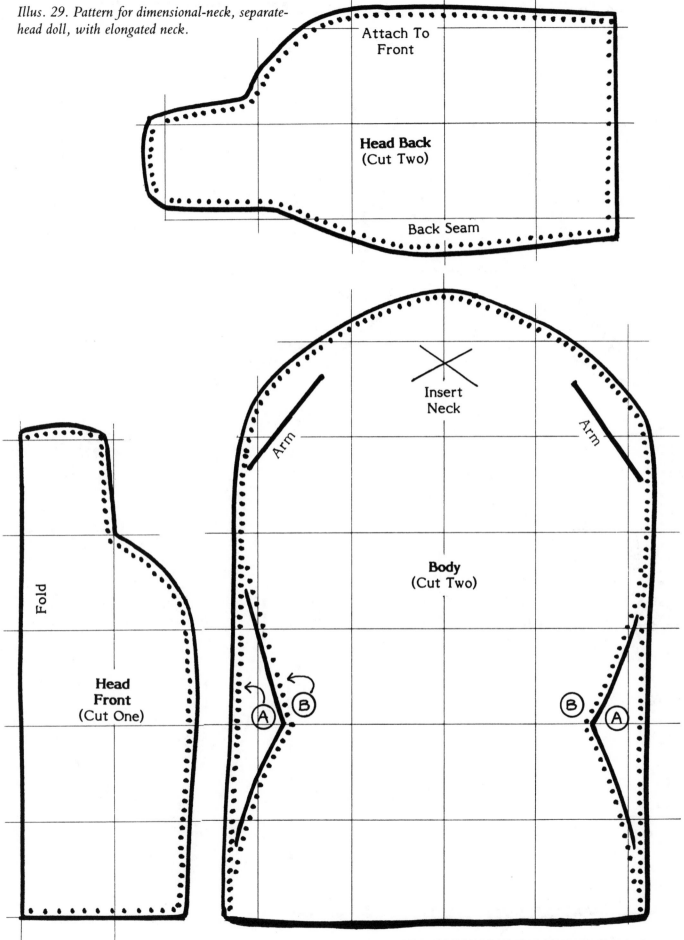

Illus. 29. Pattern for dimensional-neck, separate-head doll, with elongated neck.

Attach To Front

Head Back
(Cut Two)

Back Seam

Insert Neck

Arm

Arm

Body
(Cut Two)

Fold

Head Front
(Cut One)

Ⓐ Ⓑ

Ⓑ Ⓐ

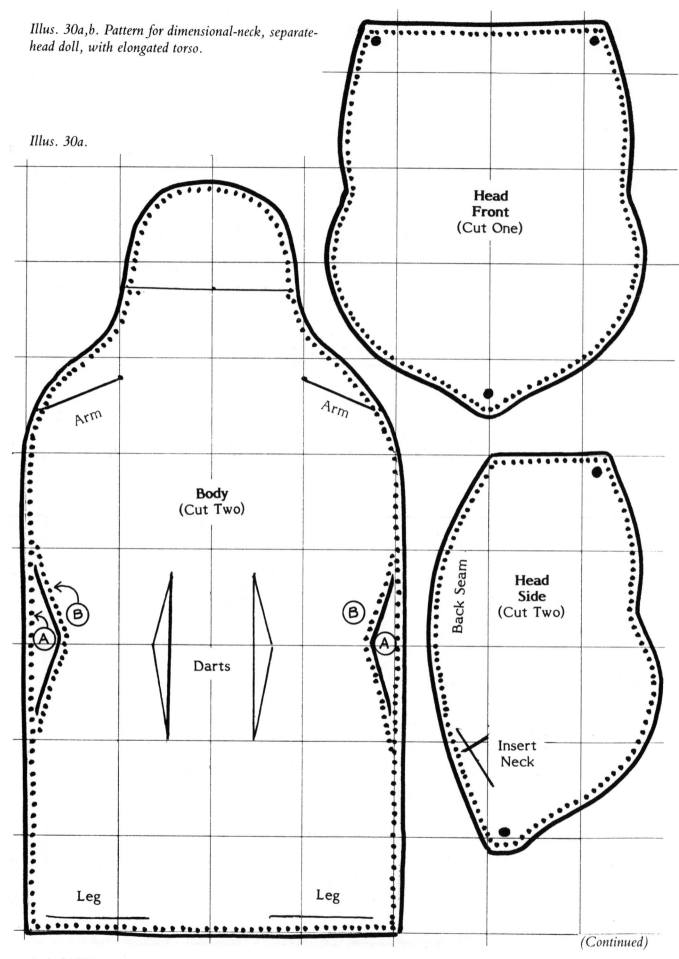

Illus. 30a,b. Pattern for dimensional-neck, separate-head doll, with elongated torso.

Illus. 30a.

Head Front
(Cut One)

Body
(Cut Two)

Arm

Arm

Ⓑ

Ⓐ

Ⓐ

Ⓑ

Darts

Head Side
(Cut Two)

Back Seam

Insert Neck

Leg

Leg

(Continued)

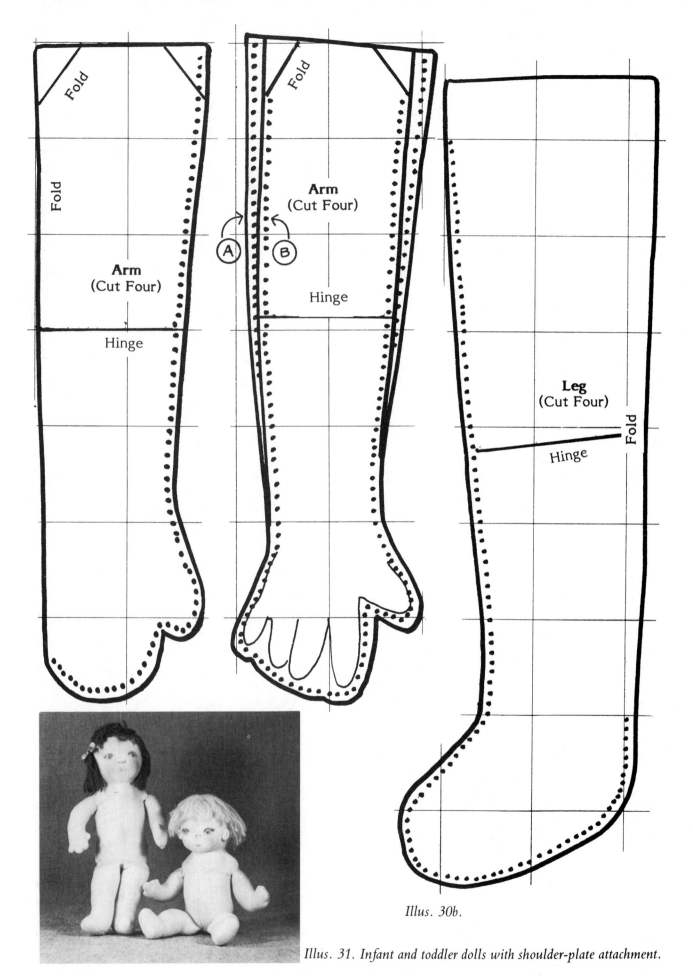

Arm
(Cut Four)

Fold

Fold

Hinge

Arm
(Cut Four)

Fold

Ⓐ Ⓑ

Hinge

Leg
(Cut Four)

Fold

Hinge

Illus. 30b.

Illus. 31. Infant and toddler dolls with shoulder-plate attachment.

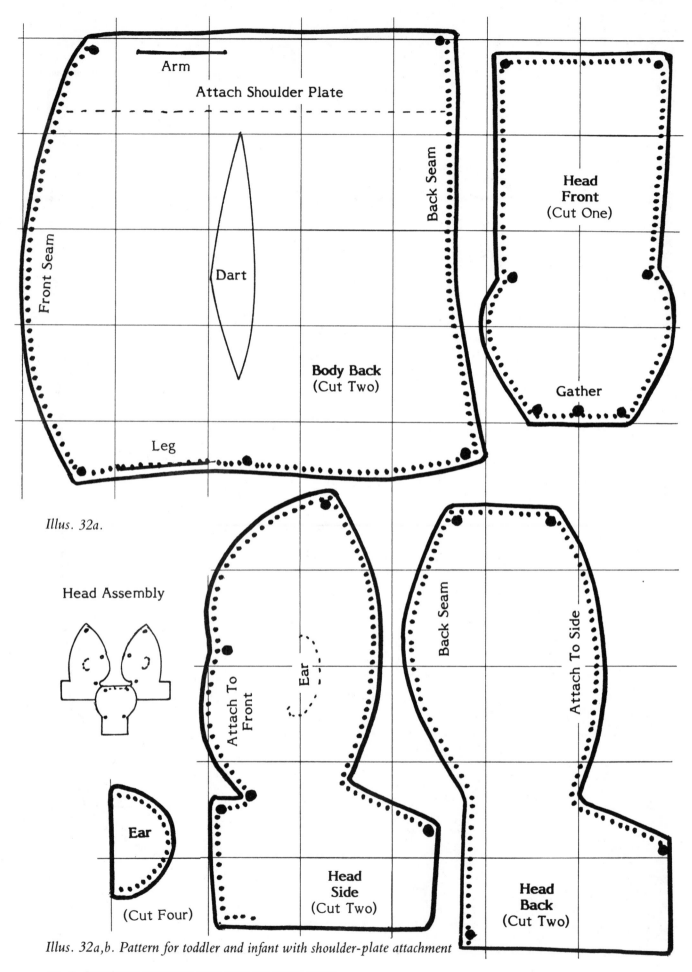

Arm

Attach Shoulder Plate

Front Seam

Dart

Back Seam

Body Back
(Cut Two)

**Head
Front**
(Cut One)

Gather

Leg

Illus. 32a.

Head Assembly

Attach To Front

Ear

Back Seam

Attach To Side

Ear

(Cut Four)

**Head
Side**
(Cut Two)

**Head
Back**
(Cut Two)

Illus. 32a,b. Pattern for toddler and infant with shoulder-plate attachment

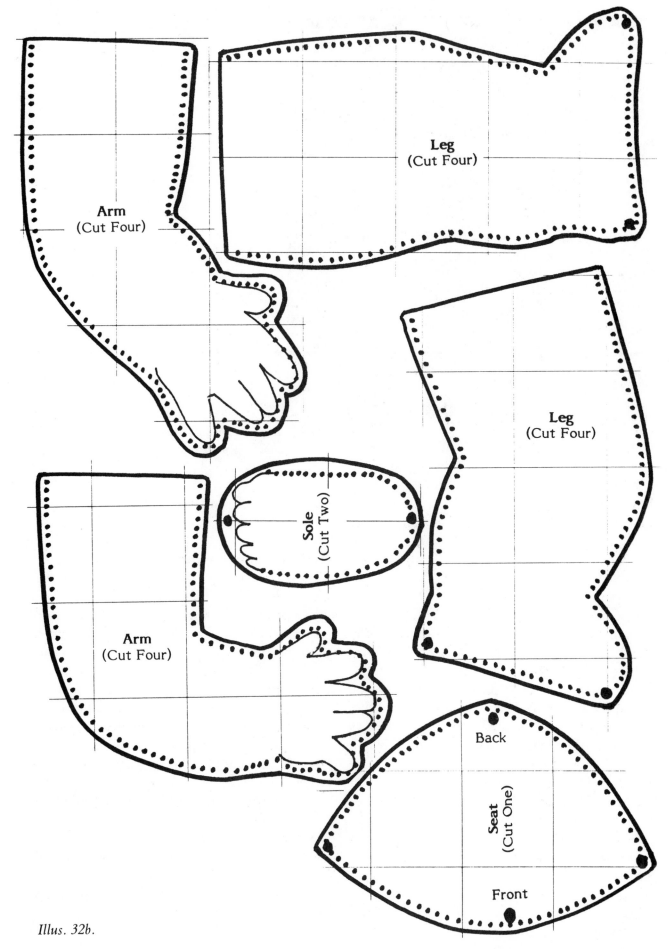

Arm
(Cut Four)

Leg
(Cut Four)

Leg
(Cut Four)

Sole
(Cut Two)

Arm
(Cut Four)

Back

Seat
(Cut One)

Front

Illus. 32b.

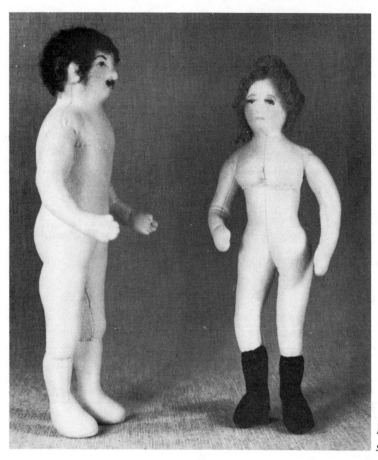

Illus. 33. Man and woman dolls with shoulder-plate attachment.

best made of knitted fabric, velour, or felt, since ravelling would present a problem and some stretch is necessary. Wire and creatively stuff these mannequins. Needle shaping further enhances them. See patterns in Illus. 34–35.

Suggestions for assembly:

• Assemble the body but do not stuff.
• Seam the front of the leg and insert the sole before closing the back of the leg. Reinforce the sole with cardboard.
• Wire and stuff the torso; simultaneously extend the wire into the lower legs and into the head.
• Position the lower legs last, making certain that the wire extends almost into the foot.
• Complete arms with wire and attach to the body before the head is attached.
• Creative stuffing is essential for realistic shaping. Needle shaping is required.
Optional treatment:
• Simulate boots by making the lower legs of an appropriate fabric.
• Faces are painted or embroidered or a combination of both.

• Make ears of semicircles of cloth and sew in place.

Body without a Head—Lenci Style

This particular Lenci-style doll (Illus. 36 and Color Illus. 1A) is designed for the attachment of a separate 4-inch head (measured from forehead to chin). The arms and legs are to be jointed with disc joints (Illus. 37). Note that the construction of the foot is somewhat unusual. The doll is best made of felt but any firmly knit fabric will also serve well. A head may be attached by sewing or made to swivel as explained on page 36. The completed doll is about 15 inches tall.

The following suggestions may facilitate construction:

• Sew the front seams of the legs and attach the foot before closing the back seam.
• Stiffen the soles by inserting cardboard.
• Join arms and legs mechanically to torso with disc joints before stuffing the body.
• Fingers can be delineated by stitching, as suggested.

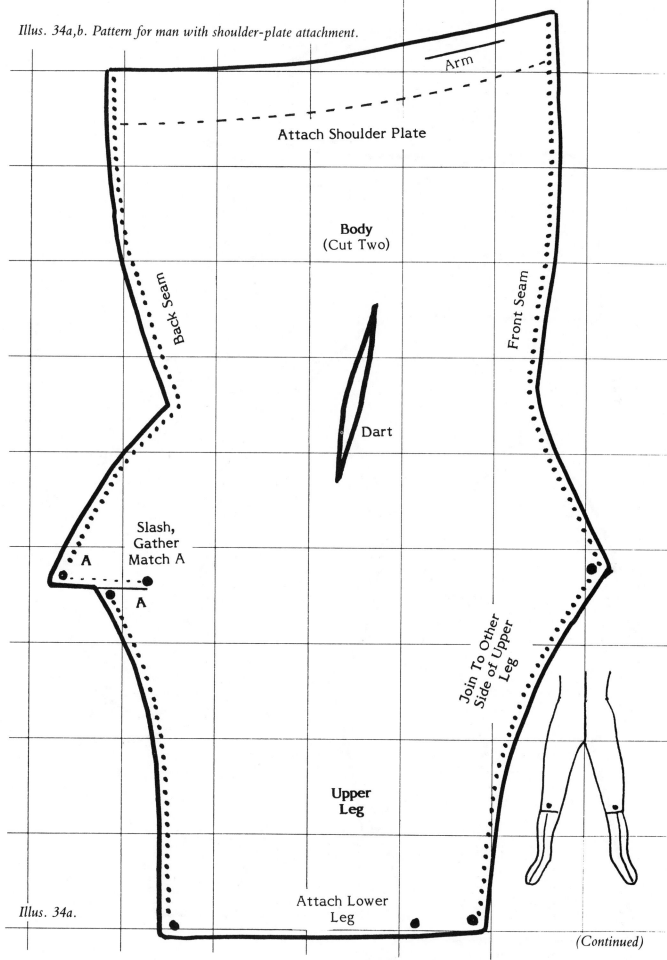

Illus. 34a,b. Pattern for man with shoulder-plate attachment.

Arm

Attach Shoulder Plate

Body
(Cut Two)

Back Seam

Front Seam

Dart

Slash,
Gather
Match A

A

A

Join To Other
Side of Upper
Leg

**Upper
Leg**

Attach Lower
Leg

Illus. 34a.

(Continued)

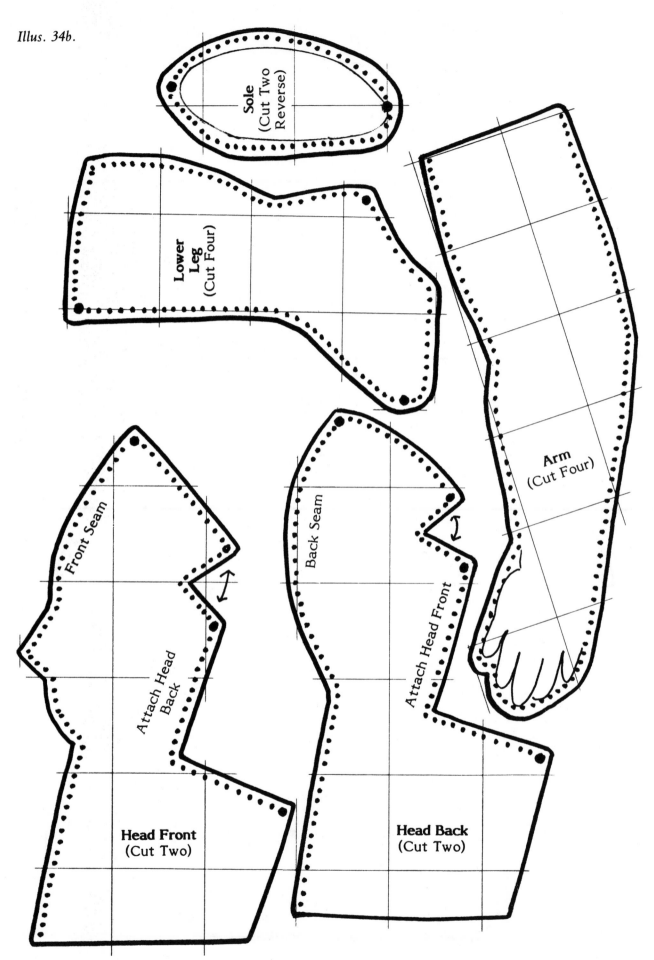

Illus. 34b.

Sole
(Cut Two
Reverse)

Lower
Leg
(Cut Four)

Arm
(Cut Four)

Front Seam

Attach Head
Back

Back Seam

Attach Head Front

Head Front
(Cut Two)

Head Back
(Cut Two)

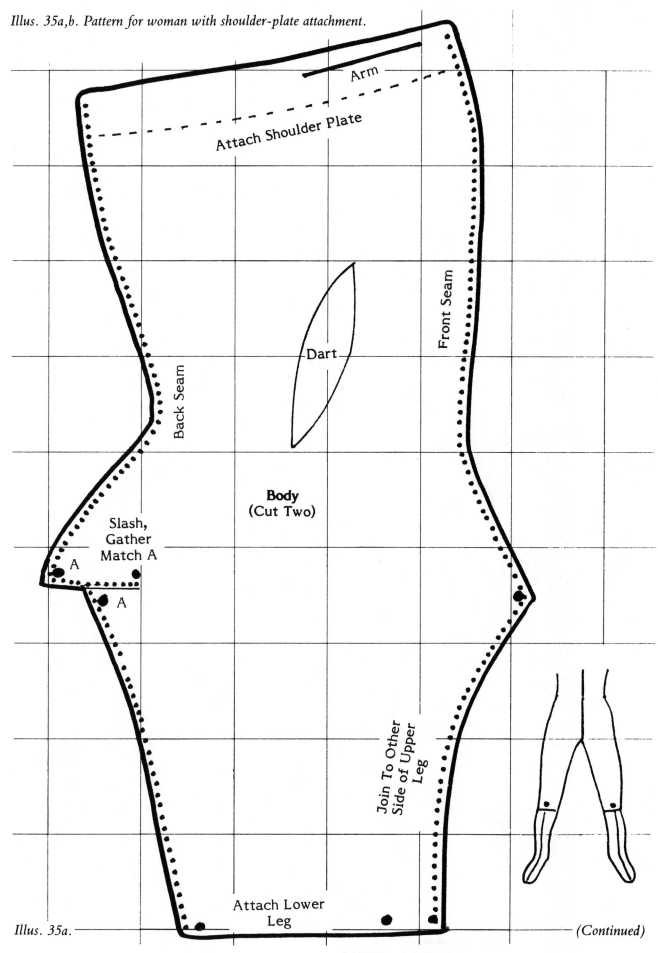

Illus. 35a,b. Pattern for woman with shoulder-plate attachment.

Arm

Attach Shoulder Plate

Front Seam

Dart

Back Seam

Body
(Cut Two)

Slash,
Gather
Match A

A

A

Join To Other
Side of Upper
Leg

Attach Lower
Leg

Illus. 35a.

(Continued)

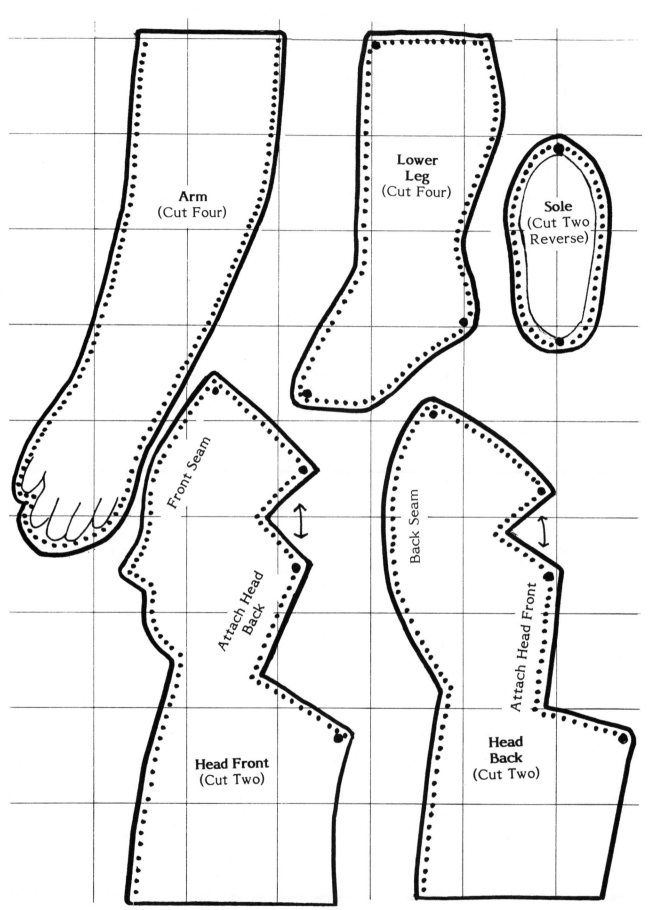

Arm
(Cut Four)

Lower Leg
(Cut Four)

Sole
(Cut Two
Reverse)

Front Seam

Attach Head Back

Back Seam

Attach Head Front

Head Front
(Cut Two)

Head Back
(Cut Two)

Illus. 36. Lenci-style doll (body without a head).

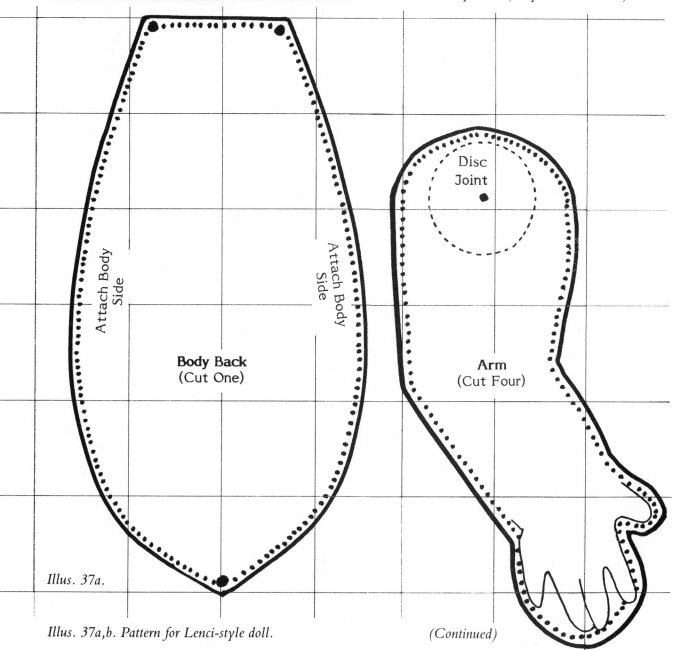

Attach Body Side

Attach Body Side

Body Back
(Cut One)

Disc Joint

Arm
(Cut Four)

Illus. 37a.

Illus. 37a,b. Pattern for Lenci-style doll.

(Continued)

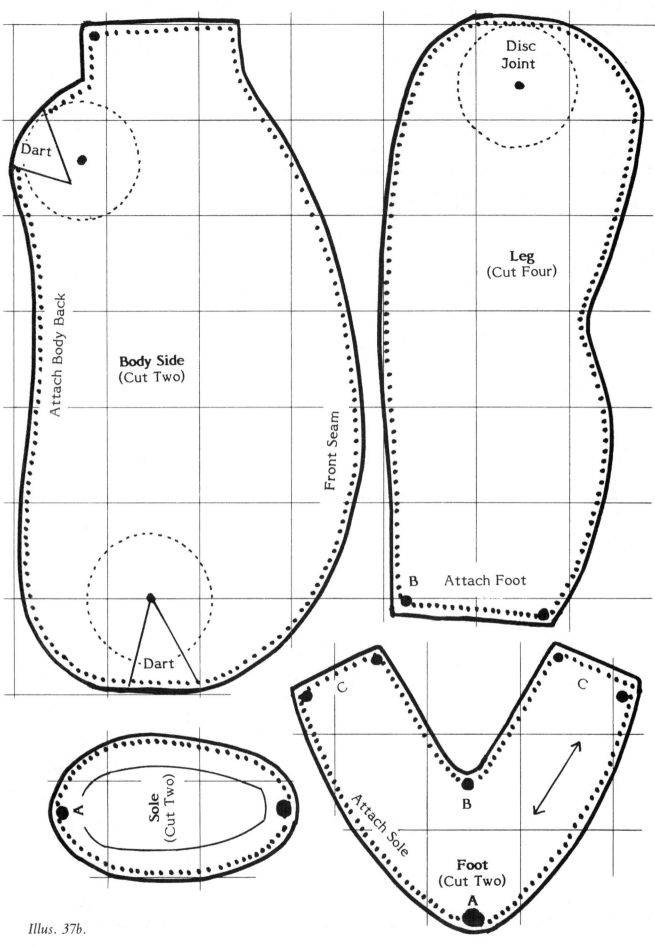

Dart

Attach Body Back

Body Side
(Cut Two)

Front Seam

Dart

Sole
(Cut Two)

A

Disc
Joint

Leg
(Cut Four)

B   Attach Foot

C

C

Attach Sole

B

Foot
(Cut Two)

A

Illus. 37b.

3 Sculpting

SCULPTURED DOLL

Whereas cloth dolls, which are made from patterns and then cut, sewn, and stuffed, achieve dimensionality from darts, gathers, contoured seams, and creative stuffing, sculptured dolls are shaped in an entirely different way. There are no patterns for sculpting. Instead, as the artist, you shape according to your own creative instincts. Aided by artists' principles of proportion and with some practice, you can learn the skill even if you are the most uncertain beginner. Sculpting is not for professionals only. Beginners can make a simple idea effective. The ballerina (Color Illus. 1A), whose Styrofoam-ball head has only a shaped and glued-on nose, is a sculptured doll.

An important alternative kind of dollmaking is making reproductions of antique dolls in porcelain. It is so important an aspect of the craft of dollmaking that many volumes have been written on that specific subject. Just as the reproduction-doll maker might benefit from some of the information that follows, the original-doll maker would do well to study the methods used in making reproductions, to examine the catalogues available from various suppliers, and to learn the skills. Many ceramics shops and recreation centers offer classes in porcelain-doll crafting. Any aspiring doll artist should certainly consider taking such a class. Mastery of that difficult material is basic to success. A wide variety of plaster moulds is available. Already fired parts, composition bodies, wigs, blown-glass eyes, and all of the materials and tools necessary for pursuit of this craft can be purchased commercially. Check your Yellow Pages telephone directory or the *Doll Reader* for supply sources.

MECHANICAL DESIGN

Before undertaking any sculpture and in fact before beginning any doll, be sure you have a clear concept of the project—its theme, required materials, and the manner in which the doll will be assembled (its mechanical design). Since handmade dolls rely on the skills of the craft as it was practiced until the beginning of this century, the study of the construction of old dolls and their reproductions will provide a wealth of information. Catalogues published by doll-parts suppliers and mould makers are valuable sources of information.

Some options in mechanical design and the manner in which the sculpture must be modified to permit the assembly are presented below.

Soft Sculpture

The entire doll can be a soft sculpture assembled only by sewing, or the soft-sculptured head can be affixed to a variety of unorthodox bodies made of cans, wood, plastic soap bottles, or cloth bodies stuffed with sand. There must be some mode of attachment, and it can be accomplished by using penetrating wires or by covering the proposed body with a cloth skin to which the head is sewn. The head can be glued to a dowel to serve as a handle and as a neck in the final assembly. A wire armature can be used.

Cloth Doll with Hardened Mask

A hardened mask will transform any cloth doll. The mask is cloth covered and can either be appliquéd in place or be used as part of the structure of the head (Illus. 38). The grain lines of the covering fabric, if they are obvious, must be straight for a quality appearance. The mask may be handcrafted or purchased plastic.

Hard Head and Hard Limbs with Cloth Body or Wire Armature Body

Usually, the head, hands, and portions of the arms are sculptured of a hard material and are attached to a cloth body or armature. Any suitable cloth torso pattern can be used, but the cloth arms and legs must be redesigned to accommodate the hard-sculptured parts. Be sure that all the appendages are securely attached. Design the limbs with a flange and a groove so that the fabric can be fastened by gluing and tying; pierce the limbs with several holes so they can be sewn on or fastened with the wire-and-button arrangement familiar to antique doll collectors. The limbs can also be hollowed or punctured by the wire of the armature, which is glued securely in place (Illus. 39).

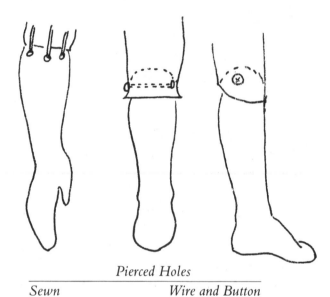

Pierced Holes

Sewn   Wire and Button

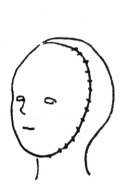

Appliquéd Mask

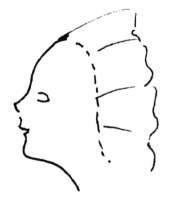

Mask as Part of the Head Construction

 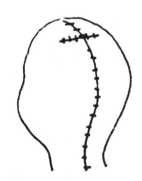 

Flange and Groove   *Punctured by Armature*
Tied and Glued

Illus. 38. Mask attachment.   *Illus. 39. Attachments for sculptured limb.*

Make the head with a flange and groove so that it, too, can be glued and tied securely in place. Pierce a head on a shoulder plate with four holes so that it can be sewn and glued to the cloth body (Illus. 40).

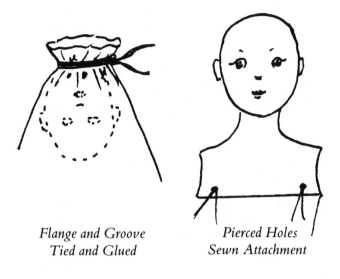

Flange and Groove   *Pierced Holes*
Tied and Glued   *Sewn Attachment*

Illus. 40. Attachments for sculptured head.

In addition, give the head mobility by using a separate head-and-shoulder-plate mechanism. Fashion the neck and the hole in the chest plate so that they fit perfectly. When the head is secured in place it rotates in the socket of the chest

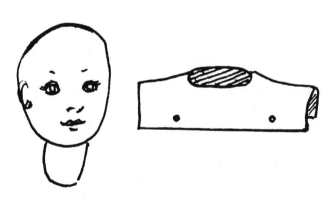

Illus. 41. Rotating-head mechanism.

plate. Join the shoulder plate and the head (Illus. 41) in a number of innovative ways: (a) glue wooden dowels into both the head and the chest plate and connect with a tight elastic; (b) insert a **V**-shaped rigid wire into the neck and attach with a tight elastic to a dowel glued in the chest plate; (c) insert flat wooden buttons into the

neck and in the neck opening (Illus. 42). Use buttons that are too large to pass through the holes and hold together with a bolt and nut. (Wooden buttons are sold by doll-parts suppliers.)

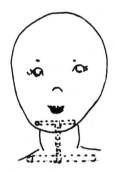

Two Dowels with Elastic

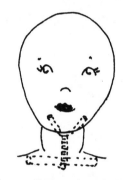

Wire and Dowel with Elastic

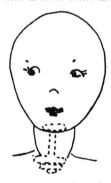

Wooden Buttons with Bolt and Nut

Illus. 42. Three methods for attaching a head to a shoulder plate.

Entire Doll Is Hard

The hard doll is usually modelled in separate parts, all designed to fit together properly upon completion. Some doll artists, however, model the doll as a complete figure and cut the parts off and modify them for the mould-making process.

The completed doll is finally assembled by stringing with a taut elastic of appropriate thickness. Stringing elastic, sold by the doll-parts manufacturers, is available in diameters from 1/16 inch to 1/4 inch, and the selection depends upon the size of the doll. In order to string, fasten hooks into the hollowed portion of the limbs and in the neck if the head is separate from the body. Use a water-based putty, such as Durham's, to hold the **S**-shaped hooks, which can be either purchased or cut from heavy paper clips and properly bent. First, fill the hollow limb with shredded paper to prevent the putty from falling inside. Let the putty dry for several days until it is rock-hard before stringing the doll. Two lengths of elastic are usually used: one to attach the arms and the second to attach the legs and the head. Pull each piece of stringing elastic taut and tie with a square knot by reaching inside through the holes in the torso (Illus. 43).

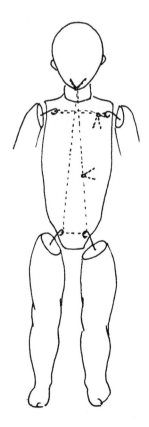

Illus. 43. Stringing the hard doll.

A nice finishing touch when stringing a porcelain doll is to line the surface of those pieces that fit together with a tiny strip of leather taken from a white kid glove or with a piece of mole-skin (sold in pharmacies for foot care). This cushions the grinding of the two hard parts and eliminates the unpleasant grating sound.

SCULPTURE PROCESS

Sculpture is the art of shaping material, and in dollmaking any material that the artist finds shapeable is worthy of consideration. Each material has its own characteristic and relies on a modification of the sculpture technique for use. Therefore, experience is the only teacher. Some guiding principles, however, apply to some degree to all materials. Although the following discussion is more appropriate for clay or plasteline, the concepts are universal.

The sculpture process begins after you decide what age, sex, size, and characteristics the finished doll will have. Basic to the sculpture is the consideration of proportion, as discussed in chapter 1 (page 11). The options are endless. The doll can be an idealized figure, a realistic portrait, or a fashion figure designed primarily for costuming; it can be an expression of any time period or state of the human condition. Options also include anthropomorphized animals or mythical creatures. Popular subjects are storytelling groups placed in an appropriate setting.

The human form is complex, and although some artists can rely on their imagination, most should use a model. A photograph is helpful, but another doll is better. By using a doll as a model not only to observe but also to "feel," you can obtain a better concept of dimension. The depths of the depressions and the heights of the projections make the anatomical structure easier to recreate. There is little danger that the resultant sculpture will be a copy; portraits are difficult to render.

In modelling the head, use an armature as the central core to support the material (Illus. 44). Paper, wire, Styrofoam, or even a light bulb can be used to support the weight of the material, to provide a convenient handle, or to give initial shape. For large clay or plasteline pieces, use a modelling stand with flexible wire (available at some art supply shops) (Illus. 45). Arms and legs do not often require an armature unless they are unusually large.

To begin, press small wads of material onto the armature to build the contour of the piece.

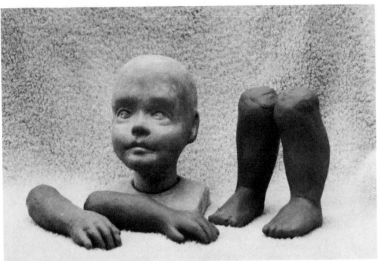

Illus. 47. Completed water-clay sculpture.

ling tools and a small wire-end tool for cutting and shaving. An X-acto knife is invaluable. You will learn by experience which tools suit best.

The following section covers two classifications of materials: those that produce one-of-a-kind dolls, such as Polyform (Sculpey), papier-mâché, air-hardening clay, and fabric used in soft sculpture; and those intermediate sculpture materials from which moulds are made, such as water clay and plasteline.

ONE-OF-A-KIND HARD SCULPTURES

New craft materials appear on the market regularly. Those that seem to be the most useful now to the dollmaker are Polyform, papier-mâché and a version of papier-mâché, as well as air-hardening clay; none of which need extraordinary equipment. All of them are used more often to shape only the head or the head and parts of the limbs that are fastened to cloth bodies or wire armatures.

Polyform (Sculpey and Super Sculpey)

Polyform is a modelling compound. Sculpey and Super Sculpey are made of the same product as Polyform but sold under separate trade names. It is the most versatile of the commercial materials. It corresponds to FIMO, which is made in Europe. Polyform is a plastic compound, which is stiff as it is taken from the box but softened into usable consistency when warmed in the hand. To harden, bake it in a home oven (or toaster oven for small pieces) at 325 °Fahrenheit from 10 to 30 minutes, depend-

ing upon the thickness of the piece. It does not shrink and can be sanded after baking, or carved or supplemented with additional material and rebaked. It is available in craft shops in 1- and 2-pound packages.

You can model Polyform with your fingers or plastic or wooden modelling tools. Cut it with scissors or carve it with a knife. Large pieces can be modelled on an armature of aluminum foil, Styrofoam, or even a light bulb (if a mould is to be made). Use acrylic paints and coat several times to cover. The disadvantages of the material are that it is heavy and thus works best if the piece is hollowed out; it is not always uniform in quality and is difficult to smooth.

Use Polyform to make one-of-a-kind dolls in which the head, arms, and lower legs are fastened to a cloth body or wire armature (Color Illus. 1B). Eyes and teeth can be inserted if the materials selected will withstand the baking temperature. A solid piece tends to be heavy; therefore the top of the head is generally hollowed to be fitted with a cloth pate. Polyform is also used for making press moulds and is especially useful for making models to be cast in plaster.

Papier-mâché and a Variation, Sculptamold

Papier-mâché is a cellulose product that can be made at home with newspapers. However, a cleaner material is available in craft shops. It needs only the addition of water to be usable. A variation of papier-mâché is Sculptamold paper-based modelling material. It is papier-mâché

Illus. 44. Styrofoam armature; sculptured nose and papier-mâché construction of Ballerina and Flower Girl.

Add material in small coils and wads and work and smooth as the sculptured piece takes shape. Keep in mind the planes and masses of the head. Think of it first as a skull and then continue to add material to shape the flesh and skin folds. When the head shape is complete, mark the longitudinal and latitudinal centers of the head and locate the features so that they are in correct proportion and position for the subject rendered. Keep certain shapes in mind: the head is an oval, and the jaw is a projection. The eyes are orbs fitted into deeply recessed sockets. The eyelids, both top and bottom, cover portions of the round eyeball. Shape the lids with rolls of material placed in position and work smoothly.

Illus. 45. Modelling stand and wire armature for working with water clay.

The nose protrudes as a bony ridge and finish[ed] with fleshy wings applied to the sculpture [as] wads of material. Form the mouth according t[o] the bony structure of the jaw and modify ac[c]ording to the muscles and flesh of the lips. T[o] form the lips, apply rolls of the material an[d] work it in place. Begin the ears by placing coil[s] of material in the space between the jawbon[e] and the skull; then shape. The sculpture is no[t] considered finished until it is perfect. All irregularities will be transferred to the mould (Illus. 46).

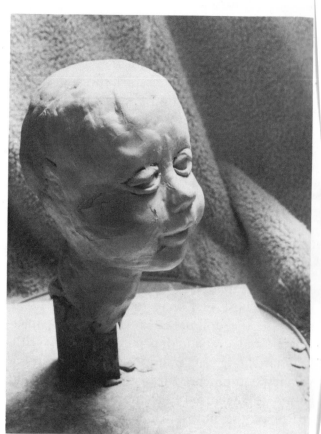

Illus. 46. Work in progress: water clay.

Although both sides of a human face are not identical, they are symmetrical. As the work progresses, inspect the reverse image of the sculpture in a mirror to help eliminate errors. Work evenly all over the piece and constantly examine all surfaces—upside down as well as sideways. It is good practice not to concentrat[e] and attempt to perfect any single detail but t[o] work evenly on the entire piece (Illus. 47).

Your best tools are your fingers. Occasionall[y] you will also use a few simple wooden mode[l]

with the addition of plaster to give the material a white color and faster hardening time.

Mix papier-mâché in bulk and keep it for extended periods of time in a tightly closed container in the refrigerator. It dries to a hard, uneven, grey surface, which is usually further processed to make it more useful in dollmaking. It does not yield fine detail and is best used to suggest simple contours or rugged features. It can be air dried or dried in a warm oven and is light in weight when completely finished.

A practical method is to apply the papier-mâché paste to an armature of wadded paper or a Styrofoam ball fitted with a rolled cardboard "neck." When the papier-mâché sculpture is complete and thoroughly dry, spread a layer of gesso (available where art supplies are sold) or acrylic latex spackling paste (available from hardware dealers) on the surface to provide a smoother, white surface. After sanding, coat the surface with acrylic varnish as an undercoat and paint with acrylic paints.

Sculptamold is somewhat easier to model and dries more quickly. It is not completely smooth when dry and requires sanding or coating, as does papier-mâché. Heads made of either of these materials may also be covered by the body fabric and may be given a swivel neck for more detail. Simplicity of the concept gives the doll its charm.

Air-hardening Clay

Air-hardening clay is coarser and less sensitive than ordinary water clay. However, its usefulness lies in the fact that it can be shaped and hardened for one-of-a-kind dolls. Use standard modelling techniques. This clay can be perfected by carving and sanding when dry. Details are sharpened with a wet paint brush during the modelling process. Air-hardened clay produces a heavy piece, which can be lightened by hollowing or by using a light armature. It dries in a few days depending upon weather conditions and can be painted with acrylic paints.

It is critical in the use of any water clay to recognize the proper working consistency. Clay should feel like putty and be readily shaped without sticking to the fingers. Place dry and crumbly clay in a plastic bag to which some water has been added. When the water has been absorbed, "wedge" or "knead" the clay to make it pliable. Let sticky clay air-dry for a while. Wrap a sculpture in progress in a wet cloth; spray it with water or enclose it in plastic to keep it moist.

Insert plastic or glass eyes into the head during the sculpture process. Because the finished piece is heavy, it is best used with a cloth body that is stuffed with sawdust or weighted so that balance is maintained.

ONE-OF-A-KIND SOFT SCULPTURES

Soft sculptures, although made of cloth, require a sculpture technique for their creation and for this reason are included with other dissimilar materials. A wide variety of lifelike faces can be created. It does require a bit of practice for success and control. Employ the same techniques to make soft-sculptured heads and bodies. The latter are much simpler in concept.

Heads for Soft Sculpture

Materials and tools. Few materials are required for soft sculptures, and the tools are simply a selection of needles. Generally, the head is made with a center core (a small Styrofoam ball, for example) around which batting is wrapped.

Use polyester filling material in batt form or surgical cotton packaged in rolls for the padding. Cotton is better for small heads because it tends to retain a firmer shape, but it is more difficult to penetrate with a needle and tends to lump. A combination of the two materials is best—one for masses and the other for fine detail.

Make the skin out of sheer nylon panty hose. Don't use the superstretch variety. Any color sheer stocking produces a startlingly lifelike skin tone when pulled over the white padding. Nylon hose are fragile, and inadvertent runs are a "battle casualty." Skaters' or dancers' tights are available in appropriate colors and are excellent second choices. They do not run easily and provide the correct amount of stretch, but transparency and skin-tone quality are sacrificed.

Use a single strand of ordinary sewing thread that closely matches the doll's skin color. To make stitches through the head, you'll need a long, or milliners', needle, and for the tiny shaping stitches, you'll need a short, or quilters', needle.

Finishing materials include buttons, plastic or glass eyes, and embroidery thread for the eyebrows. To add color, dust on ordinary cheek blush and eye shadow or draw with felt-tipped pens and acrylic paints. Make wigs out of anything at all. Use false eyelashes for a comic effect. In short, anything that defines the character of the doll is usable. When the head is complete apply acrylic craft spray to give the head firmness and protection.

Technique. To shape, pull tiny stitches with the needle and thread to indent or to extend the padding material. Reinforce these tiny stitches inconspicuously to maintain the tension. Basically, there are only two effects: indentation and extension. To indent for the eyes, nostrils, and mouth, place a small stitch firmly on the front and pull the thread through to the back of the piece until the correct tension is achieved. Repeat the stitch and hold it by overcasting.

The second effect—extension—is done by pinching the surface to raise it and holding the pinch with tiny stitches made from one side to another. The bridge of the nose, the eyelids, and the lips are made in this manner. By practising, you will soon learn to apply the correct amount of tension. The trick is to accomplish the shaping with as few visible stitches as possible, so that the skin seems to be mysteriously contoured.

Process. To form the foundation, cover a Styrofoam ball with polyester or surgical cotton until the padding is soft and smooth. The first step is to decide the age of the subject, which determines the structure and proportions of the face. To begin, envision the planes of the face (Illus. 48) and place the padding where required. The forehead protrudes, the eye sockets indent, the nose is triangular and extends, as do the chin and lips. (The child has an exaggerated indentation at eye level and protruding, round cheeks. This structure can be emphasized by tying a thread around the head at eye level to compress the padding.) Exaggerate the shaping because the skin will flatten it. The padding will remain in position but can be tacked or glued in place,

and the nose can be made more firm by saturating the stuffing material with white glue. But if you use the glue, be sure to stitch the nose before the glue dries. When the shape of the face hints of a finished contour, pull the skin over it. A dowel can be inserted into the head to serve as a neck, a handle, or the means of attachment to the body.

Illus. 48. Areas for foundation padding for soft sculpture.

Pull the skin tightly over the foundation padding and permanently fasten it on the top and bottom before you begin the needle sculpture. Since some measure of control is relinquished when both the top and bottom of the head are closed, however, another method is possible. You can pin the skin firmly in place on the back of the head but leave the top and bottom open; it will be closed as the work progresses. In this way, tiny pieces of batting can be pushed under the skin to augment the shaping and make corrections. When the top of the face is complete, close the skin on the crown and develop the bottom of the face. Closure is completed when the sculpture is finished. Draw the skin to the back so that the closure will be hidden by the wig. It is possible to move bits of stuffing with the point of the needle inserted under the skin even after closure.

To sew, review the two basic shaping stitches in Technique, above. Additionally, another stitch is useful. Make a single loop of thread and catch it with an invisible overcast stitch at the critical shaping points. This loop stitch is used to define the fleshy wings of the nostril, to locate a plump chin, and to shape parts of the body.

The first step is to locate properly the eyes and the bridge of the nose. Pinch the bridge and pull the needle from side to side using only two or three stitches on each side, reinforcing them so that they will hold. A child's nose is only slightly indented; a comic nose could have magnificent proportions. Now that the bridge is defined, make indentations for the nostrils by inserting the needle into the proper place and pulling hard through the top of the head where the stitches are anchored. It is best not to cut the thread but to design a strategy for carrying the thread invisibly through the padding to the next step. Then make the fleshy wings of the nose by using a looped thread and anchoring it identically on both sides (Illus. 49).

Make indentations for eye sockets by first pulling the thread tightly through the head and then stitching an eye shape. For an adult, pinches at both the top and bottom of the eye, sewn with tiny stitches to retain the fold, form eyelids. A recess can be made, into which beads or glass eyes are inserted. For a convincing eyelid, fold a small piece of the skin material and appliqué or glue it over the top of the protruding eye.

To fashion a smile, pull the corners towards the top of the head or make a frown by pulling the corners towards the underchin. Augment lips by pushing tiny wads of cotton under the skin and maintaining the protrusion with tiny stitches. An old face might have tuck wrinkles or loop lines on either side of the mouth. Ears can be appliquéd in position. Portraits of children require the least amount of stitching and are therefore the most difficult to render. The more sewing you do, the older the face becomes.

The finished face is brought to life by the coloring processes previously mentioned (page 36). Soft sculpture is pure inspiration with many surprises. It is only with a lot of experience that the outcome can be predicted.

Bodies for Soft Sculpture

Soft-sculptured heads are used in a variety of ways. A tiny, endearing soft-sculptured head can be fastened to a jewelry pin and worn on a lapel. They can be placed in a corked jar to render a bizarre joke. More often the doll artist requires an appropriate body. To make a soft-sculptured body, use one large tube of fabric for the body and four appropriate size tubes for limbs. The dimensions are important, and the details are stitched or tied in place. These bodies are most often exaggerated for comic effects and do not have human proportions. A wired cookie-cutter pattern can be effectively attached as shown in Illus. 50 and Color Illus. 1C.

The needle-sculptured head can also be attached to an unorthodox body, such as a can, block of wood, or plastic bottle, or it can be placed on a wire armature. A cloth body filled with sand produces a comic character. Horticultural sand, which is coarse and dust free, can be purchased in plant nurseries. Bottle or can bodies (Illus. 51, Color Illus. 1E) must be weighted so that they will not topple over. A small amount of quick-set cement or ordinary plaster also serves well. To make arms and legs, insert lengths of 14- or 16-gauge copper wire through the body and twist both ends into a mitten shape. Pad and cover the shape with skin. Cover the attachment with the sleeve. Perhaps

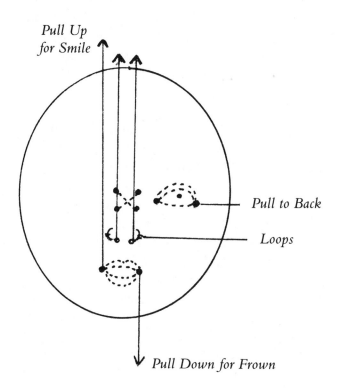

Illus. 49. Stitching diagram for a soft sculpture.

the most versatile body is made on a wire arma-ture. Complete instructions, as well as an inno-vative technique for making flexible, dipped hands, appear on pages 72–73.

Illus. 50. Needle sculpture with cookie-cutter body.

Illus. 51. Soft-sculptured people with unorthodox bodies. Old man is filled with sand, musician's body is a soft-drink can, and maid's body is a soap bottle.

INTERMEDIATE MATERIALS— MAKING MODELS FOR MOULDS

Plasteline (or plastiline) and water clay are used only for sculptures that serve as models for mak-ing moulds and for this reason are classified as intermediate materials. Moulds are necessary for shaping the fluid materials—porcelain and low-fired ceramics, composition, and melted wax. The process of plaster mould making is discussed in chapter 4 (page 75). Because plaster faithfully reproduces the surface of the model, you must consider any model unfinished if it is not perfectly smooth and exactly rendered. Those who do not wish to make sculptures can obtain excellent results by using a plastic doll as the model for the mould.

Plasteline

Plasteline is an oil-based, nonhardening clay sold in 2-pound blocks in various colors and in four degrees of hardness. The medium-firm or hard varieties serve best as model material. Plas-teline, a sensitive material, is worked much like clay but is not shaped with the use of water. It softens as it is warmed, and when used in mould making, it is left in the mould until the mould has cooled. You shape it with your fingers and with simple wooden and wire tools, as you would shape water clay. Use a wire armature on a modelling stand if the piece is large.

Water Clay

Model doll parts with fine-grained clay without grog (gritty particles) in a light color. It is sold in 25-pound slabs in ceramic supply houses and art supply shops. A light color is recommended because it makes the detail easier to see. Like air-hardening clay, water clay is best worked when it is the consistency of putty. It can be processed to this point by adding water, by "wedging" (or kneading), or by air drying. Keep unused clay in an air-tight container. Keep work in progress moist by spraying it with water or wrapping it in moist cloths and plastic. Fingers are the best tools but can be supplemented with any wooden or wire-end tools for cutting and gouging and reaching inaccessible places. For sharpening de-tails and smoothing, use wet paint brushes. Modelling stands are helpful.

Work the clay by adding coils and wads and

by gouging and cutting. Smooth and work the material into the desired contours. The most important consideration in modelling for mould making is to avoid the creation of undercuts. An undercut is any contour that fixes the model in the plaster mould so that it cannot be withdrawn. Always widen contours and recesses, therefore, towards the outer edge. Details sometimes must be eliminated to avoid the undercut but can later be recarved. (In making the mould, turn the model to eliminate the undercut or use a multiple-part mould.) This problem is discussed further in the following chapter (page 78). Let the clay sculpture dry to "leather" before making the mould. If, however, the piece becomes bone dry, apply a moisture barrier of thinned shellac.

EXISTING DOLLS USED AS MODELS FOR MOULDS

Plastic dolls can serve as models for making plaster moulds, which, in turn, are to be used for casting composition, porcelain, and wax. Because the plastic doll was originally made in a mould, all undercut problems have been eliminated, and the plastic presents a smooth and nonporous surface for the plaster. Examine the doll part for parting lines, which mark sections of the mould. Block the orifices with clay or plasteline to prevent the plaster from flowing inside the hollow parts. Plastic is flexible and is easily withdrawn from the plaster mould (Illus. 52 and Color Illus. 1C).

The amateur mould maker should never attempt to use an antique doll as a model for a plaster mould. Too frequently, the model must be broken in order to remove it from the plaster, especially if the parting line has not been accurately located. But with a little care, porcelain and plastic dolls can be used for making some varieties of press moulds and masks.

WASTE MOULDS

Advanced artists who work in porcelain consider the first model to be only a "work out" and the first mould a "waste mould." After the model is made and cast, they make the first reproduction in wax and then recarve and perfect it. The second plaster mould is cast from the wax, which will serve as the production mould.

WIRE–ARMATURE BODIES

There are two ways to make a wire armature, which serves as the skeleton inside a cloth body. The purpose is to strengthen the body construction and enable the doll to be posed, giving it an aspect of motion.

Simple Armature

The simple armature is merely an elaboration on the wiring technique previously discussed. A simple skeleton is made of wire and inserted into the cloth body for reinforcement. Another method is to use a wooden dowel or clothespin as a spine and to insert 14- or 16-gauge copper wires through holes appropriately drilled. Brass and galvanized wire are less flexible but can be used. Or insert a rigid piece cut from a clothes hanger if appropriate (Illus. 53).

Illus. 52. Porcelain body made by using a plastic doll as a model. Note shrinkage of about 20%.

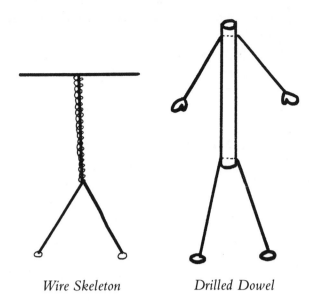

Wire Skeleton   Drilled Dowel

Illus. 53. Simple wire armatures.

Sculptured Body with Wrapped Armature

The wire armature forms the foundation for a body that is sculptured with batting and wrapped to maintain the shaping (Illus. 54).

Method. Shape lengths of 14- or 16-gauge florist wire (rigid, cloth covered wire) into a foundation. The configuration in Illus. 54 is only one of many that can be invented. The size of the doll and the proportions of the legs and arms to the body length will depend upon the concept you have in mind. See Illus. 1–7 for assistance. The armature may be complete or allow for attachment of partial legs and hands.

Bend the wires and wrap the frame with florist tape to hold it firmly. Cardboard feet can be glued in place so that the framework is balanced when standing. Wrap the frame with layers of

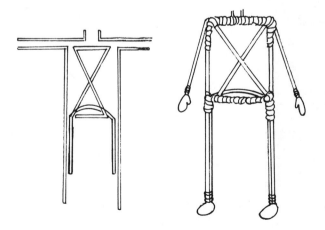

Illus. 54. Wire-armature configuration.

polyester batting to shape it, adding pieces of the padding to achieve the desired contours. Add layers of filling where fullness is desired: the buttocks, bosom, tummy for a child, and shapely legs (with rounded calves and thin ankles) (Illus. 55 and Front Cover). When the cover of soft padding appears to be satisfactory, hold it firmly in place by wrapping. Any loosely woven fabric cut in about 1-inch-wide strips can be used for wrapping. Gauze bandage is handy, and a self-adhering gauze bandage is best. One such product is Gauztex, available from most pharmacies. Additional padding and wrapping may be applied until the figure is correct and a smooth body achieved. This body can be cov-

Illus. 55. Soft-sculptured head with wrapped armature body.

ered with a knit fabric skin, cut cookie-cutter style, but since the doll will be costumed, it is not necessary to do so.

ALTERNATIVE METHODS FOR MAKING HANDS

Hands are the most difficult part of the body to fashion if some degree of realism is desired. The easiest way is to make a wire loop in a mitten shape with pipe cleaners and cover it with a padding and a "skin." Hands are most often sculptured of the hard material of the head, or they can be made by dipping.

Dipped Hands

To make dipped hands, shape five pipe cleaners, wrap them to add "flesh," dip to coat, and paint with acrylic paints. Sculpt and then pose them. All of the fingers are fashioned in the same way:

- Cut a small square of self-adhering bandage (Gauztex, 1-inch wide). Lay diagonally on the wire. Fold the corner over the end of the wire and wrap the bandage to form a finger.
- Cut a second small square of bandage and begin the wrapping below the finger tip to add more "flesh." The thumb requires a third wrapping.
- When the five fingers have been completed, bunch them together to form a hand, observing the relative lengths of the fingers and the inward position of the thumb. Note the left and right hand differentiation.
- To shape the palm, place a thin layer of padding at the base of the fingers. Hold it with a wrapping of the bandage. Pose the fingers.
- Dip the hand in Mod Podge, which is a sealer and glue. Suspend the hand over the jar to drip off.
- When the first dipping is dry, make two more dippings, but this time do it in gesso, thinned to flowing consistency.
- When dry, apply a thin coating of acrylic latex spackling paste, available from any hardware dealer, to give the hand an absolutely smooth surface.
- Sand the spackling when hard and paint the hand with acrylic paints (Color Illus. 1E).

4 Moulds

The mould is, in effect, the pattern for the sculptured doll. It enables the artist to duplicate and adapt as well as to use fluid materials—porcelain, low-fired ceramics, composition, and melted wax—in order to create dolls. There are various types of moulds that serve these functions: the press mould is used to duplicate, the plaster drain mould is used for shaping the fluid materials, and the ceramic mould as well as existing dolls are used for fabricating masks.

PRESS MOULDS

The press mould is made of Polyform modelling compound (Sculpey) into which an impression of the face (or any other part) of a hard doll or appropriate figurine can be made. This mould is used with Polyform to construct a one-of-a-kind doll, which might be classified as an adaptation. A press mould is used to make identical copies of the artist's original Polyform doll.

Making the Press Mould

Warm and knead a lump of Polyform in your hand. When it is soft, roll it on a smooth surface with a rolling pin to ensure one absolutely blemish-free surface. Press this surface hard against the desired model, which has been dusted lightly with talcum powder to serve as a parting agent and to prevent sticking. When an accurate image has been registered, bake the impression at 325 °F until hard. This is a female, or concave, mould.

Using the Press Mould

Smooth and press a larger lump of softened Polyform modelling compound firmly into the mould, which will yield a face. Shape the back of the head and add a neck and shoulder plate, if desired. Lift the Polyform carefully from the mould with an upward motion so the surface is not scuffed. The face should be perfectly reproduced. Repeat the process until a good image is obtained. The sculpture is completed by adding coils to form ears and by perfecting the shaping. To eliminate some of the weight of the material, hollow the crown of the head and the shoulder plate. Cut grooves or holes to attach to the body. Bake the piece at 325 °F. Then cool, paint, and assemble it as desired (Illus. 56).

MASK MOULDS

Adding a dimensional face mask to a cloth doll produces an amazing transformation. Cover the mask with the same knit fabric of the body and either appliqué it on the cloth head or make part of the head construction. Paint it with acrylic paints. The mask can be purchased or made by the artist herself.

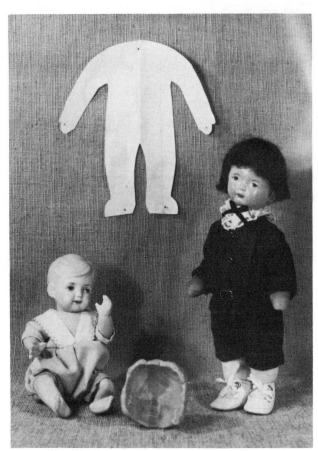

Illus. 56. Polyform head made with Polyform press mould. Taken from a porcelain doll.

Purchased Plastic Masks

Plastic masks can be purchased at craft shops and from doll-parts suppliers. When covered with the fabric of the body, the entire aspect of the mask is changed (Color Illus. 2B). An excellent adhesive to fasten the fabric covering is the aerosol mounting glue available in photography shops. One such brand is Craft Mount, which, when used according to directions, does not bleed through the fabric. With care, eye sockets can be cut out of the mask, and plastic or glass eyes cemented in place. Cut the cloth cover to accommodate the insertion of the eye.

Cutting is most easily done by piercing the center of the eye opening and slashing an **X** into the outer corners. When the opening is sufficiently large, trim the eye shape. Fit the fabric meticulously into the eye shape and fasten the cut edges with tiny dots of white glue. The cut edge may be rimmed with white glue to prevent fraying; this must be done with great care. It is important also to keep the grain lines of the cover fabric straight.

Finished Dolls as Moulds

Use existent dolls (not antiques, please!) not only for fabricating plaster drain moulds, but also for fashioning masks directly of felt or plaster-impregnated gauze that is to be covered with cloth.

Felt. Soak felt of an appropriate color and as close to 100 percent wool as possible in warm water and pull it tightly over the face of a plastic or ceramic doll. Carefully fit it into the recesses of the eyes and mouth. Held with a rubber band to dry, it will image the contours of the doll which was used. When the mask is dry, trim and stiffen it by applying many coats of water-thinned white glue to the back or by spraying several times with an acrylic craft spray. This mask can also be used to cover the plaster-impregnated mask.

Plaster-impregnated gauze. An excellent stiffened mask can be made with plaster-impregnated gauze, which is used for various medical and podiatric purposes. One such brand is Plaster Splints, which is available from medical supply companies. It is sold in rolls of various widths, but the 6-inch width is best. Thinly coat the face of an existent porcelain or plastic doll with petroleum jelly or cold cream to prevent the material from sticking. Cut two squares of the plaster gauze. Soak them in cold water until the plaster softens. Lay the pieces on the face on the bias, one over another, and press firmly on the contours. After the cloth has been smoothed, rub it gently with a moistened finger to spread the plaster, making an even surface.

When the mask is completely dry, remove it, trim to shape, and cover with the cloth of the doll's body. An opaque knit fabric works best as a cover, or a felt mask made from the same doll can be glued to the plaster cloth mask for extra stiffening.

One-Part Plaster Mould

Any plaster mould may be used to fashion composition masks or to shape ceramic materials which, when fired and glazed, serve as moulds for masks. In the first instance, the flexible composition slip is cast directly into the concave plaster mould, and when dry the mask is trimmed and covered with fabric. In the second case, low-fired ceramic material is cast into the plaster mould. When the greenware is dry, it is fired in a kiln, glazed, and refired. The end result is a convex, or male, ceramic mould used as any existing doll would be used to make a mask.

Original Clay Sculpture Used as a Mask Mould

Instead of using an existing doll as a mould for a mask, model an original sculpture of water clay. The piece is hollowed and left until bone dry. It is fired, glazed, and refired, and the end result is a convex, ceramic-mask mould (Color Illus. 3B) to be used as any existing doll is used. Any ceramic shop can assist with this project.

MAKING PLASTER DRAIN MOULDS

Plaster drain moulds are necessary for shaping fluid materials: porcelain, low-fired ceramic, composition, and melted wax. The absorbent quality of the plaster, which draws off the water as well as the ready shapeability of the plaster, makes it the ideal mould material. It is called a drain mould because the liquid is poured inside the mould through an opening, or gate, and when a thin shell has formed against the plaster, the excess material is drained off. Wax, because of its light weight, is the only fluid material that need not be drained and can be used as a solid piece. The drain mould for making dolls can be a one-, two-, three-, or four-part mould, depending upon its function. More complicated shapes require multiple-part moulds.

Commercial moulds are virtually trouble-free and are available for making reproduction dolls and some original artists' dolls. Amateur mould makers don't usually produce such perfect moulds. But serviceable moulds of original sculptures can be made even though the art of mould making is not easily learned. Although homemade moulds do not last as long as commercial moulds and the casts usually require some recarving of the greenware, it is a skill well worth learning. Should you finally produce a doll of commercial value, you can make a professional mould and use it as a production mould. Commercial mould makers live in almost every large community.

Required Materials and Tools

Model   Use a clay, wax, Polyform, or plasteline sculpture, or a plastic doll.

Water clay   Used for the "claying up"

Plaster   USG #1 Casting plaster (manufactured by United States Gypsum)

Parting agent   Mould release soap or tincture of green soap

Orange shellac   For sealing dry clay models and other porous surfaces; thinned with denatured alcohol.

Denatured alcohol   For thinning the shellac and cleaning the brushes. These materials and some of the tools are available from any ceramics supplier.

Four casting boards   Boards with Formica face on one side; average usable size is 12″ × 6″, depending upon the size of the pieces usually cast. Use these for the sides of the mould box.

Work board   With Formica face approximately 12″ × 12″. Use these for the base of mould box.

C-clamps   Four needed

Putty knife or steel scraper

Coarse metal files   For cutting gates and edges; other plaster-working tools.

Ruler and T square

Assorted soft brushes

Two natural sponges   For applying separator (parting agent)

Scale   That can be adjusted to zero

Variety of plastic buckets   One to serve as a sink, and a smaller bucket for mixing the plaster

Scoop   For plaster

Three-minute timer

Coin or tool   For cutting "keys"

Wooden wedge

Large enamel spoon

Optional Materials and Tools (not necessary for small batches)

Fixed-speed electric mixer with rubber disc on the shaft   A hand drill used at 2400 r.p.m. is a good substitute. For small batches, use a stick or your hand for mixing.

Model   Parts of the doll are best made in small, separate moulds because large moulds are heavy and difficult to handle; the head, body, and chest plate each have separate moulds; the legs are paired as are the arms, each in its own mould.

The major concern in fashioning the model is to avoid undercuts. An undercut is a defect in the design of the model, which serves to fasten the model in the plaster so that it cannot be withdrawn (Illus. 57). To avoid undercuts, design the model so that indentations and contours widen in the direction of the outer surface. Sometimes, the model may be turned, or a more accurate parting line can be selected to eliminate undercuts. Complicated designs require multiple-part moulds. The head of a doll is usually a two- or three-part mould.

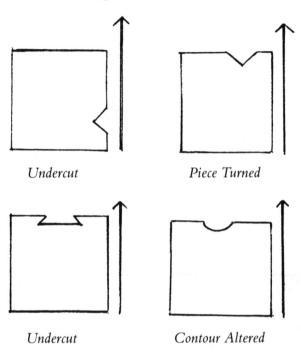

Undercut　　　　*Piece Turned*

Undercut　　　　*Contour Altered*

Illus. 57. Undercuts.

The parting line, or the line that marks the sections of the mould, is an important determination. It is the widest portion of the model so selected that the sections of the mould can be drawn off without obstruction in their separate directions. The parting line is determined both visually and by experience. Mark the line on the model with an indelible marker.

Water clay　For blocking off areas of the model that are to be reserved for a subsequent portion of the mould. This process is called claying up or clay build-up. Place the clay build-up exactly to the parting line. Since it serves to shape the surface of the mould it must be done carefully. Clay is also used to seal the seams of the casting, or mould, box.

Plaster　For mould making, use USG #1 Casting plaster. It is sold only in 100-pound bags (which are depleted faster than one would expect). Plaster absorbs moisture from the air and must be kept in a tightly sealed, plastic garbage can and stored in a dry area. Plaster has a limited shelf life, and for best results, it should not be kept much longer than 90 days. Humidity and temperature not only affect its shelf life, but also the speed at which it sets up.

The mixture of plaster is designated in terms of the ratio of the number of parts of water to be added to 100 parts of plaster as defined by weight. USG #1 is recommended for use at a ratio of 70. This means that as determined by weight, 70 parts of water are to be added to 100 parts of plaster. Table 2 indicates the amount of plaster that must be added to specific quantities of water to produce this ratio. Also, in Table 3 is

TABLE 2
RATIO OF WATER TO PLASTER

For USG #1 Casting plaster the recommended ratio is 70 parts of water to 100 parts of plaster by weight.

	Water		Plaster			
Amount	Weight		Weight		Total Weight of Mixture	
	lbs.	oz.	lbs.	oz.	lbs.	oz.
1 pint	1	02	1	10	2	12
1 quart	2	05	3	04	5	09
1½ quarts	3	07	4	14	8	05
2 quarts	4	10	6	08	11	02
2½ quarts	5	12	8	02	13	14
3 quarts	6	15	9	12	16	11

Note: Add a bit more plaster on unusually damp days.

TABLE 3
CALCULATION OF THE AMOUNT OF PLASTER MIXTURE NEEDED

To determine approximate cubic-inch measurement, multiply the length by the width by the estimated depth of the section of the mould to be cast. Example: A 4 × 5 × 3-inch mould section = 60 cubic inches. A quart of water would be ample.

Cubic Inches	Water To Be Used (70 Ratio)
Less than 40	1 pint
40 to 80	1 quart
81 to 120	1½ quarts
121 to 160	2 quarts
161 to 200	2½ quarts
201 to 240	3 quarts

It is always best to err on the side of mixing too much plaster, because augmenting a cast weakens the seam.

a system for calculating the total amount of plaster that must be mixed to make the required mould.

<u>Parting agent</u>   To form a slick film that prevents the plaster from adhering to the work surfaces, the mould box, and model, use a parting agent, or separator. Mould soap is available from a ceramics supplier, and tincture of green soap can be purchased in any pharmacy.

<u>Orange shellac or varnish</u>   Orange shellac, thinned to about half strength with denatured alcohol (sold in paint stores), is used for sealing porous surfaces of the model. Orange shellac has a limited shelf life. Be sure to note the expiration date printed on the top of the can. Brushes are cleaned with the alcohol. Thin the varnish with mineral spirits or paint thinner.

<u>Casting boards</u>   Make casting boards for box sides and the work board from scrap laminate, available from shops that fashion counter tops. The sink cutout, which has flanges already glued to the edge, is the portion required for the casting boards. The Formica face provides a nonstick surface for the plaster work. Dimensions given are for a medium size board, but you should make boards according to the size of the models you plan to work on. An alternative to casting boards is waxed or plastic-coated, half-gallon milk cartons. Since the sides of the plastic cartons are flexible, squarer moulds are made if a small frame is fashioned to fit around the carton segment to hold it firmly. Tape together pieces of 3-inch wood moulding, flat side inside. Trim the milk carton to make a 1-inch or 1½-inch tray into which the clay-up is made. Insert the shallow tray into another portion of the carton, which is cut so that the walls will extend about 1½ inches over the highest part of the model. This forms the mould box (Illus. 58). Make the second cast in another trimmed carton. It is important that the corners are always sealed with an uncut portion of the carton. This stopgap method is not the best, but it is an adequate substitute in an emergency when working small pieces.

<u>C-clamps</u>   Fasten the mould boards tightly together with C-clamps to erect the box.

<u>Scale</u>   A scale is required for accurate mixing methods. The scale must have ounce designations and a reset that permits a zero reset.

<u>Timer</u>   A 3-minute timer is most useful.

<u>Electric mixer</u>   A fixed-speed mixer is useful if large batches of plaster are to be mixed. An electric hand drill with a rubber disc on the shaft can be substituted. Hand mixing is adequate for small amounts (less than 12 pounds) of mixture.

<u>Brushes</u>   Various soft brushes are useful for brushing out moulds, applying the parting agent, and painting the shellac. Natural sponges are also used to apply mould-release soap.

<u>Plastic buckets</u>   Plastic buckets are used for mixing plaster because they can be bent to flick off particles of hardened plaster. The mixing bucket should be small for easy handling.

<u>Rubber bands</u>   Available from ceramic supply sources, special rubber bands hold the mould halves together so that they will not warp. They are also used in the casting process.

Miscellaneous: You will need a ruler or **T** square for squaring off the clay-up, a scoop for lifting plaster, and a large wooden spoon or dowel for mixing the plaster.

Working Space

Working with plaster is at best a messy job. Be sure to guard against spills. Water is necessary for mixing and clean-up, but since plaster should never be put down an ordinary drain, use a large bucket of water as a sink. Discard the plaster residue into the bucket of water and let it separate. When the plaster has settled to the bottom, drain off the water. A large garbage can

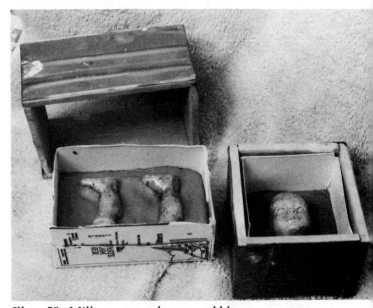

Illus. 58. Milk carton used as a mould box.

is essential; newspapers and some clean rags are needed to keep the work surface clean.

Procedure

Preparing the model. Paint the model if it has a porous surface with two or three coats of thinned shellac. Brush on the shellac and leave it to dry without rebrushing, which will cause lifting and wrinkling. Bone-dry clay or unglazed ceramic surfaces must be shellacked. Plasteline is sometimes coated depending upon its degree of hardness, but wax, Polyform, and plastic do not need shellacking.

Marking the parting line. The parting line reveals where sections of the mould are joined. It must be carefully designated to permit the sections of the mould to be drawn off the model. For the head, the parting line of the two-part drain mould is across the crown, along the outer ridge of the ears, along the widest portion of the jaw or cheeks, and along the widest portion of the neck and shoulders. The parting line of the arm extends along the sides. Turn the arm in such a way that the bent fingers will not cause undercuts. Position the legs with the toes pointing outwards, which would make the parting line through the middle of the front and back. An alternative is to make the leg mould an **L** shape with the toes pointing directly upwards. The parting line is then along the sides of the legs, along each side of the foot, and across the toe (Illus. 59–60). The shoulder plate mould is a one-piece mould, bowl shaped. The parting line

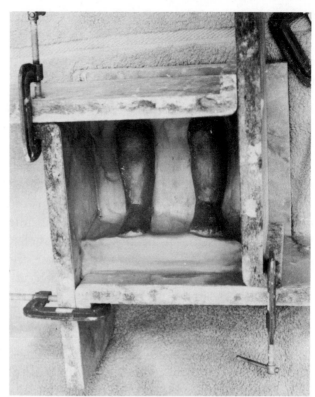

Illus. 60. Clay-up for legs in a mould box.

on the body is at the widest portion of the sides at the neck and crotch.

If the model has complicated irregularities, such as a bulbous nose or exaggerated chin, a three-part mould is required so that the portions of the mould may be drawn off to the sides. This is not more difficult but requires one more step in the mould-making process. Mark the parting line with an indelible-ink pen.

Claying-up. Put a pad of clay about 1½ inches thick on the work board and position the model on the clay. Build the clay to the marked parting line, making certain that all portions of the parting line are touched with a flat surface of the clay. To do this, roll and press tiny wads into the small irregular recesses and smooth the entire surface. It is an important step and must be done meticulously. The surface of the clay forms the surface of the mould. When the pad is entirely smooth and almost leather hard, measure and trim it carefully so that the corners are square and there is at least 1 inch or 1½ inches of clay around the model. A porous model is shellacked again. Models of other materials may be brushed with shellac at the point where the clay touches the surfaces.

Illus. 59. Clay-up for head in a mould box.

Applying the parting agent. Wipe the parting agent, mould soap, or tincture of green soap on the surface of the mould boards as well as on the model and the hardened surface of the clay-up. It can be brushed on or applied with a sponge, but any bubbles left on the surface will form an irregular surface on the mould. Brush on the parting agent several times; let dry in between coats.

Erecting the casting boards. Place the casting boards around the clay pad and tightly clamp them with C-clamps. Press the pad of clay tightly against the boards and seal the outside seams of the board with clay to prevent the fluid plaster from escaping.

Mixing the plaster. The manner in which the plaster is mixed and handled is critical to the success of the mould. Tables 2 and 3 show how to calculate the amount of plaster that needs to be mixed as well as the amounts of water and plaster necessary for the required quantity. The ratio, as explained, is 70 parts water to 100 parts plaster, as recommended for USG #1 Casting plaster.

Always add plaster to the water; never add water to the plaster. The water must be clean and at room temperature. A simple method is to measure the specified amount of water and put it in the mixing bucket. Put the bucket on a scale and place the reset at zero. Sprinkle the plaster—never dump it—into the water until the scale indicates the required weight of the plaster. (If a scale is not available, an alternative, but less accurate, way is to sprinkle plaster into some water until a mound rises above the surface of the water.) Let this mixture rest, or "slake," for exactly three minutes, then begin the mixing. Mix the plaster vigorously but without beating air into it. This can be done with an electric mixer, as described, with a large spoon or stick, or by inserting your hand and agitating your fingers under the surface of the mixture. Vigorous mixing hastens the setup time. Three minutes is sufficient time for the mixing.

Pouring the plaster. The plaster is by this time beginning to "cream." Pour it slowly in a steady stream into the corner of the mould box to prevent the formation of bubbles on the surface of the model. Fill the mould to 1½ inches over the highest point of the model. Gently nudge the table on which the mould box rests to help air bubbles escape from the plaster mixture. Begin cleanup immediately.

Removing the casting boards. When the plaster has begun to set, smooth the top surface and remove the excess water. Remove the casting boards when the plaster, which first becomes warm to the touch, has recooled. Turn the mould upside down and remove the clay. This reveals the surface of the first half of the cast. Carefully clean the model and the plaster of any particles of clay. Remove with alcohol any shellac that has adhered to the plaster. A one-part mould is now complete.

Cutting the keys. Cut shallow circles, or "keys," into the surface of the first cast by twisting a coin into the soft plaster. This indentation is filled with plaster when the second half of the mould is made, and it forms a knob. The two parts of the mould can then be perfectly aligned by fitting the keys together. Two or three keys at opposite ends of the mould are sufficient.

Making corrections. At this point you might want to correct the first cast if it has any obvious irregularities. The second cast will fit the alteration. Make corrections by sanding or carving. This critical operation should be done meticulously.

Preparing for the second cast; a two-part mould. The procedure is identical for preparing to pour the second half of the mould as it was for the first pour. Treat the back of the model and the plaster surface with the parting agent. Erect the mould boards again, seal the seams with clay, and make and pour the second plaster mixture.

Removing the casting boards. Let the plaster set until it cools and remove the boards. Trim the outside of the mould and bevel the corners to remove sharp edges.

Opening the mould. Let the mould cool completely before attempting the opening. The mould is opened by inserting a wooden wedge into the seam and tapping gently with a hammer. As soon as the first seam releases, turn the mould and use the wedge again to release the other seam.

Removing the model and cutting the gate. The model will be easy to remove if the parting-line determination was accurate, there were no undercuts, and the parting agent was used properly. A flexible model will be easiest to remove; however, many times the model must be broken to remove it from the mould. This is the reason why amateur mould makers should not use antique dolls.

Locate the necessary pour hole, or gate, and carve it out of each side of the mould. To enlarge and smooth the hole, use a coarse file and sandpaper. The gate is usually at the neck of a body mould, at the neck of a head mould, and at the tops of partial arms and legs. Place a gate at the inner part of the upper arms and legs if the entire limb has been cast. In this instance the "spare," or excess, casting material that remains in the gate can be reshaped and pierced for stringing the doll.

Preparing the third cast, a three-part mould. For models with irregular features that would serve as undercuts and prevent the withdrawal of the two-part mould, a three-part mould is best. In casting a three-part mould, cast the face in two parts with the halves divided along the ridge of the nose. An additional claying up is required to block off one half of the face (Illus. 61).

Roll a thin strip of clay with a rolling pin. Trim it and lay the ribbon of clay on edge from forehead to neck on the model. This forms the surface of the second portion of the mould. Support the barrier in a vertical position with wads of clay so that it will remain erect. The second plaster cast covers half the face. Cut the keys and pour the final portion after the clay barrier has been removed.

Drying the mould. Fit together each completed mould and band them with heavy rubber bands sold for this express purpose. Let them dry on a flat surface to prevent warpage. The mould may

Illus. 61. Clay-up for three-part mould.

be dried in the oven if the temperature can be accurately regulated so as not to exceed 120 °F. Don't use the mould until it is thoroughly dry, which could take a week or more, depending upon the weather and the size of the mould.

What Went Wrong?

Plaster mould making is not easy for beginners. Not only must instructions be followed meticulously, but often only experience can provide the appropriate timing for each step. Plaster is temperamental and responds to temperature and humidity in different ways.

Suggestions:

• Make small moulds at first. Large ones are heavy and difficult to handle. Large amounts of plaster are hard to mix by hand.

• Don't attempt any more than one mould at a time at first. The critical moments require prompt attention.

• Keep the work surface clean and uncluttered.

• Don't be in too much of a hurry to open the mould. Plaster is fragile before it has completely set. Let the mould thoroughly cool.

Common problems:

• Plaster is lumpy and sets up too slowly or too quickly even when the directions have been followed. This may indicate that the water or the plaster is contaminated. New plaster is required, or cleaner water needs to be used.

- Pinholes in the cast indicate that air has been introduced or that there was improper slaking or mixing.
- Rough surface on the mould indicates that the plaster was poured too soon after mixing. The larger particles have settled out.

Rectifying errors:

- Irregularities in the image can be sanded and carved as long as the surfaces that seal the mould are not altered.
- Mend pinholes by carving out the crumbled plaster. Place a small amount of water in the palm of your hand and sprinkle plaster into it. Mix to a thick paste and patch the hole. If the mould has dried, the hole must be moistened.
- A broken mould can be glued with Duco cement for one more cast.

The plaster mould cannot be used interchangeably for most composition materials and for porcelain. Composition leaves a residue that hinders the absorption of water in the porcelain slip. Wax casting requires a wet mould, which shortens the life of the plaster mould.

5 Ceramics and Wax

USING A PLASTER DRAIN MOULD

A plaster drain mould, when thoroughly dried, is ready to be used in the shaping of the fluid materials. Porcelain, low-fired ceramics, composition, and melted wax are all cast in the plaster drain mould although each is handled somewhat differently according to its inherent qualities. Experience is the best teacher. In general, prepare and pour the liquid material into the tightly banded moulds. As the fluid is absorbed into the plaster and the level of the material drops, pour more into the gate of the mould. When a thin shell begins to form on the inside of the mould, pour out the excess fluid, let the mould drain, and let the cast dry to the "leather" stage. When the cast is firm, open the mould, remove the cast pieces, process them, and let them dry for further polishing. (The process for wax shaping does not depend upon absorption of fluid.)

CASTING CERAMIC MATERIALS, ESPECIALLY PORCELAIN

Earthenware, which is subsequently glazed, and porcelain are the two ceramic products used in dollmaking. The latter is far more important and more universally usable to dollmakers. The discussion, then, will deal with the use of porcelain although earthenware is handled in much the same way. The major differences are the variation in firing temperatures and the painting of the fired material.

Buy porcelain slip in appropriate skin colors in gallon containers. Various other colors of porcelain are also available in pint sizes. The names for skin colors vary from brand to brand, but there are four basic colors plus pure white: light ivory, a rosier shade similar to the one used for antique dolls, an oriental shade, and brown. Porcelain slips can be mixed to achieve intermediate shades, but mixing is difficult and must be done thoroughly to prevent marble effects.

Preparing the Slip

The slip as it comes from the container is most often too thick for use. Thin it by stirring thoroughly. If thick residues remain in the container after mixing, pour the slip into another plastic container and scrape the bottom. Then the mixing is complete. If necessary, use a deflocculant (sodium silicate) to thin the slip. It is sold by ceramics shops. Be sure to follow the directions closely. Water can also be used. Stir the slip and strain it through a plastic strainer until it reaches casting consistency—which is similar to heavy, sweet cream—without lumps, bubbles, or hard particles. The slip thickens as it stands, so you must stir and strain it before each cast. The introduction of air bubbles results in pinholes in the cast. Slip must be kept free of rust or metallic particles. Using plastic containers and lids as well as a plastic strainer will prevent the appearance of black metallic spots in the fired porcelain.

Tools

In addition to the completed plaster moulds and a quantity of slip, you will need the following:
Rubber bands sold for banding moulds
Large glass mixing bowl to use for draining the moulds
Cake rack to fit over the mixing bowl (stainless steel is best)
Plastic pitcher, at least 1-quart capacity
Plastic strainer with plastic mesh (do not use metal)
Wooden dowel or wooden spoon for mixing
Rubber spatula
Clean water
Box or tray of shredded newspaper for drying the casts
Container for scraps of hardened slip
Variety of clean-up tools, including a greenware saw available in any ceramics shop and an X-acto knife; also various finger saws, and a blunt stylus
An assortment of brushes, including a fine-tipped brush

Procedure

Pouring the slip. Don't use the slip if it varies from optimum pouring consistency. Brush the mould surface to remove dust and dried particles. If the mould is bone-dry, moisten it slightly by passing the image side quickly under a water faucet. Eliminate this step after the first pour. For easy handling, pour a quantity of slip from the gallon container into the plastic pitcher. Fit the mould pieces together and band them tightly. Pour the slip steadily and continuously into the mould through the pour hole, or gate. It is usually best to pour into the face side of the mould to force air bubbles out. Interruption in the pouring produces rings in the surface of the cast. When the material appears to recede, pour more slip into the gate. From the gate you will be able to see a thin shell forming on the inner walls of the mould. The beauty of porcelain is its

translucency, which requires that the walls be thin. However, the beginner should let a thicker wall form since it will make a less fragile piece. When the cast appears to be from 2/16 to 3/16 inch thick, empty the mould and invert it on the cake rack placed over the glass bowl to drain. A blockage in the draining can be opened by carefully prodding or blowing with a plastic drinking straw.

Leave the emptied mould inverted and tilted on the work surface to complete the draining. When the cast appears to be hardening, clean the edges of the gate neatly and let the mould rest. It usually takes about 20 minutes for the cast to achieve sufficient solidity for the mould to be opened, but the time varies depending on the wetness of the mould, atmospheric conditions, and temperature of the work place.

Opening the mould and removing the cast. When the cast is sufficiently dry it will begin to shrink from the inner walls of the mould. You can open the mould easily at this time. Difficulty in opening the mould indicates that the cast is still too wet, and forcing it will result in splitting the cast. To open the mould, place it on the table and lift one half of it directly upward to avoid scuffing. The cast remains in one part of the mould. At this point much of the cleaning and recarving can be done, even when the cast is almost too soft to handle. With a sharp knife trim the spare (or the extra part remaining in the pour hole); remove the larger seams; and cut out the crown of the head, the openings in the body for the fitting of arms and legs, and the eye sockets. Cut the eyes by first making a puncture in the middle of the eye, cutting X-shaped slashes that reach almost to the corners and then completing the cutting. Smooth the cut edges and taper with a wet paint brush. Pierce holes and resculpture to sharpen details; rim the eyelids with deeper grooves, redefine the nostrils, add contour to the lips, and emphasize other fine details with both ceramic tools and a wet paint brush. Many antique dolls were made with intaglio eyes, that is, with pupils carved or incised. This recarving and shaping can be done now, if desired.

Augmenting the cast. Slip is liquid clay and can be used as creatively as though it were in solid form. With some skill, you can dot on additional slip to accentuate knuckles, to shape eyelids, to bend and reposition fingers, and to mend minor breaks. The innovative use of porcelain slip in other colors is also possible. White porcelain can be applied and carved to form teeth; matt-finished black or brown can be brushed onto feet to eliminate painting shoes. Let colored porcelain slip dry to a soft clay consistency and roll it in coils for hair decoration, shoe bands, or any other detail. The ceramist uses porcelain slip to make flowers and in lace draping. There is no reason why some of these skills cannot find their way into dollmaking.

Drying the cast. Place the cast in a box of shredded paper. It will take several days to dry, depending upon the weather.

Preparing for subsequent casts. After the first cast has been removed, clean the mould of all particles of slip that might have adhered to the plaster. Carefully brush the mould, reband it, and it is ready for the second pour. If the mould has leaked, leave the residue of hardened slip as a plug to prevent the second cast from leaking out. Use the mould for four or five casts before leaving it to dry. Drying the mould by overusing or overheating it in the oven results in premature disintegration of the mould.

After the first cast, which is frequently not successful because the mould is not at its optimum dampness, the problems inherent in the mould become apparent. With experience some recarving and smoothing of the image in the mould is possible. Always band the moulds to prevent warping. Scraps of slip can be reused if they are reconstituted, strained, and well mixed.

Cleaning the greenware. When the cast is chalky dry, the balance of the cleaning and smoothing is done. Greenware is fragile and must be handled with extreme care. Trim seams with clean-up knives and smooth with any of the following: nylon net, a piece of hosiery, paper towels and tissues, wads of cotton, and finally with a piece of fine silk. Begin with the most abrasive material and end with a soft polish. If glass eyes are to be set, bevel the inside surface of the cut edge to enable the glass eye to fit closely. Use an eye

sizer, wrapped in a piece of nylon stocking, as a buffer. Shape the eye sockets carefully so that they are identical in size and shape. Smooth the cut edges with a wet paint brush. To clean and shape the fingers use finger saws. Check and modify parts that are to be fitted together and smooth the edges.

It is at this point that many doll artists do a considerable amount of recarving. It is possible to alter each cast sufficiently so that, unless one looks closely, each appears to have been made of a different mould. If you recarve extensively, you can give the cast a pre-fire at cone 018 (see Table 4) or a china fire. This renders the piece a little less fragile, but it is still soft enough to be carved. If you choose this technique fire the finished cast on completion as you would any other porcelain cast.

The dust that results from the cleaning of porcelain greenware can be troublesome. Disposable surgical masks can be worn to filter the air. Also, much of the dust can be captured by holding the pieces as they are cleaned over a damp towel laid onto the work surface.

TABLE 4
CONE NUMBERS

019—018—010—015	1—2—3—4—5—6—7	
China	Low-fired	High-fired
Paint	Ceramics	Porcelain
1386 °F	2185 °F	2300 °F

← ———————— HOTTER ————————→

Kiln

A high-fire kiln is required for bringing porcelain greenware to a vitreous state. It is also necessary in the painting process to mature the pigments. For the dollmaker who elects to work in porcelain, the purchase or convenient access to a kiln is required. Kilns are available in a variety of sizes and are fired either by gas or electricity. Operation is simple and safe.

A kiln is an oven, lined with insulating refractory brick, in which temperatures up to 2300 °F must be reached for porcelain firing. Since all kilns operate in slightly different ways, the manufacturers' instructions must be followed closely. In general, you should use a kiln whose controls are activated by pyrometric cones that melt at designated temperatures and serve to shut off the kiln when it has reached a selected temperature. Temperatures are described by cone numbers (see Table 4).

The length of time required for the firing depends upon the kiln, but in general the recommended porcelain fire is from eight to twelve hours. Some ceramists obtain satisfactory results from shorter firing times.

Thoroughly polish the first pieces cooled from the firing before the china painting. Scrub them with grit scrubbers or polish with an ordinary household cleanser until perfectly smooth. Note: the shrinkage in firing is approximately 20 percent. It is best, therefore, to design a soft body after the head and hard parts have been completed.

What Went Wrong?

Porcelain is the most difficult to handle of all the sculpting materials because it is the most fragile. Some common problems are as follows:

- Tiny black dots in the porcelain indicate underfiring. The piece can be refired at the correct temperature to eliminate the dots.
- Discoloration of small metal particles on the surface indicate that there has been some metallic contact either from rust on the slip jar lid or on the strainer that was used. Eliminate both.
- Cracking. Sometimes porcelain "remembers" where it was mended in the greenware state. Insufficient air space left around the pieces in the kiln can result in breakage.
- Collapse. Pieces collapse or distort if there is insufficient strength in the supporting walls. Use ceramic fibre to support larger pieces in the kiln.
- Distortion. Aluminum hydrate dusted on the kiln shelves prevents the piece from sticking as it shrinks in the firing.
- Ridges in the porcelain. The slip was not poured slowly and continuously. Interruption in the pouring process causes this problem.
- Blistering. Kiln temperature was too high.

CASTING COMPOSITION

There are now several different kinds of composition materials on the market with promise of more to come. They are fluid and require plaster moulds for shaping. The casts are either air-dried or dried in a home oven. The differences lie in the formulation of the composition. Some are latex-based, and at least one is a ceramic material. Some are used directly as sold; others must be mixed with another substance to constitute a workable material.

All are useful for making doll bodies, and it is for that purpose that they are sold. But because they are so convenient to use—they don't require a kiln—you can use an appropriate composition for hard portions of the doll, for the entire doll, for masks, and for accessories. The resultant product is light in weight and also makes excellent "wooden" shoes, musical instruments, little animals, and the like.

In general, although manufacturers' instructions vary, handle the materials as you would any other fluid materials: pour the slip into the plaster mould and then decant it; let the cast mature and open the mould. Clean the dried cast of unwanted seams and dry it. Composition casts are a little more difficult to clean than are porcelain casts. They can all be painted for a usable finish.

Several companies manufacture composition, and it can be found in retail shops and through catalogues worldwide. Be sure to check your Yellow Pages (telephone directory) for a supplier nearest you. Listed below are three different types of composition.

Air Cure Flexible Slip (Douglass and Sturgess Inc.). Latex, chemicals and fillers; shrinks 20–25 percent; uses dry, plaster moulds; is air- or oven-dried at 150 °F; painted with lacquer, tempera, or acrylic paints; excellent for casting masks.

Duncan Composition (Duncan Enterprises). Blend of clays and plastic; uses plaster moulds; dried in home oven at 350 °F; uses a primer for improving surface; painted with water-based stains.

Composition from Bec Dolls. Latex-based; requires a mixture of stabilizer and activator; uses plaster moulds; air-dried or dried in home oven at temperatures up to 160 °F; painted with latex- or rubber-based enamels.

WAX WORKS

Wax is the most neglected of all of the materials that can be used to make dolls. There being no "right" wax with which to work, you must experiment with various waxes and additives. To further complicate the matter, the compounds and blends sold commercially are trade secrets and not only vary by manufacturer, but also are given different names.

In keeping with the theme of this book, which suggests the use of only those materials that are readily available from commercial sources, I have included the waxes that candlemakers use and which are easily obtainable. The moulds used are plaster moulds. The serious wax worker may wish to explore original formulations and the use of RTV (room-temperature vulcanizing), or flexible-rubber, moulds. This information can be obtained from references included in the bibliography.

Types of Wax

Waxes are made from both organic and inorganic materials. Organic waxes include beeswax and various vegetable waxes, such as candelilla and carnauba, and also waxes derived from animal fats. Inorganic waxes made from petroleum, like paraffin and microcrystalline wax are used by candlemakers. (This is not the same as paraffin used in the kitchen.) Petroleum waxes are classified according to their melting point.

Paraffin: 125–130 °F low melting point
        140–145 °F medium melting point
        150–160 °F high melting point
Microcrystalline: 170 °F or more.
The higher the melting point, the harder the wax.

Additives

To alter the quality of paraffin, to give it color, hardness, and opacity, manufacturers introduce various additives into the mixture. Stearic acid, or stearine, is used to harden the wax and make it more opaque. Polyethylene crystals are more frequently used for the same purpose. These are sometimes called hardening or whitening crystals or opaque crystals. Special colorants are used for wax. They may be in powder or solid form and are used sparingly in producing a skin tone. Minute quantities of orange and variable amounts of brown result in good skin colors. A candle whitener or white colorant is used in generous quantity to add opacity to the wax. To prevent light fading, ultraviolet-light color stabilizer can be added. The manufacturers' directions give proper proportions for additives.

Preparing the Wax for Use

All waxes must be melted in order to use them. Wax is combustible and care must be taken. Never heat waxes beyond 300 °F. Always use a wax thermometer. A seamless melting vessel is required (an old coffee pot serves well). It is best to melt wax over an electric coil instead of over an open flame of a gas burner. For safety's sake, you can also melt the wax over water in an improvised double boiler. However, this method is not always feasible because the temperature of the wax cannot be raised beyond 200 °F over water (water boils at 212 °F). Some waxes and polyethylene crystals require a slightly higher temperature in order to melt.

To facilitate melting, break up the wax with a hammer into small pieces or shave it off. Introduce colorant and additives after the wax has melted. Add the color gradually, testing on a white dish to ascertain the hue when hardened. Wax may be reused but should be strained to remove any foreign particles. A cleansing tissue anchored with a few dots of hot wax serves as an excellent strainer.

Use of Wax in Dollmaking

Wax is used three ways in dollmaking:
1. Direct modelling. For this purpose a microcrystalline wax is available from a sculpture supply house. There is also tacky sculpture wax available in white and shaping wax of the candlemaker, both of which are also used for modelling. These waxes are compounds made to increase pliability. Add whatever skin colorant is appropriate.
2. Wax-over or dipped. Heads, legs, and arms of ceramic, papier-mâché, and composition can be dipped in melted wax to alter the surface quality. I suggest using a taper wax. To maintain maximum transparency don't introduce additives or color.
3. Shaped in moulds. A high-temperature melt wax is used for casting. You may wish to formulate an original compound but try these two formulas first. (a) One is a pre-

mium candle wax, which is a high-temperature melt paraffin. Most manufacturers have already added stearine or polystyrene crystals. To increase the opacity, add a white colorant in a quantity at least 1½ times the specified amount. Twice the indicated proportion might better produce the degree of opacity desired. Gradually add to this compound minute quantities of colorant to achieve the desired skin tone. (b) A wax with a melting point of 225 °F is available. Used for creating free-form designs when cast in water, it is extremely opaque. It is not a burning or candle wax and requires only the addition of color. It is more opaque and less glossy than the premium candle wax and requires an ultraviolet-light color stabilizer to prevent the color from fading.

Direct modelling. Melt and color the microcrystalline wax or shaping wax. Pour it onto an oiled cookie sheet. Lubricate the pan with vegetable oil or petroleum jelly. Roll, twist, and work small pieces with warm fingers. Moisten your fingers with water or petroleum jelly if the wax becomes sticky. Shape with your fingers and warmed metal tools.

Waxing-over or dipping. Dip the portion of the doll to be wax coated in one continuous movement into the hot, melted wax. For this reason it is necessary to use a container deep enough to receive the piece. Taper wax is melted and allowed to cool to 155°–160 °F. Dip the pieces in a continuous, turning motion and hold them so that any drip-off will occur where it is least visible. Dipping tends to dull the colors of the underpainting as well as to smooth the contours. A small head requires only one or possibly two dippings while a larger one could be dipped several times to achieve the required effect. If the first coating is allowed to cool for subsequent coats, the wax must be heated to about 200 °F to ensure adherence of the second or subsequent dips. Papier-mâché and composition are most frequently used in the waxing-over process.

Casting in plaster moulds. A plaster mould is immersed in cold water until it is saturated and ceases to bubble. Wipe the inner surface of the mould so no beads of moisture mar the image. Melt the wax, mix with appropriate additives, and add the colorant. Let it cool to about 190 °F or a little lower. Pour the wax against the gate of the banded mould in a continuous and steady stream. Tilt the mould and pour the wax into the face side of the mould to ensure a better cast. As in casting any other material, add more wax when the material in the mould appears to have receded. Leave a solid cast to harden. However, decant a hollow piece when the wall of hardened wax appears to be about ³⁄₁₆ to ¼ inch in thickness, depending upon the size of the piece. Place the banded mould in the refrigerator to mature the wax. Wait about an hour, depending upon the size of the cast. Open the mould and remove the piece when it is hard.

Finishing the Wax Piece

As with other cast materials, smooth the seam lines, remove the crown of the head if eyes are to be set, recarve and cut out the eyes, if desired. A warmed metal tool is the most satisfactory knife. Smooth surface irregularities with an abrasive piece of nylon netting. Buff to a shiny surface with a cloth that has been dipped in turpentine or paint thinner. Reinforcing the large, hollow head is conveniently accomplished with plaster-impregnated gauze. One such brand is Plaster Splints, which is available from medical supply retailers. Cut the gauze into small pieces, soak it in water until pliable, and fasten it against the inner wall of the head for added strength. Glass eyes can be inserted and glued in place and eyelashes fastened to the eyelids.

Artists' oil paints and acrylics are most often used for painting wax. Oil paints are mixed only with turpentine but still remain slow drying. Acrylics, since they are water based, adhere with some difficulty. The most effective paints for wax, although they are somewhat unusual for this application, are petroleum-based craft paints used to decorate models and trains. Two such paints are called Floquil-Polly S and Pactra 'Namel. Each is sold with its own specific brush cleaner. Ordinary paste blush works well for coloring the cheeks and is rubbed into the wax. Assemble the doll as you would any other.

6   Painting

At this point the doll lacks only its unique characterization. Will it be realistic or stylized? You can, of course, adopt any style—from antique, with conventional eyelashes and bold eyebrows, to contemporary, with shading and accentuated facial structure. In general, a simple style and clean, clear colors will render the best effects.

MEDIA

There is a wide choice of media for painting, which depends upon the material of the doll; soft-tipped pens, brush-on cosmetics, fabric paints, and crayons, petroleum-based craft paints, bisque stains, acrylics, and finally, china paints, which are used only on porcelain. As an alternative to painted eyes, blown-glass eyes can be used in any hollow head and also in needle sculpture. China painting, because it is a unique technique, is discussed in detail separately.

Soft-tipped Pens

Many kinds of soft-tipped pens are available for art, craft, and drafting purposes. The colors most useful for the dollmaker are brown, black, reds and pinks, and blues. Some of the pens are water soluble and others are permanent. They are wide or narrow tipped—the narrow being most useful. Use soft-tipped pens to color on wood, cloth, and papier-mâché and to accentu-ate any detail. Be sure to test the pen before using it so you can ascertain its characteristics; avoid a point that produces spreading or feathering.

It is easier to draw fine detail with a pen than to paint controlled lines. You can also use soft-tipped pens to transfer color, for instance to lightly color a child's mouth. If drawing contours would render the mouth too harsh, dab the color on your finger and transfer it to the lips for a softer effect. These pens are invaluable for coloring cut edges, such as on leather shoes and for hiding small errors in sewing.

Fabric Paints and Fabric Crayons

There are many kinds of fabric paints and crayons, and new ones are introduced constantly. All are worth investigation and experimentation. Fabric paints tend to be harsh in color but nevertheless might be chosen for some uses.

Petroleum-based Craft Paints

Petroleum-based craft paints are sold for models and trains. They render either a matt or gloss opaque finish in a variety of colors. A special thinner for mixing and for clean-up is required. These paints are suitable for areas where a solid, opaque, unshaded color is desired, such as shoes. Petroleum-based craft paints are not, of course, fired but can be used satisfactorily on porcelain when the parts have already been fired. These paints are most effective on wax since they dry quickly and are compatible with the oily surface. Two such products are Pactra 'Namel and Floquil-Polly S. When painting shoes, you can achieve a perfectly even edge by dipping the foot into the paint.

Ordinary Brush-on Cosmetics

As previously explained, you can color cloth dolls effectively with dry, brush-on cosmetics. Use cheek blush on face, knees, elbows, and hands; shade the eyes with green, brown, or blue eye shadow. If applied skillfully the brown shades contour the face, shape the nose, and accentuate the chin. Paste blush is an effective colorant on wax. Cosmetics are not permanent unless fixed with a coating of acrylic craft spray but can be reapplied when needed.

Bisque Stains

Bisque stains, which come in a wide variety of colors both opaque and transparent, are available from ceramics shops. They are not permanent on hard surfaces unless fixed with a special fixitive spray sold with the paints. They can be used on any surface that has some "tooth," or roughness to it, including porcelain. 'Bisque stains produce a bright, clear, painted look. The results most closely resemble the painting of commercial plastic dolls.

Acrylic Paints

Acrylic paints are the most versatile of the coloring media and have replaced artists' oils in dollmaking because they are easy to handle and quick to dry. Acrylics are water based and are easily cleaned up with water if done immediately. They are hard and water resistant when dry. Colors are readily mixable and are brilliant and clean. Acrylic paint adheres to wood, Polyform, papier-mâché, wax, and with some pretreatment will adhere to cloth, plaster, and some plastics. Mixed with water, acrylics make a transparent wash, and mixed with medium they are given an opaque finish, either gloss or matt. These paints can be applied over modelling paste, which is used to build detail and over

acrylic gesso, which primes and prepares a smooth painting surface. Addition of retardant slows the drying process. Acrylic paints are available in fluid form in crafts shops and in tubes of pure pigment. Either may be used in dollmaking, but pure pigment is less expensive and lets you mix colors and vary textures.

To paint on cloth, plaster, and some plastics, lay a base of the colorless medium wherever the paint is to be placed. Paint the details first with the invisible medium and let it dry. Then overpaint with the pigment. Use any soft bristle brush. The widest should be appropriate for the size of the piece to be painted, and the narrowest for delineating detail. Manufacturers designate width in different ways. The smallest, just a few tiny bristles wide, are usually numbered 6/0. A crow-quill pen can also be used.

Mixing the paints. A muffin tin or plastic ice cube tray makes a perfect palette for mixing large quantities of paint. Acrylics can be premixed and stored in tight jars. Mix and transfer the pigments with a palette knife. Mix the pigment with water for transparency and with acrylic medium (gloss or matt) for opacity, or with a mixture of both to obtain a flowing consistency. Several thin coats are better than a thick coat, which tends to chip. To lighten any color, add white. To darken and subdue a shade, add a touch of black.

An adequate palette for the doll artist is Titanium White; Mars Black; Burnt Sienna (brown); Cadmium Red, Light; Cadmium Yellow, Light; and Ultramarine Blue. A ruddy skin tone is achieved with Portrayt (Red Oxide).

Mixing flesh tones. There are four basic skin tones with a variety of intensities that are used in dollmaking. The following formulas must be mixed in the order of the steps indicated. The quantities of each color depend upon the effect desired. Therefore, be sure to add pigment in small increments.

Bright, rosy flesh tone:	1. Titanium White 2. Burnt Sienna 3. Cadmium Red, Light To dull the shade, add Mars Black

A light tan skin tone:	1. Titanium White
	2. Cadmium Yellow, Light
	3. Burnt Sienna
	To dull and darken the shade, add Mars Black
A dark, rosy skin tone:	1. Titanium White
	2. Burnt Sienna
	To dull and darken, add Mars Black
A ruddy skin tone:	1. Titanium White
	2. Portrayt (Red Oxide)

Blush and Shading

Blush and shading can be accomplished in two different ways: (1) Add minute amounts of the color of the blush or shading to the base skin tone and carefully feather it onto the piece, or (2) make a thin mixture of the pigment in water and "wash" it on the piece, taking care to blend the edges. Shading of the sides of the nose, the eye sockets, the jaw, and accentuation of the wrinkles is done with a deeper tone of the skin color.

Any number of layers of acrylic paint can be applied, but the undercoat must be thoroughly dry before you apply subsequent layers.

PAINTING THE FACE

The techniques used by the doll artist for painting the face are almost as varied as those used by the fine artist who paints portraits. Some doll artists can sometimes be identified by their style. You might find the following suggestions useful, but many variations are possible. The techniques that relate directly to the application of paint do not apply to china painting, which is a unique technique.

Painting the Eye

A doll's eyes are the most critical and difficult part to paint. They bring the face to life. A realistic rendition attempts to establish the roundness of the orb. Although commercial dolls' eyes are painted simply, you may want to render them more realistically. Human eyes are never identical, but you should try to make doll eyes the same in shape and size and in the direction of their gaze (Illus. 62). The pupils and irises should be perfect circles, but the eyelids cover a

portion of the orb. The pupils usually show a "catch light" (reflection of light).

The iris of an infant's eye appears to be larger in proportion to the white of the eye than that of

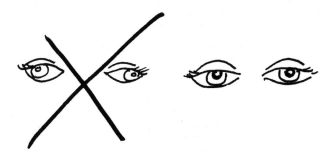

Illus. 62. Round iris and identical direction of the gaze.

an adult. Varying the amount of the iris, which is left visible, and changing the direction of the gaze are other ways to add expression to the face (Illus. 63).

The pupil of the eye is sometimes painted as a perfectly round, black circle. But if you want to add life and realism, show the pupil with a "catch light" by painting an incomplete circle or

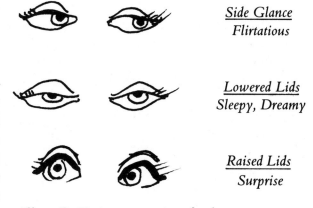

Side Glance
Flirtatious

Lowered Lids
Sleepy, Dreamy

Raised Lids
Surprise

Illus. 63. Various expressions for the eyes.

by dotting white paint in each pupil in corresponding locations (Illus. 64). A slightly off-center gaze is more expressive than a straight-on stare.

Eyes can be rendered more realistically by shading the iris from the outer rim to the pupil

Illus. 64. (Left) Pupil as a complete circle and (right) with a catch light.

and by drawing in the lines radiating from the pupil. To make blue eyes, blend various tones of blue; fleck brown with gold. You might want to outline the rim of the iris in black. Although pure black is most often used, you can create a softer effect by greying the black with minute amounts of white pigment (Illus. 65).

Illus. 65. To render a realistic eye, shade the pupil, draw lines that radiate from the pupil outwards, and then shade the white area.

Finishing the Eye

To give eyes more prominence, place a tiny red dot in the inner corners. To make eyes painted on a hard surface appear moist, apply a dot of colorless nail polish on the dried paint. You can suggest tears by judicious placement of dots of colorless nail polish on the cheeks.

The entire rim of the eye opening is sometimes blackened if glass eyes are to be set, as is the incised edge when the eye is painted. To suggest an antique style, draw fine slanted lines from the lid completely around the opening for eyelashes. Modern dolls are usually portrayed without eyelashes or with only the suggestion of a lash radiating from the outer corners of the eye. As with other uses of black for eye definition, a greyed black gives a softer effect.

Eyebrows

Eyebrows are easier to suggest than to draw sharply. Although it is difficult to make brows the same, try the following method. Paint the first brow and turn the doll upside down in order to copy it. Mistakes can be overpainted for a second attempt. A feathered brow is more realistic than a straight line. Eyebrows for children are best left undefined by painting and then blotting off the excess paint.

Nostrils

Nostrils can be suggested by two red dots, but this is optional.

Mouth

The mouth is usually light in color and soft in shape. When using acrylics, mix Cadmium Red, Light with Titanium White to produce a pleasant coral shade. A slightly darker tone of the same mixture is used to outline the center of the lips in order to give additional definition. A child's mouth is a gentle wing-shape, and the lower edge of the upper lip is accentuated. A gentle smudge is frequently used instead of a harsh outline. This is done by picking up some paint on the finger and dabbing it in place.

Practice makes perfect in painting. Before each painting session, make a trial-run. Close observation of painting techniques on other dolls is the best teacher. There are notable differences between the techniques used on antique porcelain dolls, composition dolls, plastic dolls, and those of various original doll artists.

CHINA PAINTING

China painting is the technique for coloring porcelain. Pigments are suspended in an oil medium and can be applied only in a single, thin layer at each painting session. The porcelain surface is prepared for the painting by coating with an almost invisible layer of oil, which permits the pigment to flow evenly. The oil, which burns off in the kiln, serves only to hold the pigment in place. The piece, once painted, is fired in the kiln to a china fire (cone 018 or 019), which effectively opens the pores of the porcelain to admit the pigment for permanent coloring.

To build layers of paint, you must fire in between each painting session. In general, the overlaying of color is done only to intensify the hue. Place the pigment only where it will be visible. For example, when painting an eye, you should apply the white of the eye only where it will be seen and not under the portion that is to be the iris and the pupil.

Many doll artists use a crow-quill pen instead of a brush when fine detail is desired. To use the pen, you must mix the china paint with pen oil to make it free-flowing. The pen oil makes the paint more difficult to control. You might want to try an alternative. Mix the dry pigment with a sugar solution or a soft drink made with sugar (a cola will do). The sugar mixture is used like ink—directly on the porcelain without any oil preparation. When this detail has dried, oil the surface of the porcelain and continue the painting in the usual manner. The sugar-mixture detail is not affected by the subsequent oil application. The sugar mixture does not require an oil base to be laid on beforehand. After the surface has dried, applying oil will not alter the results.

Materials and Tools

The paints, oils, and brushes used in china painting are unique to the technique and are available from ceramics shops, doll-mould distributors, and sources that specialize in china painting supplies.

Pigments. Pigments sold for dollmaking are available in either dry, powdered, or premixed form in either gloss or matt finishes. The advantage of dry pigment is that it can be mixed with sugar solution instead of oil. Also, a wider variety of colors is available. The advantage of the pre-mix is its readiness for immediate use. Dry pigments can be mixed and stored in air-tight jars. The palette for the doll artist is white (gloss and matt), black (gloss and matt), a medium light blue, light pompadour (yellow red) and pompadour (darker yellow red), hair brown or finishing brown (darker and less red), and a yellow or yellow brown for painting blond hair. The names vary from manufacturer to manufacturer.

Painting and mixing oils. Oils are designated in less clear-cut and in different ways. In general, the differences are mainly in viscosity, which influences the required drying time. You will learn by experience which is best suited to your work. The mixing oil is sometimes called mixing medium. The painting oils are oil of lavender (synthetic is less expensive than natural), oil of cloves, copaiba, or simply as medium 1, 2, or 3. The choice depends upon the speed at which the painting is to be done. The heavier oils keep the colors "open" or moist longer than do the light oils. Pen oil is a thin oil used to mix pigment to the consistency of ink, which is then applied with a crow-quill pen.

Other materials. Clean brushes with turpentine but be sure you completely remove it from the bristles, because it is another oily substance. To use economically, pour small amounts into a small cleaning vessel and discard the turpentine when it becomes soiled. Clean fingerprints off the porcelain piece before painting with alcohol.

Clean the brushes with a lint-free cotton cloth. Wrap a piece of fine, well-washed silk around a pad of cotton and use it to apply cheek color (pouncing). Two white ceramic tiles are needed: one for mixing the paint and one to serve as a palette. Mix and lift the pigment with a flexible palette knife.

Brushes and pens. A set of good sable brushes, although expensive, is a good investment. Select brushes designed specifically for china painting: an assortment of soft, pointed sable brushes in sizes from 2/0 to 6/0 (the narrowest). A separate brush for each color eliminates the need to clean the brushes while painting. The brushes are named china mop, liner, and square shaders and differ only in the shape of the bristles. Each painter must establish her own preference. A "kitty tongue" or "cat's tongue" is a longer bristled brush that produces softer, flowing curves. Deerfoot stipplers are short-bristled brushes, specified as 1/8 inch or 3/8 inch, and are used for blending and feathering edges. They are never used for painting.

Clean the brushes meticulously in turpentine after use and lay them horizontally until completely dry. A brush with "disorderly" bristles can be tamed by moistening with saliva, shaping and placing in the freezer for a day or two.

For drawing fine detail use a crow-quill, or fine-nibbed, pen. It is also recommended for use with the sugar-mixed pigment.

Mixing the Paint (Dry Pigment)

No matter what the mixing medium, you must grind the pigments and blend them so thoroughly that there are no residues of dry grains of color. Place a small dot of mixing medium on the mixing tile, and near it place a tiny mound of powdered pigment. With the palette knife lift the oil a drop at a time and mix with the pigment. When all of the dry material is mixed and the paint has the consistency of toothpaste, transfer it to the painting tile. The working surfaces must be spotless, and methods must be performed with great care so you don't muddle the colors, which are kept separately on the palette. Colors are not mixed as other paints are mixed. Instead, you blend colors in the painting process by "loading" the brush with a secondary tone.

Applying the Paint

The vehicle for applying china paints is the oil, which must first be laid onto the surface to be painted. However, omit this step when the pigments are mixed with the sugar solution. Prime some clean brushes with medium and wipe off the excess oil. Don't dip the brush but rather use the bristles to work off tiny amounts of paint, adding medium sparingly to achieve a working consistency. The bristles are rolled in the pigment to "load." Excessive use of oil will result in "burn-off" of the pigment and distortion of the color. The strokes tend to leave less color at the initial point and pull the pigment to the end of the stroke. This quality is used effectively to intensify the color of the iris by starting the stroke at the pupil and pulling to the outer rim of the iris.

In painting the lips begin the stroke at the outer margins of both the top and bottom lips and pull to the center line. Only the most skillful china painters are able to lay color that does not need additional application after firing. The beginner, in an attempt to keep the application a thin layer of paint, tends to produce pale results. An excellent remedy is simply to fire the piece and then apply more color. It can require three firings to finally achieve the desired results. Mistakes can be removed before firing with the painting medium. If the painting results after china firing are completely unsatisfactory, the piece can be high fired, or porcelain fired, once more. Most of the pigment is burned off and the painting can be done again.

Painting the Doll

There is no correct way to paint porcelain dolls. Each artist develops a technique that dictates the method. Some artists prefer to paint all in one step and fire at the end; others elect to paint in three or more steps, firing between each painting. After experimentation and careful record keeping of the details so that the results can be compared, you will adopt a style suitable to your work. In any event, before firing you can remove the paint with medium so that several attempts can be made if desired.

Basic styles. There are two basic styles of painting. The first is the most straightforward, which was used on antique dolls and therefore on their reproductions. There is no shading of skin tones and eyelashes and brows are painted in a stylized manner. The second method, used by modern doll artists, seeks to render more realism. An undercoating is used to accentuate the masses and contours of the face, and the eyes are heavily shaded.

Either mode, or a combination of both, can be elected. Review the section on face painting at the beginning of this chapter, although some of the information is repeated.

Antique mode. Careful examination of an old doll is often the best explanation.
- If the porcelain pieces have been handled, they should be polished and cleaned with alcohol.
- Line the eye rim and draw the eyelashes with the sugar-pigment mixture. Let it dry. Modify the black pigment by adding a small amount of white pigment for a softer effect. (If only oil-based paints are used, reverse this and the next step.)
- Rub the surfaces of all the pieces with a light medium (synthetic oil of lavender is a good choice). Wipe them until only a slight polish remains. The dried pigment that was laid on with the sugar mixture is not affected by the oil.
- Paint the white of the eye with white gloss, avoiding the portion to be painted later as the iris and the pupil. If gloss is not available, dot the completed and fired eye with colorless nail polish for a moist effect.
- To paint the iris pull the pigment from the rim of the pupil to the outer edge of the iris, avoiding the space that is to be the pupil.
- Paint the pupil with gloss black, making a perfect circle.
- Wipe out "catch lights" in the pupils with a toothpick that you have chewed well and moistened in your mouth.

- Paint the first eyebrow, selecting either hair or finishing brown. After the first brow is painted, turn the head upside down to copy it.
- Paint the lips with light pompadour or pompadour, pulling the strokes from the outer portion of the lips to the middle line.
- Dip a silk pad into the selected red color and dot, or "pounce," it on the cheeks. Even the edges of the cheek color with the deerfoot stippler.
- Blush all appropriate parts of the doll and outline the nails with pompadour, if desired.
- Pounce the hair color.

Fire the pieces at cone 018 after drying. The drying might take several days. If the painting appears too pale after firing, you can repaint in exactly the same way and then refire. Where only the cheek color requires supplementation, the piece can be fired at a slightly cooler temperature (cone 019). Red colors tend to burn off at higher temperatures more readily than do other colors.

Modern mode. Here is a chance for you to impart your own style. But first study the general instructions below.
- Scrub and polish the porcelain pieces as they come from the kiln. If the porcelain has been handled, clean with alcohol.
- Rub the surface of all of the pieces with a light medium (synthetic oil of lavender is a good choice). Wipe until only a slightly shiny residue remains.
- Pick up a small amount of the light yellow red or light pompadour on a lint-free cotton cloth and rub evenly all over each piece. Wipe off this undercoat evenly so that only subtle amounts of the pigment remain on the surface and in the creases. It is important to avoid fingerprints on the wet surface and to examine the piece in a bright light to ensure evenness. Much of the color will fire off so that a little darker coating is left than is actually desired.
- Paint the white of the eye with white gloss, avoiding the portion that will be iris and pupil.
- Paint the pupil of the eye with a black gloss. It is a perfect circle. When gloss pigments are not available, the eye can be touched with colorless nail polish when completed. A catch light can be wiped out of the pupil with a well-chewed

toothpick, or the catch light can later be painted in as a white dot.
- Fire the pieces in a china fire (cone 018) according to the kiln manufacturer's instructions.
- Draw the eye detail with either oil-based pigments or with the sugar-water mixture. In either case, the black pigment is best greyed with the addition of a small amount of matt white. If the oil-based paint is used, apply a layer of oil, as in the first step. However, if the sugar mixture is used, apply no oil. Load the pigment on the pen nib by scooping with the palette knife. Detail is added by drawing a fine line around the entire eye, forcing the paint into the incised rim. Draw eyelashes if you wish.
- When this application has dried, and if it has not yet been done, rub oil on the surface of the piece so that the painting can continue.
- Shade the eyelids with the addition of minute amounts of black or blue (which fires lavender) on adult faces or brown on children's faces. Blend the pigment perfectly with the deerfoot stippler so that there are no boundary lines of color, and the transition is gradual. For the faces of children and young people, shade only over the eyes; shade older faces, if appropriate, at both the top and the bottom of the eye socket.
- Create an iris for the eye by drawing pigment from the inner rim to the outer edges. To render more realistic eyes, apply pure color, and before it "closes," or dries, pick up minute amounts of either brown or black on the brush and accent the rim of the iris or differentiate one side of the iris. Shadow the corners of the eye whites almost imperceptibly with blue or grey. The same can be done to the area directly under the upper eyelid to suggest a round contour. This is more effective when painting a large eye. After the first firing, additional color can be added to the eye as can the tiny lines radiating from the pupil.
- Place dots of light pompadour in the inner corner of the eyes.
- Paint the first brow lightly with either of the brown colors and turn the head upside down so you can make the second brow identical. Eyebrows are sometimes painted in two sessions with an intervening firing. The first

painting is to lay a pale arch, and the second painting places the darker hairs.

- Paint the mouth with the choice of red by pulling the pigment from the outer edges of the lips to the center line. A softer, deeper red can be achieved by using a minute amount of hair brown in the initial mixture.
- Make another application of medium on the cheeks if the first one appears to have dried. Dip the silk-wrapped pad in the red color, dot it, or pounce it, on the cheeks, and smooth and blend with the deerfoot stippler so that the transition of color is even and gradual.
- Blush the knees, hands, and feet and define the fingernails if desired. Accentuate wrinkles and creases.
- Paint and shade the hair.
- Let the pieces dry and fire again at cone 018.

The painting can be considered complete unless you want to make the colors more intense. When deeper hues are required, the painting process is repeated and the firing done once more.

SETTING GLASS EYES

Usually reproduction artists, rather than original doll artists, choose glass (or plastic) eyes over painted eyes. But there is no reason why any hollow composition, porcelain, or wax head cannot be made with set eyes. Eyes, available from doll-parts distributors, are made of either plastic or glass, and are either flat oval or round and stemmed. Only the artist's preference determines which is selected. Plastic eyes are less expensive than glass ones, and round eyes are easier to set than flat ones.

Eyes are measured in millimetres across the widest horizontal distance of the socket. They are usually designated in even numbers. The size of a glass eye selected not only relates to the eye-socket opening but to the artist's preference with regard to the amount of eye white and colored iris that is to be shown. A larger eye with more color and less visible eye white would change the appearance of the face. It is best to have an assortment on hand so you can select the appropriate size by trial and error.

The eye is fitted as the last step in the completion of the head and just before the wig is made. Because the inside of the eye socket has been rounded and prepared before the head was fired and the eyelashes and rim have been painted, the eye need only be fastened in place.

Permanently fasten the eye in place with either plaster or an epoxy-type glue. The former is preferred because the plaster can be removed and the eyes reset, if desired, but the latter is easier to use. Before the eyes are permanently fixed they must be held in position to ensure proper placement and exact matching in the direction of the gaze. To temporarily set the eye, place generous dots of petroleum jelly on each side of the eye socket in the inside of the head. Holding wax is used in the same way and serves an identical purpose. A wad of florist clay or modelling clay fastened partially to the outside of the eye and to the cheek will also hold the eye. Put a few tablespoons of water in a paper cup and sprinkle plaster in the water until it mounds. Leave it for a few seconds and mix thoroughly. When the plaster appears to be "creaming," transfer it with a wooden stick or palette knife and apply over the back of the eye, extending around the surface of the eye to the periphery of the socket.

To preserve the luminosity of the round eye, don't cover the stem with plaster. Lay the head face down on a towel until the plaster hardens. When dry, clean the excess plaster, wax, or petroleum jelly on the outside of the eyes with a toothpick. (Never put plaster down a household drain.) While most artists position and plaster both eyes at the same time, it is easier to complete one eye, plaster or glue it in place, and let it dry. Then match the second eye to the first. If you make an error while using plaster, place a moistened wad of paper on the plaster. It will, in time, soften and let the eye be removed. Eyes set with glue or epoxy cannot be removed.

The doll is now ready for assembly and costuming.

★   ★   ★

In the same way that a theatrical designer costumes the characters in a play, the dollmaker costumes a doll. Just as the characters on a stage tell their story at a glance, so must a doll reveal at a glance the idea that the dollmaker intended to convey. The doll itself—including the wig and clothing, hat and shoes—should present the following characteristics: sex, age, chronological period, occupation, fictional or historical perspective, and the emotion that the dollmaker wishes to elicit from observers. The doll artist usually has some idea in mind initially, but the idea may also develop as the project unfolds. The inspiration for the costumer comes from everywhere: the study of historical costume and people, from magazines, movies, television, cartoons, books, famous paintings, and even greeting cards.

Part II deals in separate chapters with the five major crafts under the costumer's direction: wigmaking, dressmaking, pattern drafting, millinery, and cobblery.

Part II
THE COSTUME

7 Wigs

The hair style and material of a doll's wig are important aspects of costuming. The wig should be consistent with the chronological period, age, and sex portrayed by the doll. But more important, the wig should reflect the concept—realistic or fantastic—that the artist has in mind. It can be consistent with the material of the doll or a contradiction of it, for instance using human air on a stuffed cloth doll. The wig can be beautiful or comical. Anything goes.

MATERIALS

Many materials are available for making wigs. Those most commonly used are yarn, mohair, crepe hair, and fur. You can purchase wigs that have already been made from a doll supplier in sizes from 5 inches to 18 inches in circumference (as measured around the head at the hairline). Purchased wigs can be restyled, simplified, and thinned.

Yarn, Rope, or Cord

A variety of yarn colors, textures, and thicknesses (or plies) are available and include worsted, bouclé, mohair, and angora—all of which produce different effects. One-ply yarn, or fine yarn, is available from weavers and embroiderers; brushed-out embroidery thread and candlewick yarns are particularly good for small

dolls. Ravelled burlap, ravelled hemp rope, and macramé cord brushed to a magnificent mane can be used for unusual effects. Roving, raw material from which yarns are spun, is available from weavers and is good for unusual effects. (Your Yellow Pages telephone directory should list weavers.)

Mohair

The source of mohair is goat hair. Purchase it in strands by the yard and in small curls from a doll-parts supplier. Mohair makes excellent hair material for small dolls. It was used widely for antique-doll wigs because the texture is finer and thus more to scale than human hair. It is available in many colors.

Theatrical or Crepe Hair

Available from theatrical-goods and makeup shops, this hair is braided on a cord and sold by the yard. You can purchase it in every hair color, and although wavy when unbraided, it can be straightened by applying a warm iron. It tends to be wiry and kinky.

Fur

Fur, both real and fake, provides interesting hair material. Real fur (karakul and Persian lamb) rescued from a secondhand store can be fitted to a doll's head for a short coiffure. Fake fur sold in craft shops is available in blonde, orange, black, grey, white, and brown shades and is especially suitable for wigs for a child or an old-person doll. The hair can be trimmed and brushed into whimsical wisps. It is then fitted to the head and sewn in place. Fake furs that are used on sewn garments can sometimes be used effectively.

Reworking Wigs and Weaving Hair
Human wigs of either real or synthetic hair can be reworked into diminutive wigs. Strands of hair or mohair can be woven, or wefted, onto strings and used in the same way that wefts taken from commercial wigs are used.

INITIAL TREATMENT OF THE HAIR
Alter various hair materials by pretreating them prior to the construction of the wig. A weft of hair can be pretreated and curled, if desired. You can also curl the hair on a finished wig.

Yarn
To alter the quality of most yarns, brush or ravel them. Make curls by wrapping the yarn tightly around a knitting needle, chopstick, or dowel and spraying several times with a firm-hold hair spray or acrylic craft spray. When thoroughly dry the curls are cut from the long strand and used in vertical falls. A loose curl becomes a kinky strand if pulled with your fingers until straight and then released. This technique applies to wool and cotton yarns as well as macramé cords that have been ravelled. You can also ravel an appropriate colored knitted garment to provide kinky hair.

Synthetic Hair
The quality of synthetic hair can be altered by boiling it in water or by steaming. To make curls, tightly wrap the hair on a wooden skewer, wire bag-ties, or metal (not plastic) curlers. Boil the curls for a few minutes or suspend them over the boiling water in a vegetable steamer for about an hour. (You can use the steamer again for cooking.) After it has dried, unwind the curl; it remains a permanent spiral. Cut and weft small segments of the curls by stringing them on heavy, waxed thread, as beads are strung.

Mohair and Theatrical Hair
To straighten mohair and theatrical hair, press with a cool iron. Do not use steam.

WIG STANDS
A wig stand can be made easily and enables you to work with both hands. Insert and glue a dowel or chopstick into a Styrofoam ball that fits inside the wig. Wrap a piece of the top of a pantyhose around the Styrofoam, cover with a plastic bag, and fasten tightly to the dowel with a piece of thread. The resulting wig stand can be anchored on a block of clay or in a narrow jar weighted with sand. A small C-clamp fastened to the edge of the table frees one hand for other work. Make wigs that are to be wet or sprayed separately from the doll and fasten them to the head later.

BASIC WIG CONSTRUCTIONS
There are six basic constructions used in wig-making for dolls, and you can use any combination of them. They are: glue-on wigs, fur caps, embroidered hair, sewn strips, topknot and pate, and woven or wefted hair sewn to a cap.

Glue-on Wigs
Both simple and complex coiffures can be made by just styling theatrical braid or mohair and gluing the hair in place. The wig may have a stitched part or just be pushed into shape. It can be a ring of hair exposing a bald pate. The wig may be augmented by gluing a bun and tiny tendrils of hair tucked underneath and fastened in place. It is a simple method and most suitable for small dolls. In applying the wig, place tiny dots of white glue with a toothpick to fasten the underlayer of hair to the scalp. It is important to use the glue sparingly so that it does not ooze through the outer layer.

Fur Caps
Fit real or fake fur to the doll's head in much the same manner that you would cover a ball with fabric. Arrange the fur backing in the front to create an appropriate hairline and pin it firmly (Illus. 66). Then draw the fur backwards and fit and trim to the head. Cut out overlapping wedges, fit the edges together, and sew so that stitches are invisible on the outside.

A pattern can be made in the same way, if desired, and the fur cut from the pattern. Suggest a softer hairline by brushing and trimming the fur or by augmenting with separate curls and tendrils of other hair materials that match in color. If the head is cloth, curls may be embroi-

Illus. 66. Fur cap wig; (left) *fitting the fur and* (right) *the fur wig in place.*

dered around the edges. Persian lamb hair can be adorned with little black pigtails inserted into slashes in the fur to add a whimsical touch. Brush and trim fake fur into style or pull it into small wisps and tie with ribbons for a charming baby hair style.

In using fur, it is important to observe the direction of the hairs. The fur is usually placed so that the hairs lie forward around the face. To cut any type of fur, hold the point of the scissors close to the backing to avoid cutting the individual hairs.

Embroidered Hair

Two embroidery techniques are used to represent a wig: the hair is stitched directly to the scalp to cover it and simulate hair, or the yarn is sewn in strands to the scalp, simulating the growth of human hair, and then the long strands are styled. To cover the scalp of baby dolls, stitch with satin stitch in a circular pattern in which human hair grows. Make a slightly irregular hairline. Introduce variations by leaving loops instead of pulling the stitch tightly. These loops are fastened with small reinforcing stitches so that they will not pull loose. To stitch a curly top, first wrap the yarn around your finger for three or four turns. Sew the curls to the scalp

with the same yarn. It is best to use a continuous thread while the process is repeated to cover the entire scalp. Augment the curly top with French knots or loose curls made in the same manner (Illus. 67).

An alternative technique is to sew long strands of yarn to the cloth head, observing a realistic hairline. When all of the long strands are stitched in place, pull them to the crown and fasten into a bun or braid. This method is best utilized with embroidery thread or finer yarn. The strands of yarn can be sewn to a band

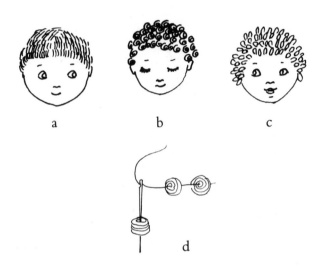

Illus. 67. Embroidered wigs; (a) *overall satin stitch,* (b) *stitched ringlets,* (c) *loops,* (d) *sewing curls to the scalp.*

instead of to the head, and the band is then glued or sewn in place. This is the basis for the Gibson Girl hair style, which can also be used in conjunction with long curls (Illus. 68).

Illus. 68. Embroidered wig with stitched strands: (left) *sewing the strands;* (right) *styling the strands.*

Sewn Strips

To make another simple wig construction, lay down strands of yarn (or any other wig material) and stitch them together in strips with a single row of tiny machine stitches. You can fashion an entire wig or make small strips for bangs. Glue or sew the strips to the head in your choice of hair style. Glue or tack the hairs to the sides of the head to hold them in place (Illus. 69).

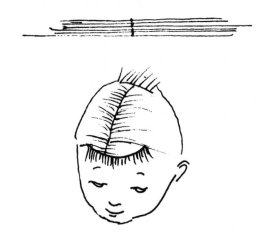

Illus. 69. (Above) *Sewn strips for* (below) *wig construction.*

If the feed-dog of the sewing machine engages the hair strands, place a piece of tissue paper over the strands and later tear it off. After the strips are sewn, securely tie the thread.

If you need strands of yarn the same length, wind the yarn around a book or piece of cardboard that will yield the correct length. Then cut the yarn to remove it from the cardboard. The resultant strands will be identical in length. Strips of curls are fabricated by winding yarn around a yardstick and securing the loops with a tight outline stitch before slipping the strip off the stick. The strip method produces a wide variety of hair styles (Illus. 70).

Topknot and Pate

The topknot and pate was frequently used on small, antique dolls. It is most readily adaptable to any doll with an open crown, but a modified version can also be used on a cloth doll. It is used to supplement the wefted wig. To make a topknot, tie a bundle of hair in the center and pull it into a small hole in the stiffened buckram crown. Glue the hair firmly in the pate and then glue over the opening in the head. Spread the

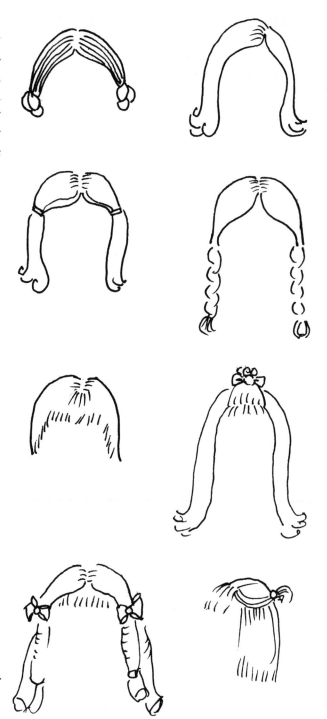

Illus. 70. Hair styles made with sewn strips.

hair in a circle around the head and trim. You can use yarn instead by making a pompom and fastening it to the scalp.

Pates, an oval of brown buckram, are available in various sizes from a doll-parts supplier. Pates may be improvised by using Drape N' Shape, a coarse fabric that has been coated with sizing and then dried. Cut two or three circles of Drape N' Shape and wet and shape them on a light bulb or Styrofoam ball. Paint the material and glue several layers together. Make a small hole in the purchased or improvised pate and pull the topknot into it and glue it (Illus. 71).

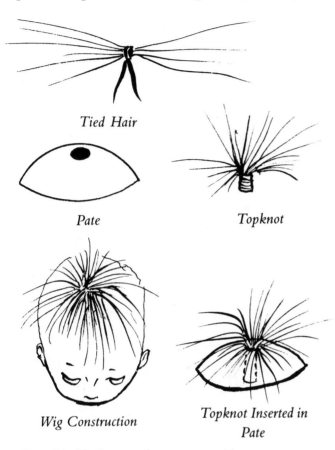

Tied Hair

Pate

Topknot

Wig Construction

Topknot Inserted in Pate

Illus. 71. Topknot and pate construction.

Woven or Wefted Hair Sewn to a Cap

Most human wigs and purchased doll wigs are made by sewing strands of woven or wefted hair in a spiral pattern to a net cap. The wefts can be made of yarn, mohair, or human or synthetic hair.

Weaving frame. You can either buy a professional weaving frame or construct a simple frame yourself. For a simple frame, all you really need is a smooth board on which two strands of heavy thread are stretched and held taut while you weave on the threads. The thread should match the hair color. A simple frame is shown in

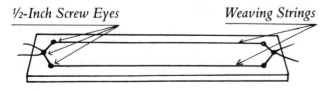

½-Inch Screw Eyes   Weaving Strings

Illus. 72. Homemade weaving frame.

Illus. 72. Insert three ½-inch screw eyes into both ends of the board in a triangular pattern. String heavy, waxed thread between the two weaving eyes and tie the thread ends to the third eye to keep the string tight (Illus. 72). A more sophisticated frame would no doubt make the job easier, but for the occasional weaver, this improvised loom will serve well.

Weaving the hair. Twist or weave small bunches of hair on the two weaving strings as shown in Illus. 73. Push tightly each successive twist towards the preceding one until the weft is the desired length. Then knot the ends of the weaving string, trim closely, and fasten with a dot of glue. Weave yarn and mohair when dry, but human and synthetic hair are more easily handled when they are wet. Human hair is resilient and does not bend easily.

Therefore, anchor each of the woven strands in place on the weaving strings with a tiny stitch using a fine matching thread, as shown. You can now sew the weft onto the net cap. The length of the required weft depends upon the size of the wig, the material used, and the fullness desired. An average wig, which measures 9 inches around the head at the hairline, requires about 1¼ yards of weft if four spirals are needed to cover the cap.

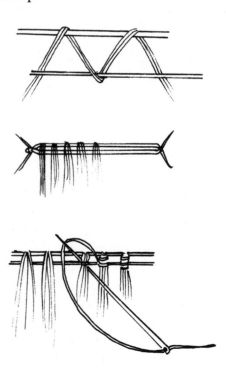

Illus. 73. Weaving stitch.

Reworking purchased wigs. If weaving hair seems like too much trouble, here is an easier and completely satisfactory method. Buy a human wig in a secondhand shop. After careful washing and rinsing with a creme rinse, dry the wig and prepare for the next step.

With a seam ripper or razor blade, carefully rip the machine-sewn wefts from the base to which they were sewn. The wefts can be used just as they are, or if it appears that the top edge is too bulky, it can be modified. Close examination will reveal that commercial wefts are stitched, folded, and resewn. Rip out the second line of stitching and carefully press the weft to flatten the folded edge.

It is now ready for application to the net cap. Interesting effects are obtained by using almost imperceptibly different colors of hair together to give a natural appearance. Human hair may also be bleached and dyed, but it is easier to seek out the right colors in the first place.

Wig cap. A wig cap is made of either blonde or brown cotton vegetable netting, which you can buy by the yard from a hair products supplier. Cut a circle of the net that is large enough to cover the doll's head to the hairline. Because this process is somewhat messy, you should proceed with a wig stand. Moisten the fabric and fit it to the head shape by folding small darts and shaping to the wig stand. Place a piece of cloth over the wet cap and fasten tightly with a rubber band to hold it in shape. When the cap dries, trim it more precisely and sew a ⅜-inch matching ribbon around the edge of the cap to maintain its shape.

Constructing the wig. Now sew the wefts by hand with a tiny overcast stitch in a spiral pattern around the cap, being careful to catch the weaving string. It is important to start the spiral at the bottom of the cap and work towards the crown so that the strands of hair will not fall in the way of the needle. How closely you apply the strands of hair depends upon the bulk of the wefts, the size of the wig, and the appearance desired. Discontinue the spiral almost at the crown so you can add the finishing topknot. To fashion a topknot, tightly roll a coil of weft that is 6 inches to 7 inches long. At each turn, tightly sew the

top of the weft so that it will remain coiled. To make a pate, cut two layers of vegetable net in a circle about 1½ inches in diameter. Insert the topknot into the center of the pate and glue and sew the pate to the top of the cap. Continue the spiral of the weft around the pate to cover the edges (Illus. 74). When completed, spread the topknot of hair to hide the last weft application. Use the cap-and-weft technique with yarn, synthetic and human hair, and mohair. One of many alternatives is to use the weft only along the lower edges of a cap and make the top of the wig with an overlapping stitched strip.

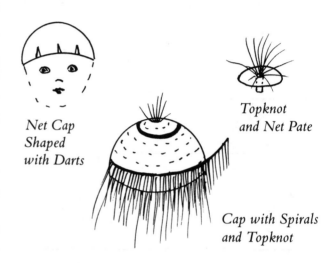

Net Cap Shaped with Darts

Topknot and Net Pate

Cap with Spirals and Topknot

Illus. 74. Construction of a wefted wig on a net cap.

A curly-top wig is fabricated in much the same manner, but instead of using a weft of straight hair, small ringlets are woven. To make ringlets, as described on page 104, immerse coils of synthetic hair in boiling water, cut the resultant curls when dry into inch or larger segments, and string them on heavy, waxed thread. Bring the needle through the curl and repeat the stitch so that each curl is tightly attached. The weft of curls is used as any other weft, by sewing with tiny overcast stitches through the net cap, taking care to catch the weaving thread. In the case of the curly-top wig, begin the spiral at the crown and continue to the bottom edge of the cap. A weft of curls can be used to augment any coiffure.

Now the wig is ready for trimming and styling, which is done in the same way that a hairdresser would. Glue the finished wig to a stiffened pate or glue it directly onto the head.

8 Clothes

These techniques for dressmaking for dolls have been simplified to eliminate unnecessary seams and excessive bulk. Therefore even a beginning seamstress can achieve immediate success. Doll clothing, with the notable exception of historically accurate costumes, is basic in construction. The only problem initially is in working on tiny garments, but even that can be overcome with practice and the use of a few tricks.

TWO KINDS OF COSTUMING

There are two kinds of costuming: (a) one in which the clothing is not removed, which eliminates many construction details; and (b) one in which the clothing is removed and requires the construction of complete garments. If the clothing is not to be removed, it can be sewed to the doll or be made part of the construction of the doll. Often this kind of costuming is effected by applying pieces one over the other to simulate a complete outfit. For example, you could sew on only the front of a vest and suggest a shirt by showing only its collar. Then the only complete item would have to be the jacket.

The only requirement is that the illusion be so carefully preserved that the observer is unaware that the garments are incomplete. This kind of dressing relies most on intuition and inspiration. This technique is discussed in detail on page 120.

Most doll garments are made with workable closures. This chapter covers these types of clothing with special emphasis on sewing techniques that differ from those for larger garments.

SEWING METHODS UNIQUE TO DOLL CLOTHES

Patterns for the front and back of simple doll garments are identical except for the neckline definition (Illus. 75). Differences in the garment are created by darts, trimming, and finishing.

Use untrimmed darts for shaping. Unless the garment is unusually large or the fabric exceptionally fine, eliminate seams for shaping; they add bulk and tend to ravel (Illus. 76).

Eliminate separate facings and bindings on the neckline and other edges by using edge-to-edge lining either of the complete garment or only a portion of the garment (Illus. 77 and page 115). This technique eliminates visible stitching.

Even the smallest hand stitches and the tiniest sewing machine stitches can be out of scale with a doll's garment. Therefore, make every effort to conceal the sewing. For this reason it is sometimes best to glue a hem rather than to sew it. Construction strategies, like adding lace or trimming on the sewing line, are designed to disguise stitches.

Eliminate buttonholes by sewing buttons over a snap closure.

Make back closures with a placket that is stitched and pressed to the wrong side (Illus. 78).

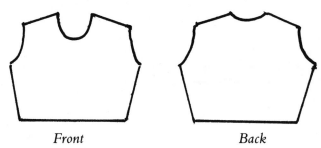

Front   *Back*

Illus. 75. Bodice pattern.

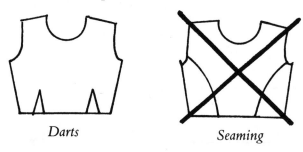

Darts   *Seaming*

Illus. 76. Shaping with darts.

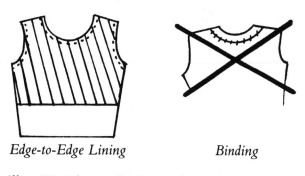

Edge-to-Edge Lining   *Binding*

Illus. 77. Edge-to-edge lining eliminates bindings.

The strip is a narrow piece cut along the selvage (lengthwise) to eliminate ravelling.

In the process of assembling garments, do as much work as possible when they are flat. Sew side seams last (Illus. 79).

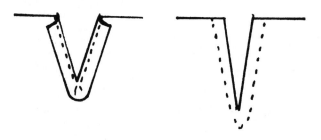

Illus. 78. Placket construction. (Left) Sewing placket (right side) and (right) finished placket (right side).

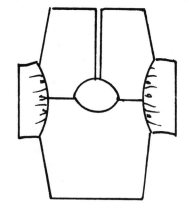

Illus. 79. Assembly of a garment.

PATTERN ADJUSTMENTS

Pattern pieces are marked with notches, letters, and dots. Do not cut these designations into the piece or mark the piece accordingly; simply note them during sewing. (Seam allowances in dolls' garments are too narrow to permit slashing.) The patterns are marked so you will know where to join identical pieces.

Lengthening and Shortening

To enlarge a pattern, cut it in two and add a strip of paper of appropriate width or length. To make it smaller, fold out excessive length or width (Illus. 80).

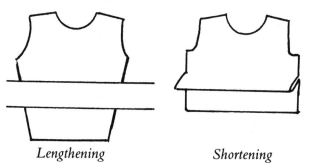

Lengthening   *Shortening*

Illus. 80. Adjusting the pattern length.

Adding or Removing Fullness

Patterns can be enlarged to fit larger dolls or to provide more fullness. Gathering and pleating of the bodice requires adding width. Widening the sleeve would permit a fuller cap. Fullness is removed from the pattern piece when necessary by placing the pattern piece beyond the fold of the fabric (Illus. 81–82).

Add-On Facings

Seldom will you need separate facings. Widen the opening, either in the front or the back of the

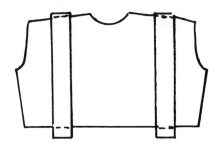
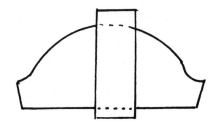

Adding Fullness to Bodice
Providing for Side Pleats in Bodice
Adding Fullness to Sleeve

Illus. 81. Adding width to a pattern.

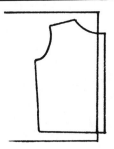

Illus. 82. Removing width from the bodice pattern.

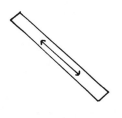

Illus. 84. Bias cutting.

garment, so that the facing is part of the pattern. Fold the facing to the inside (Illus. 83).

Always cut patterns lengthwise with the grain of the material, as indicated by an arrow, unless otherwise stated. However the pattern is laid out, cut all pieces in the same direction. Napped fabric and fur fabric, which have a right and wrong side, must be reversed so that there are left and right sides.

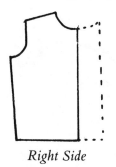
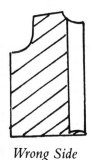

Right Side   *Wrong Side*

Illus. 83. Add-on facings.

BIAS

To cut on the bias, place the pattern piece diagonal to the grain of the fabric (Illus. 84). Bias cutting results in maximum drape, but because bias edges stretch, they must be handled gently or stay-stitched. Cut bindings and facings on the bias so that they will fit curves better. A flared skirt cut on the bias will drape more gracefully. An overskirt on a Victorian costume, for exam-

ple, should be cut on the bias. Bias cutting is used extensively in hatmaking.

HAND AND EMBROIDERY STITCHES

Sewing can be by hand or by machine. Some useful hand stitches are running stitch, back stitch, stab stitch (for felt), oversewing, and ladder stitch. Embroidery stitches include satin stitch, chain stitch, outline, French knot, and turkey work. (Stitches are shown in Illus. 85.)

NEEDLES AND THREAD

Use heavy thread (like that used for carpets and buttons) for construction details on the doll itself. It is heavy enough for attaching appendages and closing openings. The beeswax coating strengthens the thread and makes sewing easier.

Achieve the best results by attaching garments with stitches that are invisible on the outside unless the stitching is to be decorative or to simulate a construction detail. Choose thread that is one shade darker than the fabric to hide the stitches. Select the finest thread available. Either polyester or silk thread is suitable.

To prevent kinking and fraying, cut the thread on a slant and thread the needle with the cut end as it comes from the spool. Fine sewing machine needles No. 11 or No. 14 (the lower numbers designate thinner needles) will produce smaller

Illus. 85. Some useful hand stitches and embroidery stitches.

Running Stitch

Back Stitch

Ladder Stitch

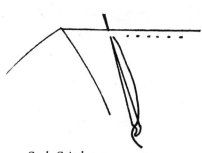

Stab Stitch

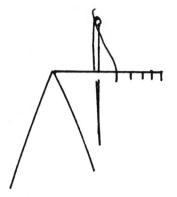

Oversewing

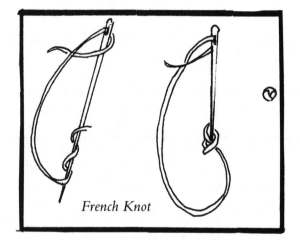

French Knot

Chain Stitch

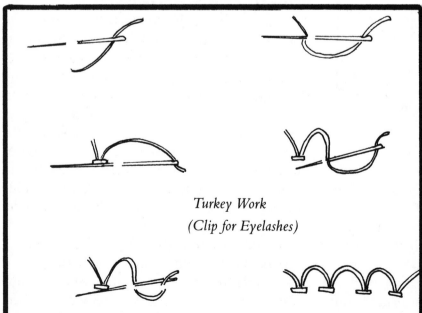

Turkey Work
(Clip for Eyelashes)

Outline Stitch

Satin Stitch

Satin Stitch
(The Eye)

punctures. For hand sewing use quilters' needles in sizes 5 to 10 (betweens), which are not only thin but short. These can transform the ordinary seamstress into a needle artist by enabling her to make the tiniest of stitches.

When you want decorative hand stitches and you are having difficulty producing perfectly even stitches, try this trick. Run the fabric through the sewing machine with the needle unthreaded. The needle will produce a row of absolutely even punctures into which your hand stitches can be placed. This method is also used for trimming shoes.

STAY STITCHING

To stay-stitch, place a row of stitching just inside the seam allowance to hold the fabric firmly. This technique is helpful for sewing a V-shape and when slashing is necessary in order to make a turn (Illus. 86). This is often the case in stitching doll bodies. Stay stitching is frequently used to maintain the shape of a bias-cut piece and prevent it from stretching, for example around the neck, on a circular ruffle, or along a bias-cut waistline (Illus. 87). Be sure to stay-stitch before you sew the seams.

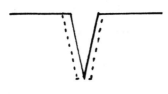

Illus. 86. Stay-stitching in the V shape.

Illus. 87. Stay-stitching the bias.

EASING

Easing is a process in which two fabric edges of slightly different lengths or contours are smoothly joined. Fabric, within certain limits, can be shaped with your fingers. Gently push the longer portion with your fingers while you stitch, compressing the fibres so they match the shorter portion. The desired result is a slightly full side without wrinkles or pleats.

SEAM ALLOWANCES

Use narrow seam allowances, not more than ¼ inch wide, on small garments and on doll bodies. Not only does the narrow seam allowance permit easier turning, but it also eliminates the need to trim seams. The width of the toe of a regular sewing machine foot is just ¼ inch wide. If additional assistance is necessary, place a strip of adhesive on the sewing machine plate to mark the correct width. Unlike directions for other kinds of sewing, it is best not to notch or slash seam allowances in order to mark them since they are narrow. A fine pin or barely visible pencil line serves just as well as a marker. Since neatness does count, and since the garments and the doll bodies will not be washed upon completion, take care not to soil or smudge the fabric.

NOTCHING SEAM ALLOWANCES

A sharp concave or convex curved seam, especially one in which one or both of the fabrics joined are heavy, needs slashing or notching of the seam allowance after stitching so it can be turned easily. It is important not to cut too close to the stitching. When a broad curve is to be fitted to a straight piece, as in the construction of shoes, remove the excess of the curve by cutting small wedges out of the excess. Notched seams lie flat (Illus. 88).

Illus. 88. Notching a curved seam.

MATCHING SEAMS

On a small garment even a tiny irregularity in the matching of seams is glaring. Perfect matching is accomplished by piecemeal stitching. Pin together the critical matching points and start the stitching from that point. Then reverse the piece, insert the needle into the same critical match point, and continue the stitching in the opposite direction. Thus, the unevenness will end up where it is least noticeable. This technique enables you to ease the excess gradually, especially where the fabric has some stretch, as

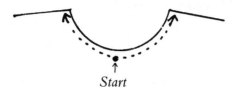

Illus. 89. Piecemeal stitching.

on a bias edge. Apply collars in this manner to ensure correct centering (Illus. 89).

HEMS

Hems are usually made by folding up the raw edge and then folding up the proper hem allowance. This results in a bulky, triple thickness of fabric. To eliminate bulkiness, try these alternative hems.

If the fabric does not ravel, all you need to make is a single fold. The single-fold hem may be glued rather than sewn if the garment is small. Place a scant dot of water-thinned white glue at intervals along the hem and hold it together with metal pin-curl clips until dry.

A tailor's hem is stitched so that it is invisible on the right side. See Illus. 90 for this easy method.

A decorative hem is made with narrow lace or braid. Turn as little of the raw edge of the hem to the right side of the fabric as possible; press to ensure evenness. Cover the raw edge on the right side with lace either sewed flat or slightly gathered. In this way the raw edge is covered, and the hem is without bulk. Adjust the length of the garment if a wider hem allowance has been given.

Fur trimming is applied in the same manner as the decorative hem. Either sew the fur over or glue it over the folded raw hem edge that has been brought to the right side.

Stitch bias strips to sleeve hems or around necklines. Do not, however, sew the strip to the wrong side but press it to the inside and leave it unfinished. It is best not to stitch through to the outer fabric.

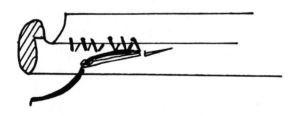

Illus. 90. Stitching a tailor's hem.

Cutting the edge with pinking shears is a historically correct finish for bonnets and ruffles. Ravelling is prevented by spraying with a resinous craft spray, but the fabric must be tested first for color fastness.

APPLYING ELASTIC

The conventional method for applying elastic is to make a narrow casing through which the elastic is threaded. The elastic is then fastened at the seams. This method, however, does not work well on small garments. You might find the following techniques more suitable.

You can sew elastic to a small garment more easily when the garment is flat; therefore only one seam is sewn initially. Turn and press the raw edge to be covered with the elastic to the wrong side of the garment. Anchor a narrow, soft elastic to the seam allowance and place it over the raw edge. Machine stitch the elastic with a wide zigzag and pull it hard as you advance. Sew the end of the elastic into the seam as the garment is closed. The right side of the garment will show a regular pattern of stitching and even gathers. This method is used on pantaloons and panties.

On a large garment try another technique. Cut the elastic, slightly stretched, to size. Seam it to form a circle. Mark the elastic circle and the garment opening with the seams completed into four equal parts with straight pins (Illus. 91).

Illus. 91. The circle technique for applying elastic.

Match the first pin markers and begin the zigzag stitching. Pull the elastic so that the second and subsequent markers match. Complete the stitching. This method is also used for applying neckbands to sweaters and T-shirts.

Use elastic cord on sleeves and tiny garments. Hem or trim the sleeve with lace. While the underarm seam has not yet been sewn, lay the cord in position on the wrong side and place a wide zigzag stitch over the stretched cord. The result is a stitched casing that is decorative on both the wrong and the right sides of the sleeve.

LINING

A well-made doll's garment, unless it is too small to detail, should be at least partially lined. The bodice of a dress, jacket, trousers, and sometimes a skirt need to be lined to eliminate hemming, binding, or other constructions that require visible sewing. Linings also preserve the shape of a garment.

Skirt

Line the skirt with a layer of tulle or net if you want a perky, stiff look. Tulle is used more effectively to line china silk to give this soft material some additional body. To make the lining, duplicate the skirt pattern and use the lining as a separate underskirt. Stiffening is also accomplished with the use of iron-on fabrics and woven or nonwoven interfacings.

Edge-to-Edge Lining

This technique is the most useful lining method for doll garments. Although difficult to explain, once attempted, the technique proves to be a simple one with many applications. Follow these steps to line a bodice:

- The lining material selected should be fine and consistent in color with the garment. If nothing is available, use a piece of the outer fabric as a lining.
- Cut the lining and outer layer identically.
- Sew shoulder seams of the bodice and press them open. Then sew and press the shoulder seams of the lining.
- Place the two layers together with the right sides on the inside and the wrong sides on the outside. Always place the pieces this way for stitching.
- Stitch the neckline and the bodice openings.
- Turn the bodice to the right side and press carefully so that the lining does not show.
- Gather the cap of the sleeve to fit the armhole and sew to the bodice, treating the two layers of the bodice as if they were one layer.
- Close the side seams to complete the bodice.

Line the jacket in the same way with the following modifications:

- Use the same material for the lining as you use for the outer layer of the jacket so that the lapels will match.
- Sew together the necklines, front edges, and hem of the jacket and lining before you turn and press the garment.
- To line the sleeves, join the layers at the cuff, right sides together on the inside. When the stitching at the cuff is complete, turn the lining to the inside and use the layers of fabric as though they were only one.

Lining the trousers requires some variation.

- Lining should be lightweight.
- Separately stitch and press the center front seams and center back seams of the outer fabric and of the lining.
- Place the outer layer and lining together with the right sides on the inside and the wrong sides on the outside.
- Stitch the layers a short distance on the sides to form a placket and then across the front and across the back.
- Stitch the hems.
- Turn the front and back pieces of the trousers right side out and press.
- Close the side seams and the crotch seams, treating the layers of material as if they were a single fabric.

Be sure to match the intersection of seams perfectly to obscure the construction method.

ASSEMBLING THE DOLL GARMENT

Assembling any doll garment depends on the complexity of the garment. Before you start, decide which techniques and patterns you'll use. Some general suggestions might lead to more effortless garment making and eliminate the need for step-by-step instructions.

Since it is difficult to sew and press a tiny garment when the side seams are closed, it is best to leave the garment open and flat until the end (Illus. 92).

- Prepare all pieces that are to be lined.
- Assemble and decorate the entire front and entire back. Complete the back placket.
- Sew and press the shoulder seams.
- Make the sleeves, attach and decorate cuffs, but don't close the side seams.
- Sew the sleeves into the armhole.
- Sew the collar in place.
- Close the side seams by stitching from cuff to hem on each side.
- Make the hem and finish decorating. Apply snaps.

You can use the same procedure with necessary modifications for making a coat or pair of trousers. The key to success is to keep the garment flat until the end. It is difficult to manipulate tiny seams in restricted spaces.

When making several garments of the same kind, set up a production line to save time. Repeat the same stitching operation for each identical piece. In between stitching operations, do not cut the machine thread so that the pieces remain attached and cannot be lost before final assembly.

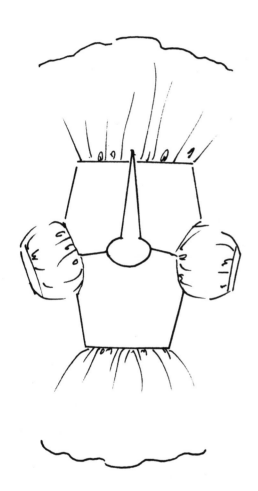

Illus. 92. Assembling a doll's garment, side seams are sewn last.

"SEWING" A SWEATER

Hand-knit garments for dolls can be very attractive, but dollmakers who don't have time to knit can take advantage of this short-cut method. Recut and resew discarded sweaters and socks to make small pull-overs, baby-doll rompers, hats,

and even booties. Pastel-colored baby sweaters have many applications as do sweaters with border patterns. Machine-knit garments can be cut and sewn without developing runs. Sew by hand using small, loose back stitches. Some of the ravelled yarn could serve as matching thread.

Take apart an old sweater and remove the neck ribbing for later use. Cut a paper pattern for the doll garment and lay it on top of the sweater so that the waistband and sleeve ribbing are utilized. Use any decorative motif. Retrim the neckline with the ribbing that you removed earlier.

If the head of the doll is too large to fit through the neck ribbing, leave one shoulder open. Close it with crocheted loops and small buttons. An overcast or crocheted edge will prevent the cut edge from running.

PRESSING

Proper pressing to give a finished look is as important on a small garment as it is on a large one. Although some fabrics can be "finger pressed" and will fold or flatten neatly with a bit of coaxing, others require ironing. Take the same precautions as you would with any pressing: carefully set appropriate temperatures and press with a light hand. Iron heavily napped fabrics on a needle board—a canvas strip pierced by rows of blunt-end needles—so the piles don't flatten.

A well-padded sleeve board is a real addition to the workshop of the dollmaker. A wooden edge presser used in tailoring provides a 1-inch wide ironing board for the doll seamstress. Both are available in most fabric shops. You can also use a seam roll. It can be made by simply rolling up a thin magazine tightly and taping it securely (Illus. 93). Cut a piece of heavy cotton fabric large enough to cover the roll plus a few inches in length. Wrap the cotton fabric tightly around the magazine roll, sew it securely closed, and force the ends into the side edges of the taped magazine. Insert the seam roll into a tiny garment and use an improvised ironing board.

The iron can also be used to mark hems or indicate straight seams. Press seams open on the wrong side after you sew them. Make folds crisp and press pleats firmly after hemming. A well-made garment can be spoiled by omitting the pressing.

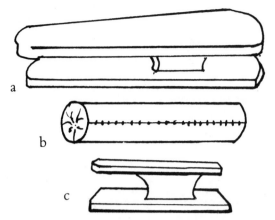

Illus. 93. Pressing boards: (a) *sleeve board,* (b) *seam roll,* (c) *wooden edge presser (use handle).*

TRIMMINGS

If the clothing is not to be washed, you can apply a wide variety of unusual trimmings in addition to those that are commonplace. Cords, braid, rickrack, and lace are available for ordinary sewing, but trimmings that are generally used in egg decorating and in making Christmas ornaments can also be used. These more glamorous trimmings come in multitudinous patterns and include gold and silver for period costuming. Some trims should be applied with glue, but most must be hand-sewn. Ribbon of all kinds is available in a variety of widths, including ⅛ inch, and in every color, even stripes. Embroidered tapes and tiny buttons are versatile trims. Narrow tubing is available, which when gathered with a cord becomes an unusual shirring. Hand embroidery, tatting, and crochet make interesting effects. Beading is a possibility. Strips of real or fake furs add luxurious touches. Tiny flowers can be purchased. Ordinary feathers can be gathered from a canary, or elegant feathers can be purchased from a fly-fishing shop. Doll shoe buckles are available from a doll supplier, and somewhat larger buckles are available from a shoe repair shop. The list is endless.

Making a Variety of Trimmings

Here are several techniques that you will find useful in costuming.

Bows. Sometimes a tied bow results in too bulky an ornament. To fashion a flat bow, loop one piece of ribbon and then fold a second piece over the center portion and stitch (Illus. 94).

Rosettes. To make ribbon rosettes for shoes or bonnets, gather a ribbon on one edge. Pull the gathering thread tightly so that the short length of ribbon forms a circle (Illus. 95). Two layers of ribbon in graduated sizes and varying shades make attractive flowers.

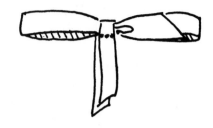

Illus. 94. Sewing a flat bow.

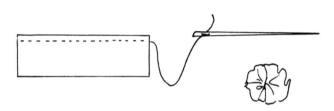

Illus. 95. Making a ribbon rosette.

Shirred braid. Purchase tubing from a sewing shop or trimming supplier. Fasten a thread to one end and then bring it through the length of tubing. Pull the thread tightly to shirr it and fasten it off (Illus. 96).

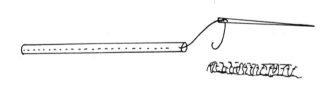

Illus. 96. Making a shirred braid.

Shell trim. Ribbon gathered in a wide **V** pattern with a tightly pulled thread produces an attractive scalloped trim (Illus. 97).

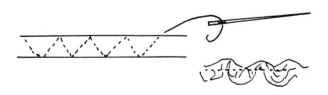

Illus. 97. Making a ribbon shell trim.

Ribbon rosebuds. Rosebuds are made by rolling a narrow ribbon around itself. Make the initial roll and then at each half-turn fold the ribbon downwards on a diagonal, making repeated twists. The folds appear to be the unfurled petals. You can easily make a device to facilitate the fabrication of rosebuds. Force a large darning needle into the end of a short length of dowel, which serves as the handle. Cut off the top of the eye of the needle with a hacksaw. The remainder of the needle forms a V-shaped holder for the first roll of the rosebud. After three or four turns, sew the base firmly or twist it with fine beading wire, and remove the rose from the holder (Illus. 98). A snip of green ribbon provides the leaves.

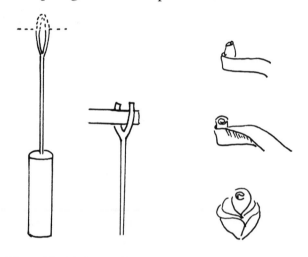

Illus. 98. Making ribbon rosebuds.

Applying lace, rickrack, and braid or ribbon on curved surfaces. You can make an insertion of lace by machine-sewing it to a fabric in a narrow zigzag path along each side of the lace. Then cut away the fabric under the lace (Illus. 99–100).

To attach a flat tube, ribbon, or braid to a curved surface, first shape the braid on the ironing board by pressing it into the appropriate curve (Illus. 101). The pressing will ease and stretch and make the application of the trim easier. This technique is also used in preparing hat trims.

Ruffles. See Illus. 102 for various types of ruffles that are appropriate to doll clothing.

Tucks and shirring. Other types of useful needlework, like pin tucks, shirring, and smocking, are shown in Illus. 103.

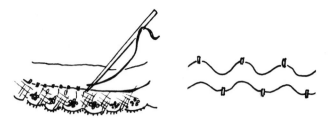

Illus. 99. Applying lace and rickrack.

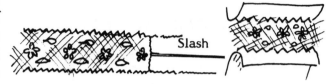

Illus. 100. Stitching lace insertion and then cutting fabric away.

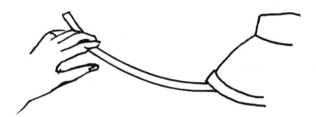

Illus. 101. Shaping ribbon with an iron.

EVEN PLEATS WITHOUT MEASURING

Pleating in the conventional manner involves careful measuring along the length of the material to be pleated. The even distances are marked and the pleats pinned and pressed. Once pleated, the top of the strip is stay-stitched to hold the pleats. For doll clothes, you can make a simple device, which with some practice can more easily accomplish the same thing.

Hair rakes or wire combs (or onion holders) have narrow-spaced wire prongs placed at approximately ⅛-inch intervals (Illus. 104). Cut a length of material approximately two and one-half times the desired pleated length. Place it on a padded ironing board and lay the hair rake on top. With a crochet needle draw up a loop of the fabric and carefully pull to reach the adjacent wire. Pin it at the top and at the bottom to the ironing board. Raise and pin a second and third loop. When the segment is complete slip the rake out and press the pleats. Continue the process until the length of material has been pleated.

SIMULATED DETAIL

Sometimes you must simplify construction details either because the garment is too small or

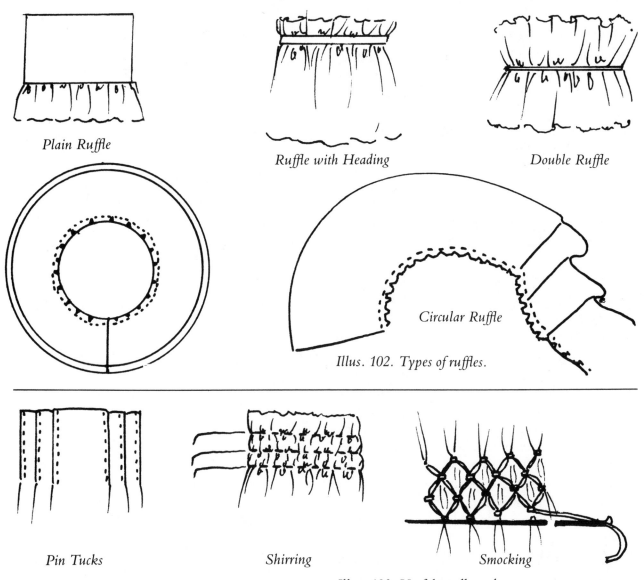

Plain Ruffle

Ruffle with Heading

Double Ruffle

Circular Ruffle

Illus. 102. Types of ruffles.

Pin Tucks

Shirring

Smocking

Illus. 103. Useful needlework.

because suitable material is not available. You may find the following tricks useful. When it is not feasible to use a yoke construction, suggest one by sewing cord, lace, or trim onto the bodice in the position of the yoke to suggest the detail. It adds style, does not require excessive seaming, and disguises the simplicity of construction. A yoke can also be appliquéd onto the top of the garment. Ribbon and trim can be glued in place to suggest detail. Suggest openings by trimming a folded vertical panel with lace or ruffle. An overskirt can be suggested in the same manner. Simulate elaborate sleeves by sewing puffs on top of a straight sleeve. Stitching suggests construction detail that is in reality not there.

Illusion is the name of the game, and simplification is frequently the only way in which tiny garments can be made. The skills of miniature enthusiasts have reached unbelievable levels, and as one becomes accustomed to such minutia, skills do develop. If detail is desired it is worth trying even though the effort ultimately ends with a simulation.

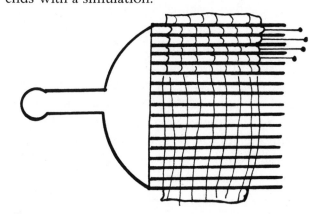

Illus. 104. Making even pleats with a hair rake.

SHORT-CUT COSTUMING

As discussed at the beginning of this chapter, short-cut dressing techniques are appropriate for dolls that will never be undressed. Garments are only suggested and may also be sewn to the doll. The following illustrations show techniques for dressing a doll so that raw edges are concealed and detail is suggested. The method is similar to that for attaching hard limbs and a hard head to a cloth body (pages 62–63).

Prepare the skirt by cutting a rectangle about two and one-half times the width of the waistline. Close the back seam and hem. Position the skirt inside out with the raw edge pointing towards the legs. Gather the top and sew or tie it securely to the body of the doll. Then pull the skirt down into position. The raw edge is now concealed (Illus. 105).

Seam the trousers and leave them inside out. Gather the leg bottoms and place them on the doll with the raw edges pointing towards the head. Adjust the gathers and sew the trouser legs or tie them in position. Then draw the garment upwards so that the raw edges are concealed and secure the waistline in position. This device is used for making suits for clowns, knickers, and bloomers when a neat finish is desired (Illus. 106).

You can make sleeves by using this technique as well. Seam the sleeve and leave it on the wrong side. Place it in position with the raw edge towards the head. Make the gathers and fasten the sleeve by sewing or tying in position. Then draw the sleeve upwards and sew invisibly by hand to the bodice (Illus. 107).

Note to the hand knitter: By using finer yarn and thinner needles than knitting directions indicate and by establishing the proper gauge, you can turn almost any pattern for a baby sweater into a doll's garment.

Note on fabric selection: Costuming is simplified by selecting appropriate fabrics—those that are lightweight, fold gently, and do not ravel excessively. Select prints that are in scale with the doll. Real finds in a thrift shop include old silk, crushed velvet, and babies' dresses. Salvage the fine lace and embroidery and use the fabric for elegant costuming.

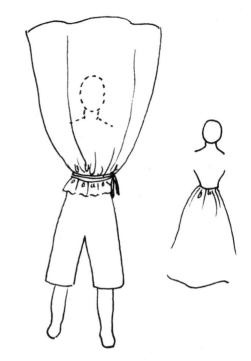

Illus. 105. Attached gathered skirt.

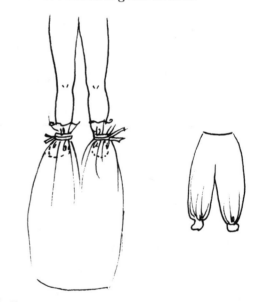

Illus. 106. Attached gathered trousers.

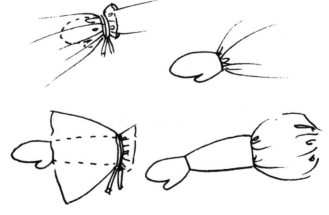

Illus. 107. Attached gathered sleeves.

9   Patterns for Clothes

The science of pattern drafting for the construction of human-size clothing is complicated and depends on many measurements. Garments must be constructed for ease of movement, wearability, and comfort. Pattern drafting for dolls is much simpler—the clothing does not have to please the customer, the doll need not move or be comfortable or ever remove her clothing. But dressing dolls is complicated because details and seams add bulk and because designs must be simplified and yet suggest detail.

Since doll sizes vary more than humans', almost every pattern must be individualized for the doll wearer. In this chapter I describe a basic technique that eliminates the need for having a pattern in hand for every project. You could, of course, purchase patterns, but this doesn't eliminate the need to try them first. The process of pattern drafting for doll clothing is a trial-and-error process.

Be sure to review the dressmaking techniques described in the previous chapter before you actually begin drafting a pattern.

BASIC PATTERN SHAPES
The first step in pattern drafting is to note the basic pattern shapes. All trim and simulated detail deleted, most doll garments are made from only a few basic patterns.

Bodice
The bodice pattern can be made either with separate sleeves or with bodice and sleeves in one piece. The latter shape, or T-shape, is used for small garments in which sleeves cannot be easily set or excessive seaming would overpower the tiny garment. It is used with minor changes to make a long or short garment, one that is open or closed in the front, or a garment that is gathered or belted. The more conventional bodice shape has recessed armholes for setting in sleeves. This bodice can serve as only a yoke, a waist-length or hip-length garment, or it can be extended to make a full-length garment. The sleeves are usually gathered at the top to facilitate fitting into the armhole. Unclipped darts can be used to fit the waistline.

Skirt
The skirt is generally a simple rectangle, which leaves room for attachment to the bodice and for a hem. Regardless of the style, whether pleated or gathered, the usual width is about two and one-half times the circumference of the waist. A sheer fabric would require more fullness; a

heavy or stiff material would require less. To eliminate bulk, cut the skirt on the bias so it will hang more gracefully. A flared or gored skirt requires more fitting. A full or partial circle serves as a perky, stand-away skirt.

Trousers

Trouser patterns can be modified for fullness and length to make knickers, panties, and pantaloons as well as some types of rompers. These garments are all derived from the same basic pattern.

The foregoing applies to making most doll garments. The simplified method for drafting patterns does not apply to complicated garments, like historical reproductions. Susan Sirkis, Estelle Ansley Worrell, and Dorothy S. Coleman et al. have all written excellent and definitive works for period costumes. For this reason the broad subject of historical costuming is treated only briefly in this chapter.

DRAFTING THE PATTERN PIECES

The second step in pattern drafting is, unfortunately, less a scientific than a trial-and-error process. Although you can make and record measurements, a more forthright and simple method is just to forge ahead and use "lay-on" measurements. First, envision the shape of the required pattern piece—will there be inset sleeves, how will the bodice close, and will the bodice be lined. (A closure requires a fold-over facing, but a lined bodice does not require a facing.)

Cut a rectangular piece of paper towel or other soft paper, which, with appropriate seam allowances, approximates an ample measurement for the bodice or dress you have designed. Place it on the doll and, keeping in mind the shape of the required piece, trace the doll's dimensions, noting especially the required width and the length of the piece. For a bodice, the critical measurements are the widths from underarm seams, the waist measurement, the length of the bodice, and the shape of the neckline in both front and back. Be sure to fit the pattern over whatever the doll will wear underneath.

Now that you have approximated the pattern piece, fold and cut the paper to ensure that the sides are identical. Carefully reshape the shoulder line, armholes, and neckline. Make provisions for any construction details, like shirring or pleating, that you might want. Cut the sleeves, adjusting for desired fullness in the cap. Be sure the sleeves fit over the hands.

If it is a simple pattern, pin and fit it to the doll and, when it is finally satisfactory, transfer it to heavier paper as a permanent record. Precious fabric or a complicated pattern requires a trial garment. Adjust and fit the trial garment, then rip it apart. Draft the final pattern from the trial garment. Record all information for future use. Although this may seem like a lengthy and difficult process, you will be developing a library of basic patterns for like-sized dolls, which will also serve for many adaptations for the same doll. Most often even purchased patterns must be refitted. Most dolls, except modern commercial ones, do vary in size.

The key to doll costuming without the use of commercial patterns lies in the visualization of the basic shape of the garment. The following is a catalogue of infants', children's, and adults' garments that demonstrates how they can be made with the pattern shapes defined and shown. Refer to the preceding chapter on dressmaking techniques for details that will transform a simple construction into a unique garment.

See Color Illus. 1A, 1–3D, and 1G for dolls made from the patterns given in chapter 1 and clothed in costumes made according to the following techniques. See also the soft-sculpture boy with a wrapped armature body that appears on the cover.

CATALOGUE OF PATTERN SHAPES

Infant

Use the T-shape (Illus. 108) for drafting simple garments for an infant doll. This shape, in which the sleeves and the garment are cut in a single piece, can serve as a sacque, dress, or coat. You can modify it and create a petticoat. The conventional bodice shape is derived from the T-shape and, with several minor changes, is the basis for a variety of styles.

The gathered raglan sleeve is a variation of the set-in sleeve. There are unlimited ways that these pattern shapes can be put together to design a variety of garments. By adding trimming, insertion, embroidery, and lace you can vary the garment. And yokes of lace can be applied to simulate construction detail. The choices are endless.

Toddler and Child

The T-shape is useful for dressing a toddler or a child doll. It serves as the basis for petticoat, pinafore, dress, and coat designs where a set-in sleeve is not feasible. The front can be widened to set pleats or to gather. The same pattern is suitable for a dress or as an overblouse to be worn with trousers and a below-the-waistline belt by a Victorian boy. With a facing, it can be opened to serve as a jacket, blouse, or coat (Illus. 109).

The bodice shape provides most of the pattern possibilities. Use the bodice with a gathered or pleated skirt. Abbreviate it to serve as a yoke. Make a laced peasant bodice by fitting it closely and eliminating sleeves. Widen and extend it to the hips, then trim it elegantly to serve as a costume for a turn-of-the-century French *bébé*. As for the infant, the cap of the sleeve is usually gathered and therefore will fit into the armhole with no problem.

See Illus. 109b–c for skirt styles and alternative sleeve styles—all of which are based on simple shapes. An armhole ruffle may substitute for a sleeve. In Illus. 109d are alternatives to a simple neckline ruffle. In addition, pattern shapes are shown for a combination, romper, and pinafore. By combining simple pattern variations with your choice of trimmings, you can make similar styles appear vastly different (Illus. 110–111).

For hosiery use tubular bandage sold by pharmacies and medical supply houses. One such brand is Surgitube, which is sold in white or tan. The small size is most appropriate. Stockings and socks can also be purchased from a doll supplier or sewn with a back seam from cast-off socks.

Adult

This discussion of adult-doll pattern designs has been abridged because three excellent and definitive works (by Sirkis, Worrell, and Coleman et al.) have already been written on accurate historical costuming of dolls. The subject is so broad that to attempt to abstract from them would be impossible. But I have supplied some basic pattern shapes, which will serve in many instances to suggest a desired historic period. The same technique applies to adult-doll clothing and to children's doll clothing, although adult costumes are much more complicated. It is necessary to envision the basic shape—for the woman it is the same T-shape and the bodice shape—and to build the costume from that point. Again, much of the detail must be simulated because of the infeasibility of multiple seaming. The pattern shapes and suggested applications follow.

For the male dolls, trouser shapes, a shirt pattern, and a simple suit jacket in the Victorian mode are shown. The books on costuming mentioned above will present detailed patterns for historical accuracy in depicting male attire for other periods (Illus. 112).

Pattern Shapes	Suggested Garments

The T–Shape

The Bodice

Coat Front

Collar

Sleeve

Gather

Gather

Sleeve Band

Pattern Shapes	Suggested Garments

Gather

Raglan Sleeve

Yoke

Gather

Gather

Sleeve

Diaper Shape

Pattern Shapes	**Suggested Garments**

*The **T** Shape*

Bodice or Dress

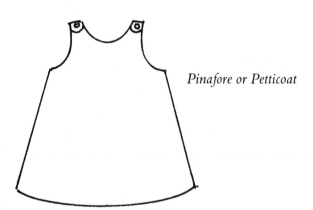

Pinafore or Petticoat

Pinafore

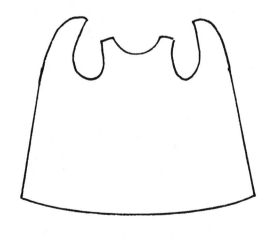

Pattern Shapes	**Suggested Garments**

Bodice Shape

Bodice or Dress

Sleeve

Yoke

Gather

Skirt

Pleated Front

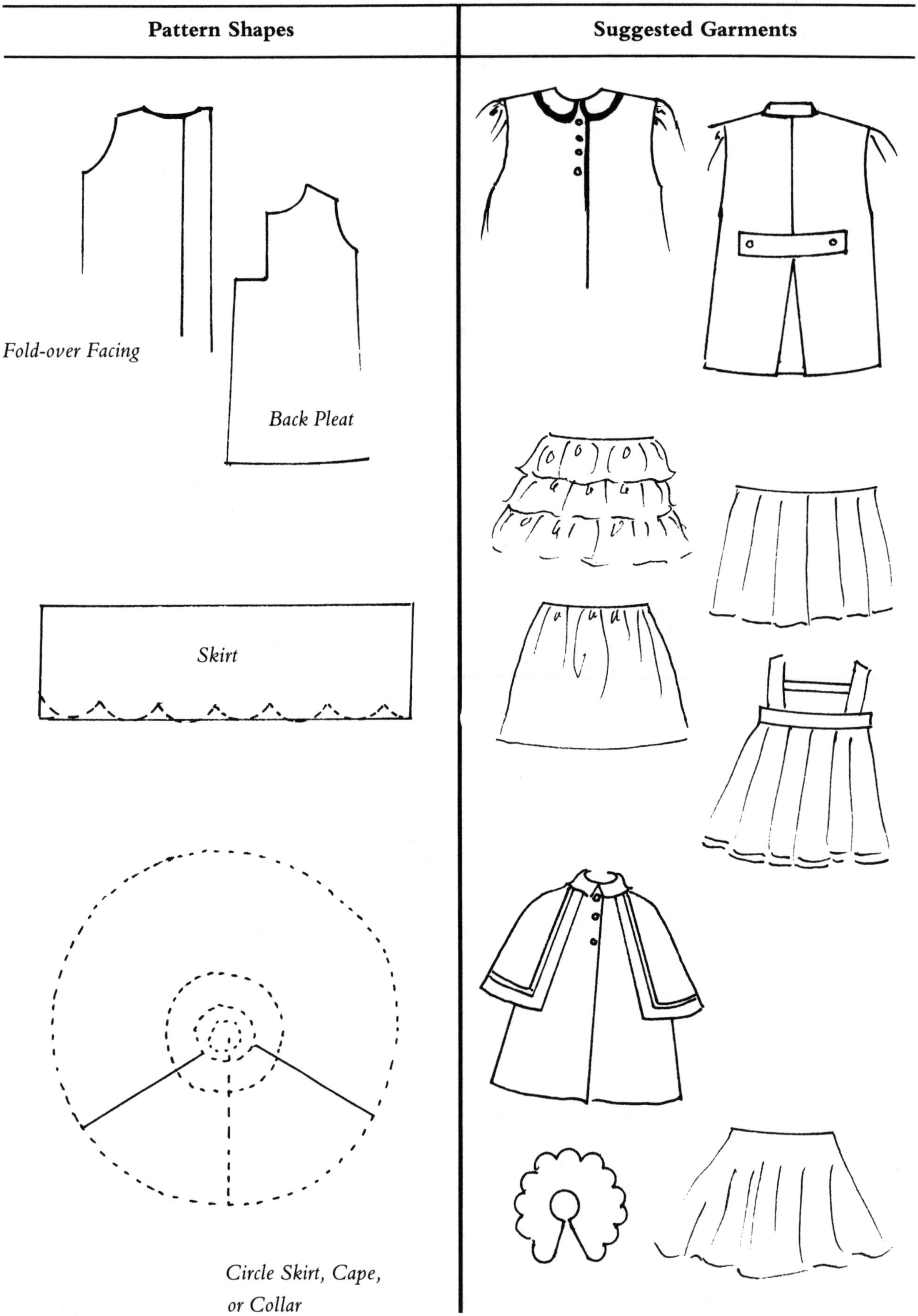

Pattern Shapes	**Suggested Garments**

Fold-over Facing

Back Pleat

Skirt

Circle Skirt, Cape, or Collar

Illus. 109d.

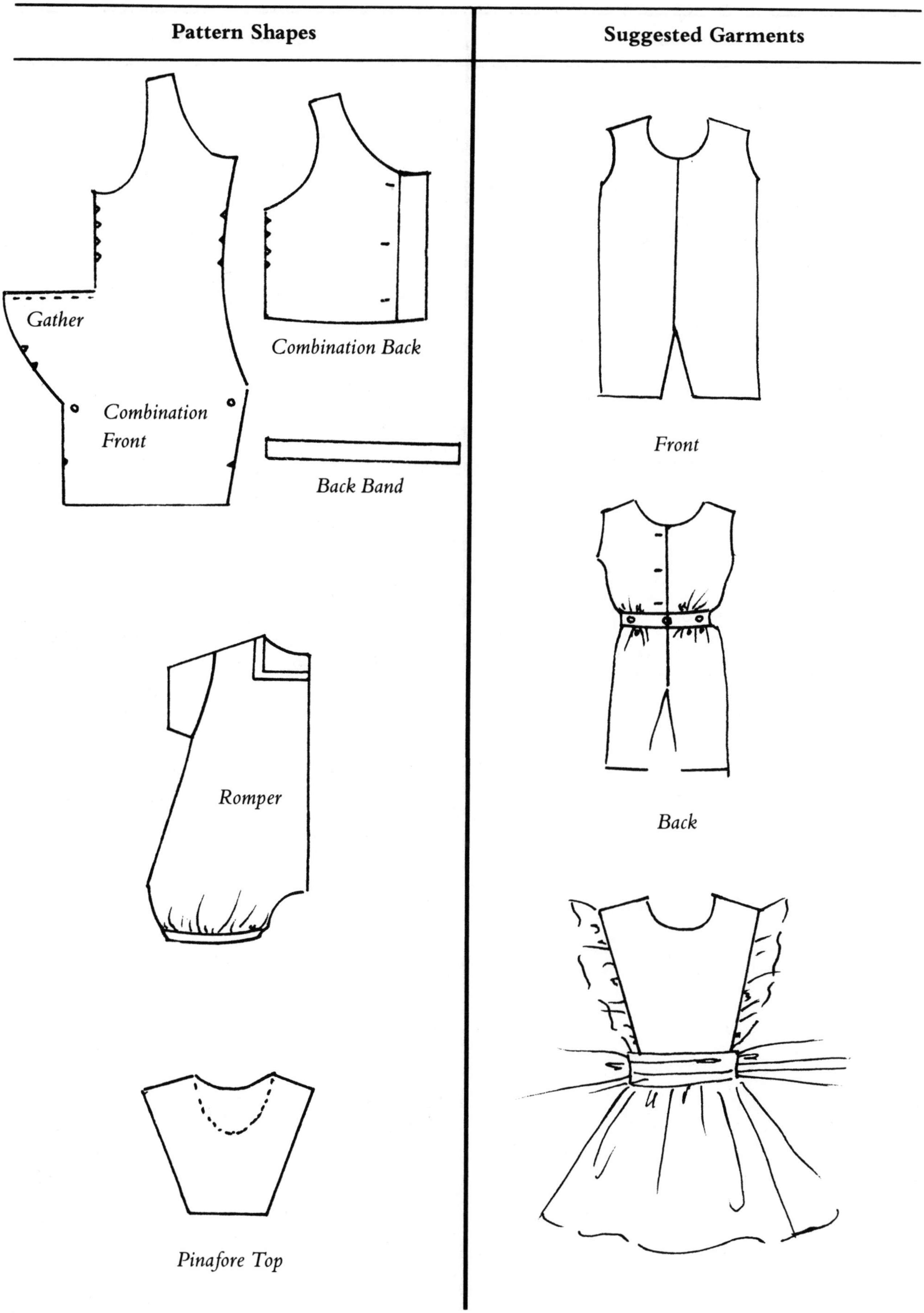

Pattern Shapes
Suggested Garments
Gather
Combination Front
Combination Back
Back Band
Romper
Pinafore Top
Front
Back

Illus. 110. Pattern shapes for trousers.

Pattern Shapes	Suggested Garments
Trouser	*Panties*
Bib, Strap, and Belt	*Knickers* *Overalls*
	Pantaloons

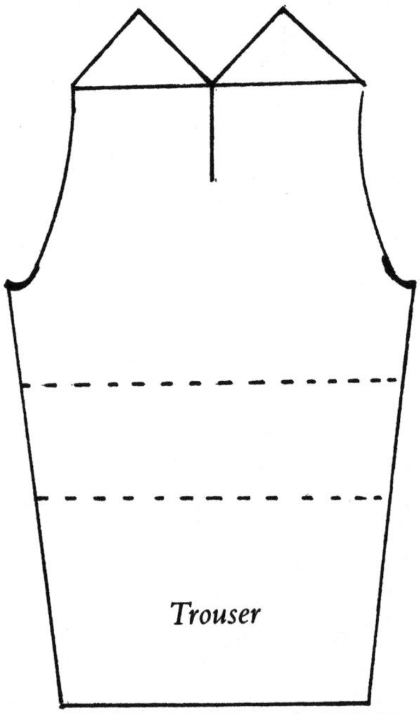

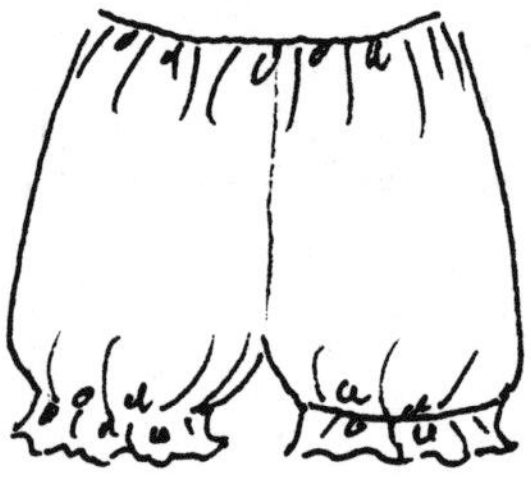

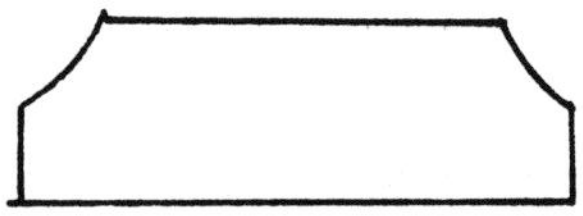

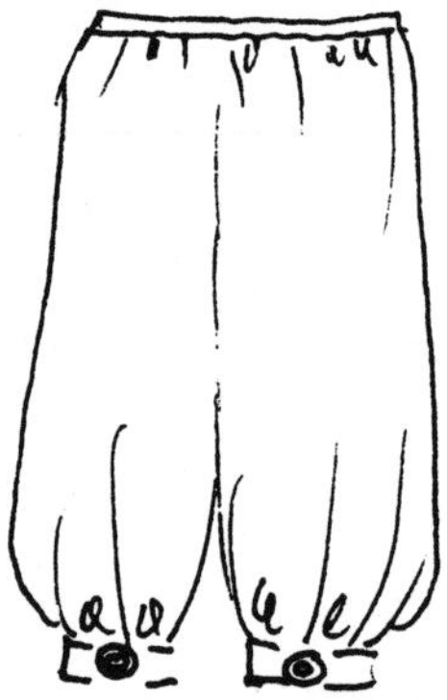

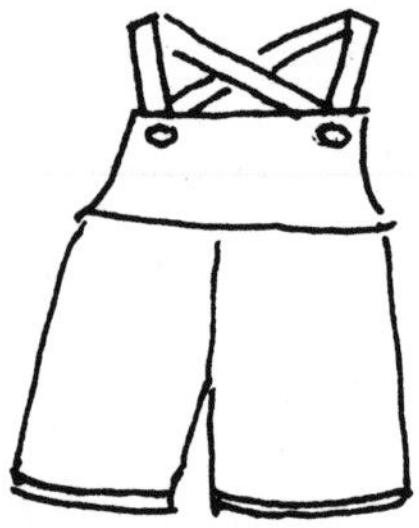

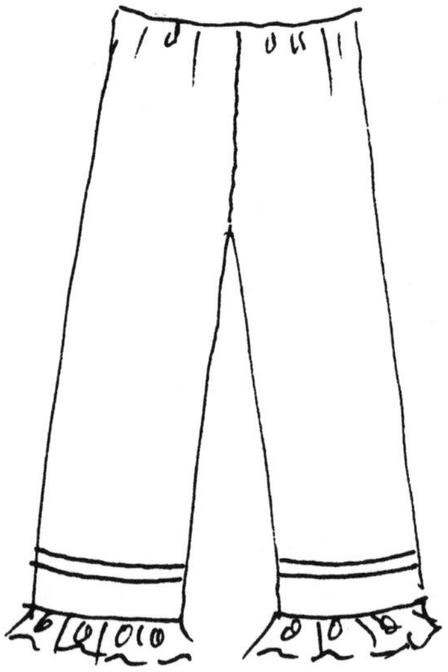

Illus. 111. Pattern shapes for collars.

Pattern Shapes	Suggested Garments

Collars

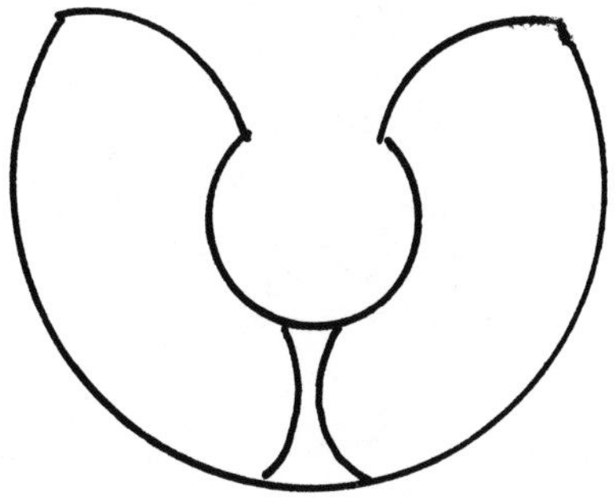

Round Tailored

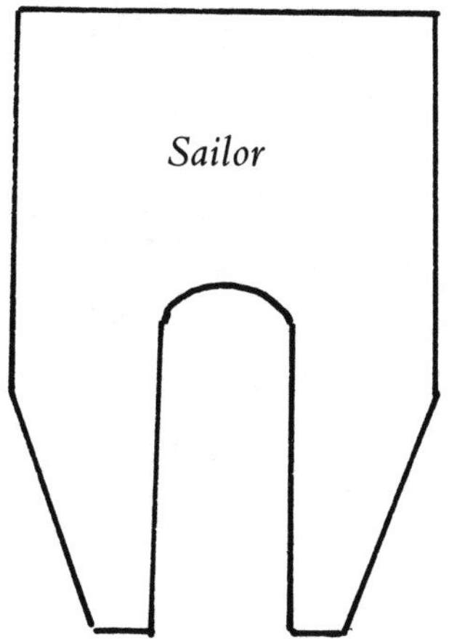

Sailor

Cross-over

Collars are always made in two layers, sewn, and then turned. Firm pressing improves their appearance. A simple ruffle of lace also makes an attractive collar.

Illus. 112. Pattern shapes for men's clothing.

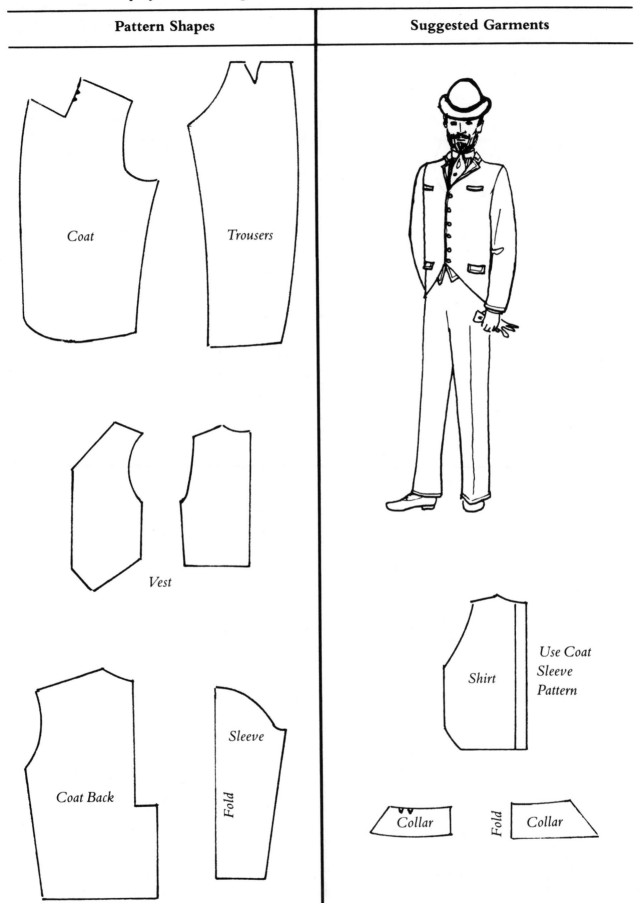

Pattern Shapes	**Suggested Garments**

Coat

Trousers

Vest

Coat Back

Sleeve

Fold

Shirt

Use Coat Sleeve Pattern

Collar

Fold

Collar

Pattern Shapes	Suggested Garments
	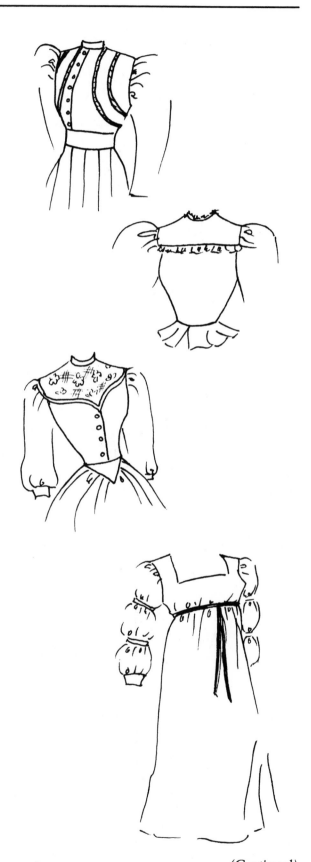

Bodice and Dress

Detail Can Be Simulated on Simple Bodice.

(Continued)

Pattern Shapes	Suggested Garments

Detail Can Be Simulated on Simple Bodice.

Pattern Shapes	Suggested Garments

Skirts

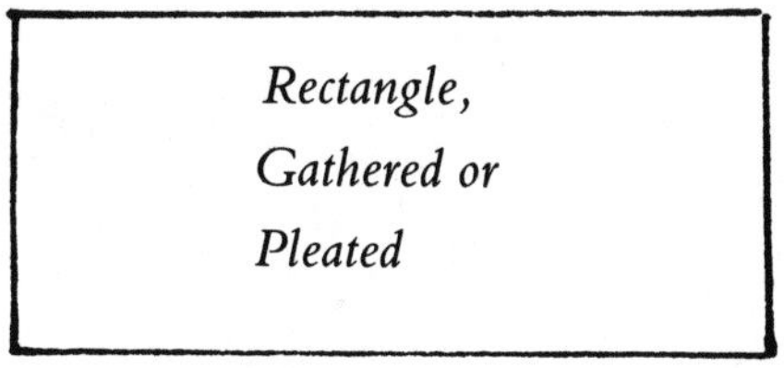

Rectangle,
Gathered or
Pleated

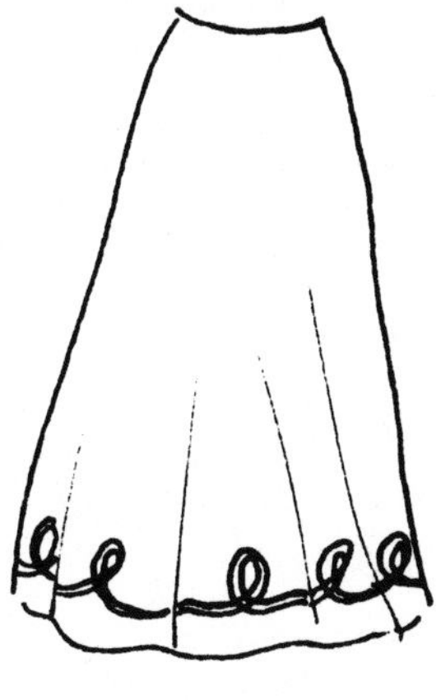

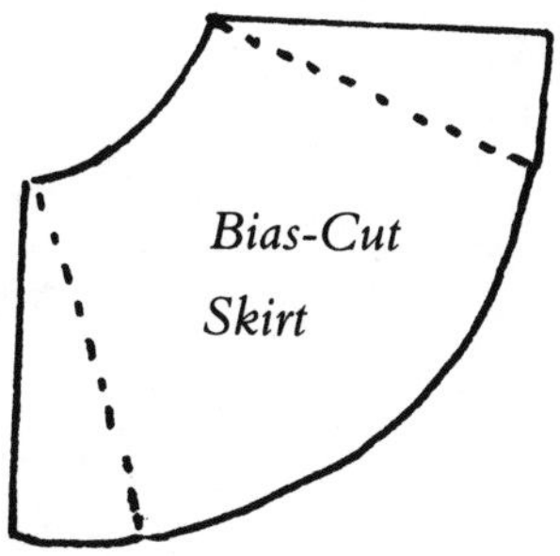

Bias-Cut
Skirt

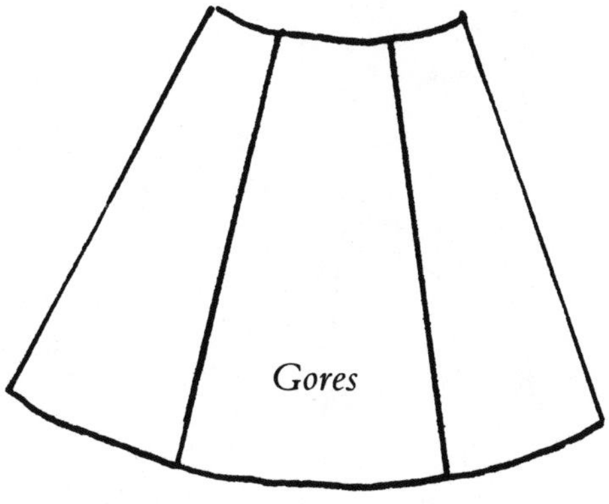

Gores

Insert Simulated
by Pleat

(Continued)

Pattern Shapes	Suggested Garments

Sleeve

10 Shoes

VARIETIES OF SHOES

Unshod dolls are incomplete. Mastering the cobbler's skills, therefore, is necessary for doll artists. Footwear can also be simulated. Porcelain and other hard dolls are sometimes made with modelled and painted shoes instead of feet. And as an alternative, a modelled shoe can be covered with thin leather or plastic, which is glued into position and finished with a leather sole to resemble a removable boot. A cloth leg can include the shoe as part of the construction. The shoe construction sometimes is, in fact, the foot, and it is attached directly to the leg with a wire. But usually dolls wear removable shoes.

Provide a cloth doll with a shoe pattern derived from the applicable portion of a leg pattern. Doll-parts supply houses sell a variety of shoe styles and sizes. But you may want to make a particular kind of shoe that is not available otherwise. The art of the cobbler requires, more than for any other costuming skill, a high degree of accuracy in measurement and fabrication in order to obtain satisfactory results. Tolerances are small in the tiny shoes, which rarely measure more than three inches in length.

The system for drafting shoe patterns of various sizes, which appears on page 144, was designed to eliminate much of the mystery of trial-and-error shoemaking.

SHOE MATERIALS

In the choice of shoe material—leather, plastic, or felt—thickness and pliability determine suitability. Shoe materials can be salvaged from old purses, discarded wallets, soft-sided luggage, and leather gloves. Purchase plastic material by the yard. Of course, the best material is leather, which is readily available from a leather wholesale or retail distributor. The most appropriate leather for doll shoes is glazed kidskin, which is available in black, brown, or white (which can be dyed). The skins measure about 2 feet by 2½ feet, are not expensive, and suffice for many pairs of shoes. Purchase calfskin, classified as 1½ oz. to 2 oz., by the pound. It is sold in scraps and is perfect for soles. A very thin leather, called skiver, which is less durable but lightweight (only ½ oz. to 1 oz.), is perfect for the smallest of shoes. Kid gloves serve well for diminutive shoes but require some stiffening if used for larger ones. To stiffen the glove kid, glue on (never iron on) organdy or a sheer stiffener to give it more body.

TOOLS AND OTHER SUPPLIES

Cardboard for inner soles and for making the pattern

Sandpaper for smoothing the edges of the cardboard pattern as well as the leather

Glue; Leather Weld is a white glue that dries transparent; Elmer's Glue-All is also good
Matching thread
Leather needle for the sewing machine
Glovers' hand-sewing needle (the smallest size available)
Sharp scissors or X-acto knife
Ruler marked in 1/16 inches
Piece of string for measuring
Soft-tipped pens that match the leather for touching-up
Tiny buttons, ribbon rosettes, tiny buckles, large beads
Bevel-edger for bevelling the leather-sole edges—size 1 (smallest)
Leather hand punch for making tiny holes, size 00 or 0
Block of balsa wood, 1″ × 1½″ × 12″ for carving a shoe block
Optional: draftsman's French curve for smoothing curves

BASIC PROCEDURE FOR SHOE CONSTRUCTION

Although the following instructions have been written for working in leather, the procedure is substantially the same for plastic or felt. Again, accuracy is essential, and this is one place where neatness does count.

Pattern

To accurately trace a pattern on the leather, first mount it on cardboard. Smooth all irregular edges and imperfections on the cardboard pattern with sandpaper. Trace the pattern on the wrong side of the leather. The decorative stitching line can also be marked on the wrong side as a guide. Reverse the pattern for a left and a right shoe if there is to be a difference between the two. Mark the center back and center fronts both on the upper and inner sole.

Cutting the Leather

Cut leather with sharp scissors or an X-acto knife. Notch or cut the toe and heel portion of the upper with pinking shears to remove some of the excess material.

Preparing the Leather

To smooth and remove imperfections, lightly sand the edge of the leather uppers and the soles. Bevel the wrong side of the sole with the bevel-edger to thin and remove the roughness on the back of the leather. Color the cut edges with matching soft-tipped pens. The sole can also be darkened along the edge if desired. Trim the leather sole a fraction smaller than the pattern. A heel can be constructed by using the appropriate portion of the sole pattern.

Cutting the Inner Sole

Make an inner sole of cardboard identical to the pattern and sand the edges smooth. If there is a difference between the left and the right shoe, mark the outside of each to avoid confusion, *L* and *R* respectively.

Decorative Stitching

A professional finish on the uppers is a perfectly stitched trim. This is more easily done on a sewing machine than by hand, but either is appropriate. Select a machine needle made specifically for leather, and the stitching should pose no problem. But you do need perfect control. To facilitate the stitching, use the guide line on the wrong side. For many sewing machines, a transparent plastic embroidery foot is available, which is useful because it enhances visibility. A medium-size stitch is best in order not to cut the leather.

Shaping the Upper—The Shoe Block

Shaping the upper by stretching it on a shoe block is optional but worth the effort. To make a simple shoe block, carve a piece of balsa wood into a shoe shape. Select a block of wood 1″ × 1½″ × 12″. Shape each end of the block into a rounded toe.

Lightly dampen the underside of the leather upper with isopropyl alcohol (rubbing alcohol) and stretch the toe section on the block (Illus. 114). Stretch gently until the appropriate shape is obtained. Water may also be used for this purpose but alcohol is preferable because it does not harm the leather and because it dries more quickly.

Assembling the Upper

To assemble the upper, stitch either by hand or by machine. Carefully match seam edges and

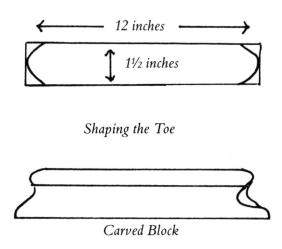

Shaping the Toe

Carved Block

Illus. 114. Carved shoe block.

begin stitching in the most visible place so that the alignment will be perfect. Sew back seams on the wrong side, press seam allowances flat with your fingers, and glue them on the inside. In more complicated constructions, completely assemble the upper before sewing the back seam. Sew or glue toe caps on the outside of the upper.

Gluing the Upper to the Sole
Glue the leather upper to the cardboard inner sole. Insert the inner sole into the upper, matching center back and toe markings. The cardboard inner sole fits snugly and may have to be sanded at the toe to get a perfect fit. Apply glue sparingly with a toothpick to the part of the leather upper that is to be folded under. The sides are glued first and are held in position with hair-pin clips. Fold under, fit, ease, and glue the toe and heel. The toe is the most critical part of the construction and must be perfectly round and smooth. Snip off the overlapping wedges of leather at the toe and heel where necessary. Lastly, fit and smooth the heel. Some of the back seam may also be snipped off to eliminate bulk. Press the leather edges with your fingers until they adhere to the inner sole and then set aside the shoe to dry completely. If a thin leather sole is to be used and indentation is obvious, a cardboard filler inserted under the leather sole will provide a smoother surface. Finally, glue the leather sole into place and glue the heel, if desired, into position.

Finishing the Upper
Trimmings, buttons, ties, laces, buckles, and rosettes are added last. Sew on buttons and fasten the cut thread with a dot of glue. A decorative inner sole can be inserted. Fashion shoelaces by dipping the ends of braid or heavy string in white glue to stiffen them. Large beads may replace buttons and, if sewn on with a long shank, can be buttoned. Touch up cut edges of the leather or tiny imperfections with soft-tipped pens.

PLASTIC SHOES
Using plastic requires careful experimentation since it varies greatly in character. The block can be used to shape the toe, but wetting is probably not necessary. Choose a fine sewing machine needle that will make small punctures in the plastic. Flexibility as well as thickness, just as in the choice of leather, will determine the choice of plastic.

SEWN AND TURNED SOLE
As a variation to the glued sole, a flexible sole may be sewn directly to the upper. This technique is best suited to a larger shoe. Assemble the upper as you would for any other shoe but leave it inside out. Then sew the upper to the wrong side of the sole, easing the two edges together with care so that the backs align perfectly. Then turn the shoe right side out. It is difficult to maneuver but must be done with exactness for the shoe to be attractive. Insert a rigid reinforcing sole so that the construction is covered by an inner sole. The selection of pattern size for this type shoe is complicated by the fact that the turning results in a finished shoe that is smaller. Be sure to add ¼ inch to the desired finished shoe size.

USING FELT
Felt shoes can be constructed in the same way that leather shoes are. It is preferable to use two layers of felt either glued together or attached by iron-on stiffening. No stretching or blocking is necessary. The soles may be stitched on as described earlier, or a hard sole can be made and glued on. To make a hard sole, wrap the cardboard outer sole with felt. Hold the fabric in place on the wrong side by stitching across from

one side to the other to fasten it. Make heels by cutting several layers of cardboard and gluing them together. Glue the shoe material to the outer surface and glue the sole material to the inner surface. Affix the finished heel to the sole.

PATTERNS FOR BASIC TYPES OF SHOES

In Illus. 115–19 are patterns for moccasins and three hard-sole constructions: a one-piece, two-piece, and three-piece upper. Assemble the hard-soled shoes as explained previously, after the uppers have been assembled. An infinite number of styles can be made with these three patterns only by changing the toe design. The moccasin will fit a 2- to 2½-inch-long foot—a size appropriate for a 14- or 15-inch baby or Indian doll. The hard-sole patterns are for a 2⅝-inch sole, but directions are given at the end of the chapter for drafting patterns of any size.

Moccasin

The moccasin is the simplest type of shoe construction because fit is not critical and there is no left and right designation (Illus. 115). The shoe is best made of felt or a soft leather glove. The edge is finished with a tiny contrasting buttonhole stitch.

Suggestions for assembly. To ensure perfectly even hand stitches, first stitch the cut pieces on an unthreaded sewing machine. Then place your hand stitches inside the perfectly spaced needle-puncture marks. Close the back seam by sewing the seam, matching the B's as marked. Then fold the back horizontally, and stitch along the line that forms the heel. Gather the upper and insert and stitch the toe.

One-Piece Upper—Two Styles

The inner sole, which is made of rigid cardboard, determines the shape and look of the shoe (Illus. 116). Although purchased shoes are not designated left and right, handmade shoes may be. This is done in several ways: by shaping the inner side of each sole, by making the sole triangular, or by reproducing the hourglass shape of an antique shoe, which is not really

Illus. 115. Moccasin pattern.

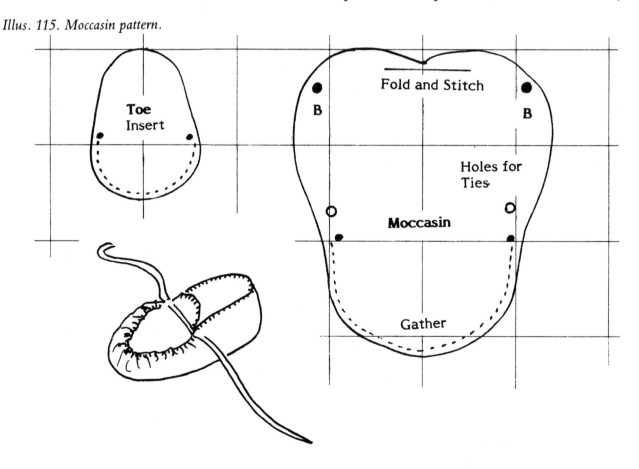

Illus. 116. Pattern for one-piece upper; two styles.

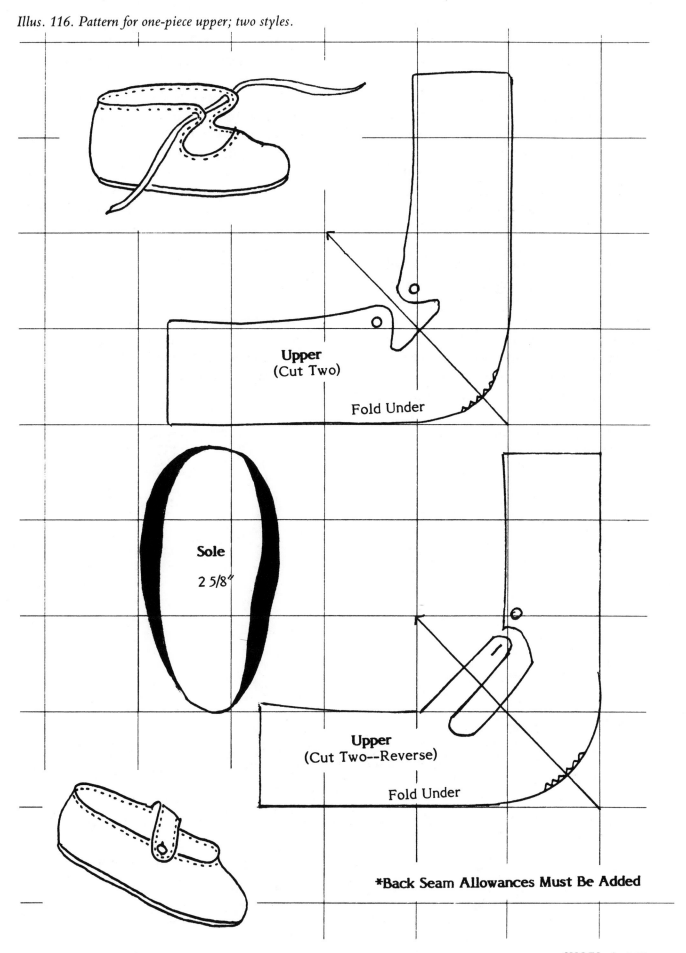

Upper
(Cut Two)

Fold Under

Sole

2 5/8"

Upper
(Cut Two--Reverse)

Fold Under

*Back Seam Allowances Must Be Added

different for right and left but is gracefully ambiguous. Before beginning construction, select a sole pattern.

Two-Piece Upper

To assemble the two-piece upper, overlap the toe and back sections and join the two along the seam allowance by stitching or gluing on the outside (Illus. 117). Then construct the shoe as you would any other. Decorate the toe with leather ornaments, rosettes, or any other confection.

Three-Piece Upper with Shaped Sole

The three-piece upper pattern is an old-fashioned, side-buttoned high shoe with a left and right differentiation (Illus. 118). It is a little more complicated to construct than the other patterns, but the following suggestions will facilitate the assembly. An additional measurement must be taken to ensure an adequate fit around the ankle.

Suggestions for assembly:
- Cut out the sole and the flap and then cut them out in reverse for a left and right shoe.

- Stitch the front seam with right sides together, matching *A* to *A*, *B* to *B*, and stitching seam. Flatten the seam and make a tiny slash to facilitate the turn. Turn the piece right side out.
- Then lay the upper flat and place the toe piece in position on the outside and match *B* to *B*. Sew seam *B–C*. The sewing is more easily done by hand. If desired, the decorative stitching can be done on the sewing machine, and the toe then glued into position instead.
- Sew the flap to the inner sides so that it will overlap the opening and button on the outer side of each shoe.
- Finally, close the back seam and continue the assembly as for any other shoe.

Oxford Pattern (Three-Piece Upper)

Overlap the toe and stitch it to the upper. Close the back after the toe has been applied. Be sure to add the back seam allowance (Illus. 119).

Illus. 117. Pattern for two-piece upper.

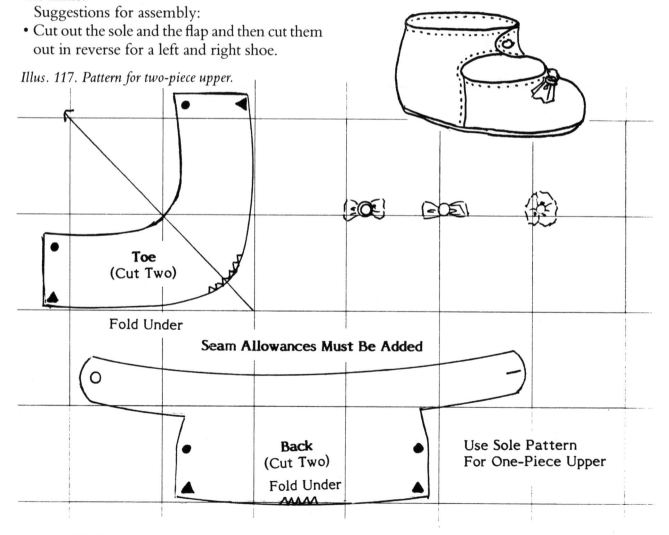

Toe
(Cut Two)

Fold Under

Seam Allowances Must Be Added

Back
(Cut Two)

Fold Under

Use Sole Pattern
For One-Piece Upper

Illus. 118. Pattern for three-piece upper.

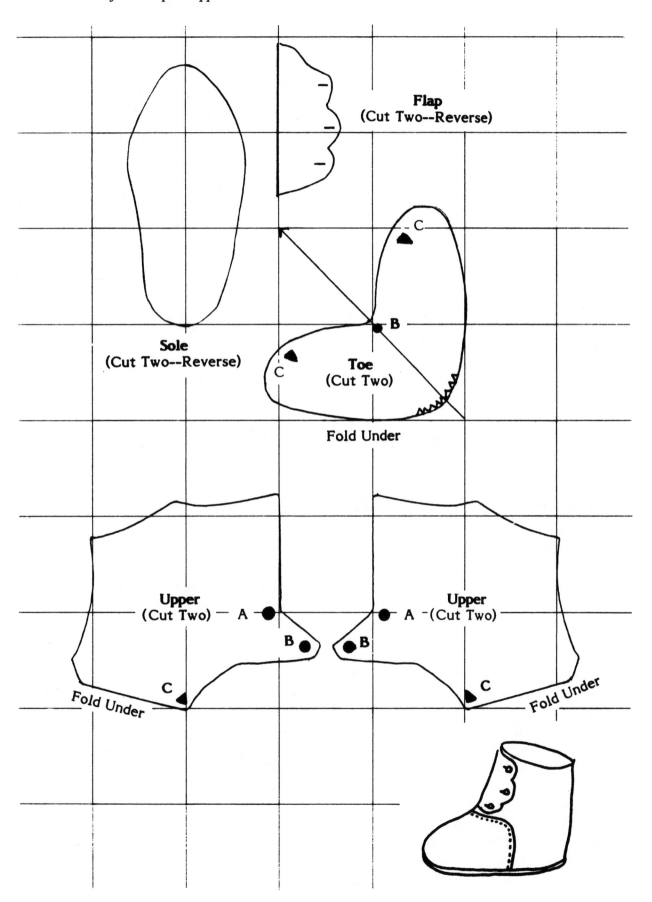

Flap
(Cut Two--Reverse)

C

B

C

Sole
(Cut Two--Reverse)

C

Toe
(Cut Two)

Fold Under

Upper
(Cut Two)

A

B

C

Upper
(Cut Two)

A

B

C

Fold Under

Fold Under

Illus. 119. Pattern for three-piece upper; oxford-style shoe.

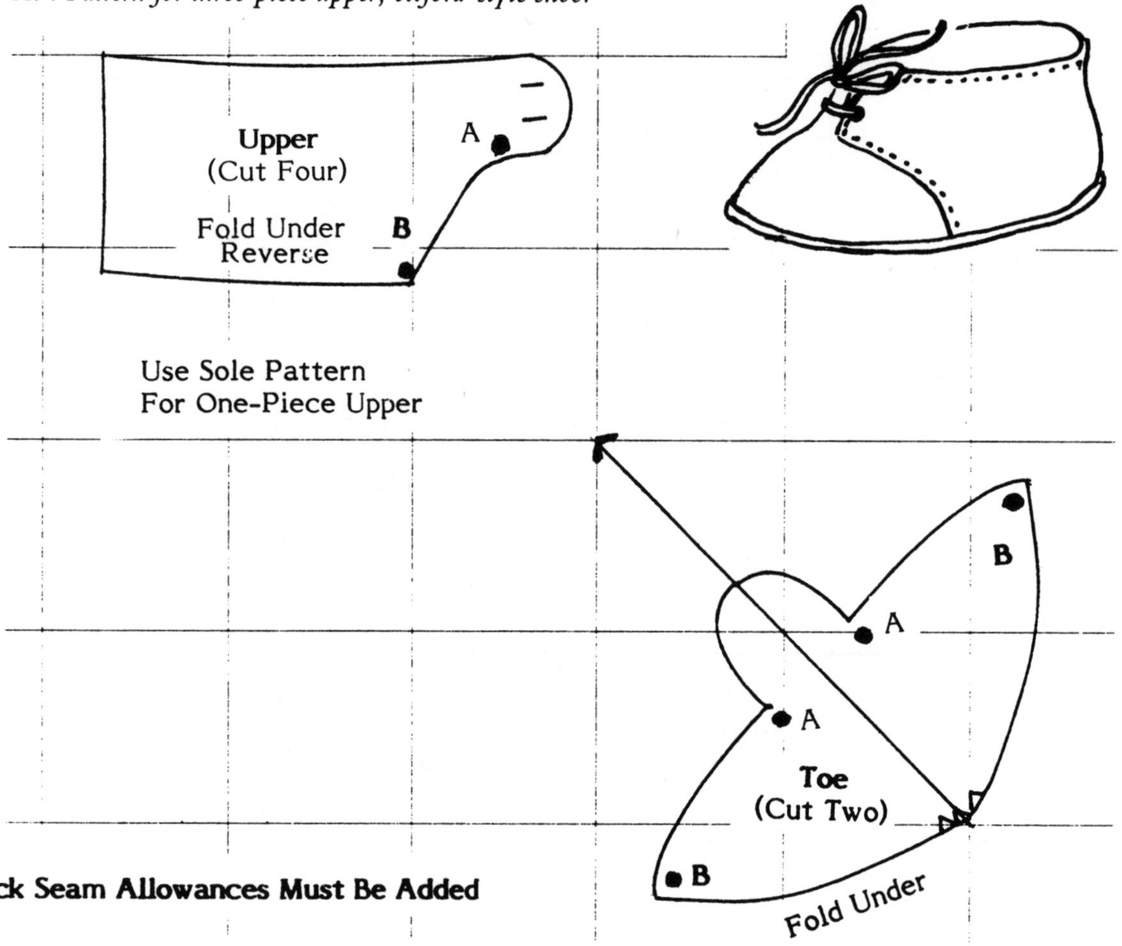

Upper
(Cut Four)
Fold Under
Reverse
A
B
Use Sole Pattern
For One-Piece Upper
B
A
A
Toe
(Cut Two)
B
Fold Under
*Back Seam Allowances Must Be Added

DRAFTING SHOE PATTERNS FOR CUSTOMIZED SHOES

Making specialized doll shoes does not have to be frustrating. The following pattern-drafting system eliminates most beginning errors.

Steps for Pattern Drafting

- Select a sole shape from Illus. 120 and a size from the chart in Illus. 121; it should closely approximate the size of the doll's foot, allowing for ease. Redesign the sole into the desired shape.
- Select the size from the master pattern in Illus. 123 or 124 that corresponds to the length of the sole that you have determined to be the correct size.
- Trace off the pattern given and *add seam allowance*. This is your master pattern. Design the shoe by modifying the contour of the sides and the style of the toe. Add straps or other construction details as desired.
- Cut the trial pattern from a piece of stiff fabric, assemble it, and check for correctness of fit and design.

Make the permanent pattern from the trial pattern.

The master pattern (see Illus. 123–24) can also be used to design two- and three-piece uppers by measuring the appropriate parts against the master pattern and adjusting for the necessary seam allowance.

Selecting a Sole Size and Redesigning the Sole

A doll's foot, like a human foot, needs space inside a shoe. Measure the foot over the stocking that will be worn. For a foot less than two inches long, choose a sole from the chart in Illus. 121 that is ⅛ to 3⁄16 inches longer and at least ⅛ inch wider than the foot. For a shoe more than two inches long, select a sole from ⅜ to 4⁄8 inches longer and from ⅛ to 2⁄8 inches wider than the foot.

For example, a foot measuring 2 inches long

by ⅞ inches wide would be best fitted by a sole that is 2¼ inches by 1 inch or 2¼ inches by 1⅛ inches, depending upon the design of the shoe. The sole can be altered by widening or narrowing, by pointing the toe, by drafting a triangular sole, by differentiating the left and right shoe, or by giving the sole an ambiguous hourglass shape (Illus. 120). These changes do not materially change the size of the upper.

The chart in Illus. 121 presents the dimensions of commercially made shoes. The soles are to be used as the basis for measuring sizes as well as to redraft other sole shapes. This is the inner sole of cardboard. Trim the leather sole a fraction smaller.

Using the Master Patterns

The master pattern in Illus. 124 is for a small shoe (sole length under 2 inches) and in Illus. 123 for a larger shoe (sole length over 2 inches). They have been designed for the average width doll's foot. *Because these patterns have no seam allowances, be sure to add an appropriate amount for the style you select.* The master pattern is used to determine the correct size of the shoe upper. Any style can be designed from the master pattern by changing the contour and height of the sides and modifying the toe design.

You can duplicate the shoe styles given for a 2⅝-inch sole in any size by using the master pattern, or you can design a totally original style. Trace the correct size from the master pattern chart, design the shoe, and when you are satisfied cut a trial shoe from a stiff material. Assemble the shoe and make corrections. Trace on cardboard to make the final pattern.

It is a good idea to compare the measurements of the shoe pattern with the measurement of the instep of the doll's foot. If the foot is exceptionally wide, the lower edge of the shoe can be broadened as shown in Illus. 122. A wide baby shoe would require a generous curve: a dainty slipper or high-heeled shoe would be best made by narrowing the curve. If, however, the shoe is closed or ankle length, the instep must be compared with the pattern and at least ⅛ inch ease added to the pattern.

To add seam allowance on a one-piece shoe, you must lengthen both edges of the back seam. On a two-piece upper, lengthen each cut edge for a total of four additions.

The design of the shoe and the shape of the doll's foot determines the height of the sides (Illus. 123–24). A diminutive shoe (under 2 inches long) might have a back with a finished height of from ½ to ¾ inches and a toe length

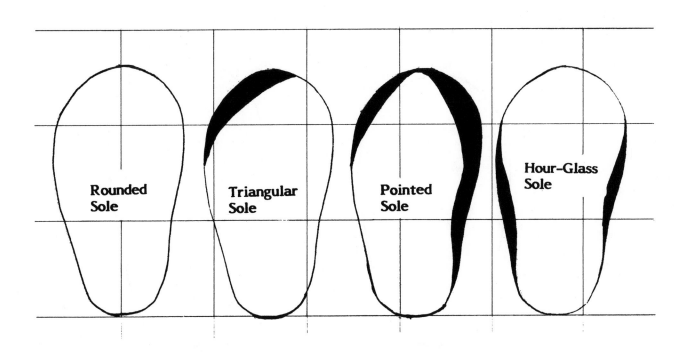

Illus. 120. Four types of sole shapes.

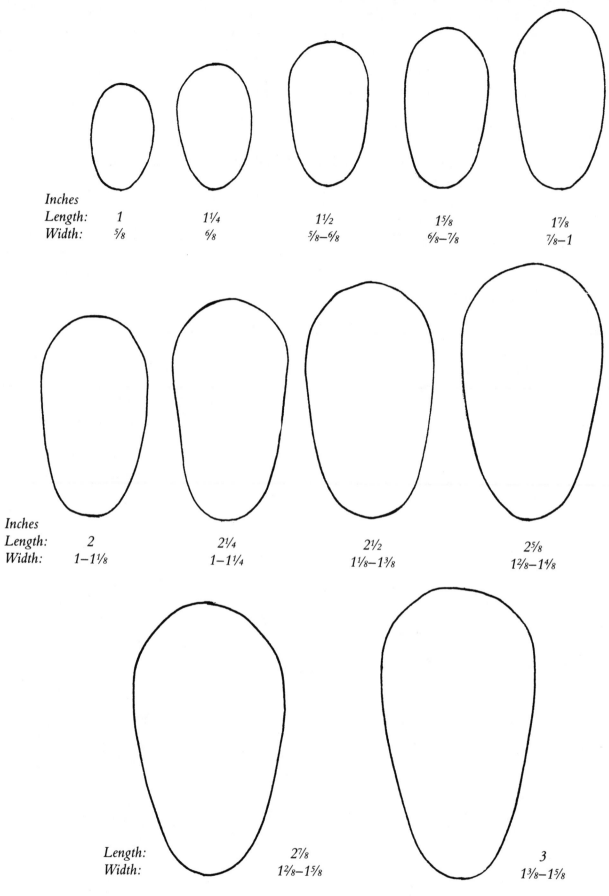

Inches
Length: 1   1¼   1½   1⅝   1⅞
Width: ⅝   6/8   ⅝—6/8   6/8—⅞   ⅞—1

Inches
Length: 2   2¼   2½   2⅝
Width: 1—1⅛   1—1¼   1⅛—1⅜   1²/₈—1⁴/₈

Length: 2⅞   3
Width: 1²/₈—1⅝   1³/₈—1⅝

Illus. 121. Chart for shoe sole sizes.

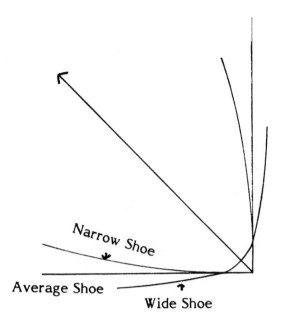

Narrow Shoe

Average Shoe

Wide Shoe

Illus. 122. Master pattern for shaping the narrow,
average, and wide shoe.

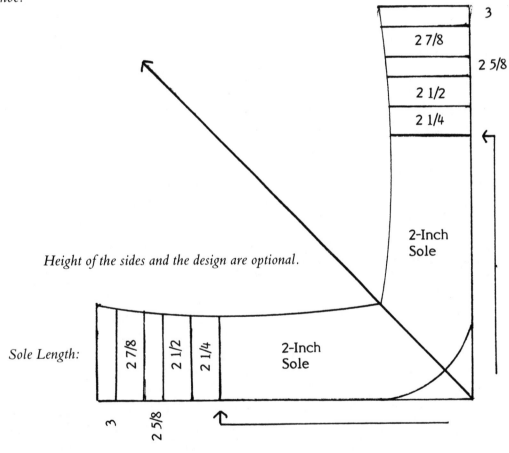

3

2 7/8

2 5/8

2 1/2

2 1/4

2-Inch
Sole

Height of the sides and the design are optional.

Sole Length:

2 7/8

2 1/2

2 1/4

2-Inch
Sole

3

2 5/8

Trace Pattern For Selected Sole Size.

Seam Allowances Must Be Added

Illus. 123. Master pattern for average-width shoe;
2- to 3-inch sole. Trace pattern for selected sole size.
Seam allowances must be added.

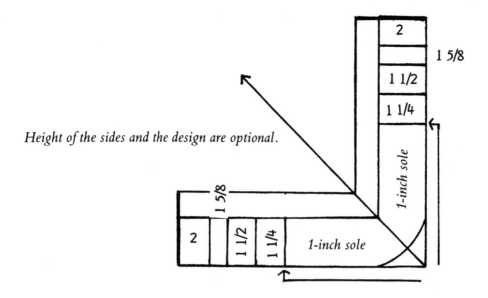

Height of the sides and the design are optional.

Illus. 124. Master pattern for average-width shoes;
1- to 2-inch sole. Trace pattern for selected sole size.
Seam allowances must be added.

from ½ to ¾ inches. A larger shoe might be from ¾ to 1 inch in height, depending on the size of the foot. The pattern must be fitted to the foot to ascertain the most attractive design.

The upper is two and one-half times longer than the sole. (See Table 4.) Therefore, for each

TABLE 4
LENGTH OF SHOE UPPER AND SOLE
(as given on master patterns)

Length of Sole (from toe to heel) (Inches)	Length of Upper★ (excludes seam allowance) (Inches)
1	2⅛
1⅛	3⅛
1⅝	3⅝
1⅝	4⅛
1⅞	4⅝
2	5
2⅛	5⅝
2⅛	6⅛
2⅝	6⅝
2⅞	7
3	7⅛

★Measure along the bottom edge of the shoe upper. The obvious question arises: How can the length of the upper be measured when the toe is a curve? An easy method is to lay a string along the bottom edge of the upper, rounding the toe carefully, and then to measure the string—another version of the "lay-on" measurement.

increment of ¼ inch in the length of the sole, increase the upper a total of ⅝ inches. Be sure to add seam allowance.

See Illus. 125 for a variety of suggested toe designs scaled for a larger shoe. To use them, trace on the shoe pattern. The designs can be adapted for a small shoe as well.

HIGH-HEEL SHOE WITH A SHAPED SOLE

Period costumes often call for shoes with high heels and shaped soles (Illus. 126). These can be made in the same way as any other shoes except that you apply the upper to a rigid, bent inner sole and you must construct a heel. Select an inner sole and redesign it to fit the doll's foot. Cut it, not in cardboard, but in Drape N' Shape sizing composition, which is available in craft shops. It is a woven material that is softened with water and is rigid when dry. Bend the sole to the desired shape and let it dry thoroughly. Glue together several thicknesses to provide the correct degree of rigidity. When the inner sole has hardened, construct the shoe as you would any other. The heel can be easily carved from balsa wood and covered with the leather. Then glue the heel in place.

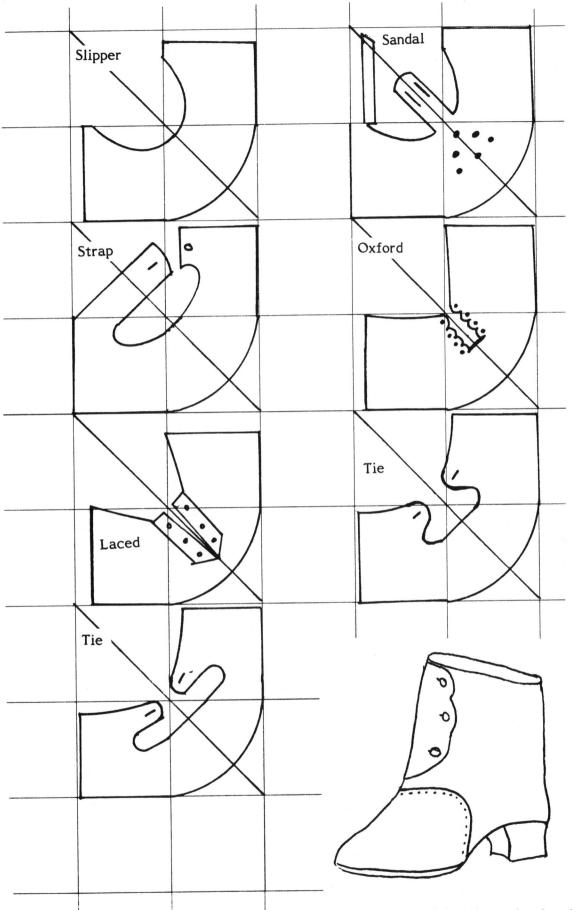

Slipper

Sandal

Strap

Oxford

Laced

Tie

Tie

Illus. 125. Suggested toe designs.

Illus. 126. High-heel shoe with a shaped sole.

SHOES ♦ 149

11　Hats

An important member of the costumer's team is the milliner. Although dolls frequently do not wear hats—and for many the head covering is more fanciful than realistic—hats can be used to define a character. A hat might be a wreath of flowers, a large bow, or a knit cap made of the cuff of a sock. But sometimes a well-made bonnet, a felt hat, a straw sailor's hat, or an infant's cap is necessary to complete a doll's costume. You can purchase doll hats made of straw or felt in a variety of styles and sizes. They can be restyled by folding, bending, and retrimming with ribbons, flowers, or feathers. But to make an original hat is a challenge and provides an opportunity to exercise the imagination.

In keeping with the theme of this book, I have included patterns that are to be used as the basis for your redesigns and innovative styling. Sizes 6 through 12 indicate the circumference of the doll's head in inches at the hairline. For example, size 12 indicates a head circumference of 12 inches.

TYPES OF HAT CONSTRUCTION

There are two types of hats: those that perch on the head and those that fit the head. Perched hats are not sized to the head but are designed in proportion to the doll. Head-sized hats need to fit closely and, therefore, are more difficult to execute.

There are also two types of hat constructions: supported and unsupported construction. Supported construction is made by building a frame of wire or wired buckram and covering the foundation with the desired fabric. An unsupported hat, though it may use some stiffening and wire, has no understructure. Poke bonnets are supported hats. Unsupported hats come in various styles and can be made of fabric, felt, or straw. The doll-hat milliner can be much more versatile than the human-hat milliner; a soft bonnet can be transformed into a rigid one by replacing the stiffening with wire, or vice versa.

MATERIALS AND TOOLS

Many of the materials used in hatmaking are also used for dressmaking, although some are unique to millinery. They are available from a distributor for millinery supplies via mail order. Here are some of the most common materials used.

Foundation Materials

The foundation materials are buckram, crinoline, and woven and nonwoven iron-on stiffenings. Buckram is a coarsely woven, stiff, heavily sized material. It can be sewn, wet, and shaped and is the most common foundation material. It is sold by the yard in both black and white. One-ply buckram is lightest in weight.

Unsized buckram is called flexible buckram, and it can be cut on the bias and used for rolled brims.

Crinoline is a fine, open-mesh material resembling stiff cheesecloth. It can be cut on the bias and is used for binding edges. It is sold by the yard in either black or white.

Woven and nonwoven interfacings are sold in fabric shops. There are a variety of weights and kinds, including fusible interfacing that can be attached on one or both of its sides.

Outer Fabrics

Outer fabrics and linings for supported hats can be made of any material that works. Taffetas, silks, fine cottons, and velours are good choices. Fur felt is most desirable but is generally available only in thrift-shop cast-offs. Pure wool felt is a second choice. If the felt is less than 60 percent wool, it will not prove to be completely satisfactory. Craft shops sell ½-inch straw braid, which is used for making large straw hats. Narrower braid is available from a distributor for millinery supplies or in miniature shops. If neither is available, you can make excellent "straw" from crepe paper. Cut the paper in 1-inch widths, pull, and braid it.

Wire

There are three kinds of wire used in millinery construction: brace (frame) wire, lace wire, and ribbon wire. Brace wire is a special silk-wrapped wire that is sold by a millinery supplies distributor. Use sizes No. 19 and No. 21; the latter is lighter in weight. Use brace wire to reinforce the brim and crown edges and to make wire foundations. Lace wire is a finer silk-wrapped wire used where only slight stiffness is required.

Ribbon wire is a fine wire enclosed in buckram and is available in widths ranging from ¼ inch to 1 inch. It is used to reinforce or support bows, for reinforcing the brims of doll bonnets, and anywhere slight stiffening is required.

Use wire joiners—metal tubes about ½ inch to 1 inch long—to join wires into a circle. In the absence of joiners, the ends of the wire can be overlapped, wrapped, and tied with thread or fine jewelry wire.

Sizing

For stiffening use fabric sizing, liquid starch, milliners' sizing, or clear acrylic spray.

Tools

Useful tools include wire cutters, a needle-nose plier, a kettle for steaming, and a variety of objects or blocks for shaping the crown of a felt hat.

Additionally, as a doll milliner, you will need to draw perfect circles. Plastic styluses for drawing small circles are available from a drafting supplies shop, but for drawing large circles, a simple compass is an essential. (Patterns that depend on large circles include appropriate compass settings.) Milliners' needles, which are longer than other hand-sewing needles, are useful in sizes 8 and 10, the latter being the finer.

SEWING TECHNIQUES FOR THE DOLL MILLINER

Many of the milliner's techniques are the same as those of the dressmaker. However, some of the methods previously described are important enough to repeat.

Bias Cutting

For maximum drape, cut woven fabric to be used in hatmaking on the true bias. Cutting on the true bias means cutting at a 45° angle to the crosswise or lengthwise thread.

Clipping and Notching Seam Allowances

Whenever you turn or fit a curved edge to a straight edge, you must clip or notch the seam allowance. Removing the excess allowance in the seam or easing the turn by clipping after stitching produces a smoother joining.

USING WIRE

A variety of techniques for the use of wire are unique to hatmaking.

Springing the Wire

This refers to the process which prevents kinking when a new coil of wire is untied. Hold the coil firmly and cut the ties so that the wire can gently relax. Keep the coil tied loosely so that the pieces can be pulled from the coil without distortion.

Straightening the Wire

Once the wire is cut it must be straightened, or it will resume its curl. To straighten the wire, run your thumb and forefinger firmly against the curl.

Joining the Wire

A wire can be joined with tubular wire joiners that are fitted to the ends of the wire and clamped with pliers. Wire ends can also be over-lapped about an inch and tied with thread or fine jewelry wire. Always cut, shape, and join the wire that is used in shaping the bonnet before sewing it to the hat.

Sewing the Wire

Wire can be sewn to a foundation with a ma-chine zigzag stitch, but it is easier to attach it on the buckram or felt by hand with tiny, loose overcast stitches. Wire can be slipped into a casing or placed between two layers of fabric.

Gathering with Wire

Use a fine jewelry wire for shirring a lining or gathering a bonnet. Sew a narrow casing and thread the wire through it. Arrange the gathers evenly along the wire. Sew the wire securely at the ends.

PRESSING

Always press a hat over a curved surface to shape it. Use a pad if you can't lay the hat on a flat ironing board.

CIRCLING

Circling is a process in which ribbon edging, bias finishes, or braid is shaped before you sew it onto a curved surface. To curve them, press in an arc with the iron. Another method is to wet the edging and wrap it around the edge of a plate that is approximately the same size as the circle desired. When the edging dries curve it to sim-plify application. Of course you must test every material before wetting it.

MAKING A SUPPORTED HAT

A supported hat is one in which the shape is established and maintained by a wired buckram foundation. Regardless of the style of the hat the method is the same. A bonnet, for example, consists of three parts: a crown, sideband, and brim. Cut them out of buckram and then wire and assemble them by notching, slashing, and sewing. Cover this foundation with the interlin-ing of muslin and then cover with the outer fabric and fit with a decorative lining. Then trim the hat in whatever manner your imagination dictates. It is a lengthy procedure but yields a bonnet that is recognizably superior. Sugges-tions for making a supported bonnet follow. Large sizes are easier to make.

Preparing the Pattern

Whatever the source of the pattern, redraft it so that you don't cut it on the fold. Measure it on the doll's head and examine the pieces to make sure they will fit together.

Preparing the Buckram

Cut out the three buckram pieces (crown, side-band, and brim). Measure, cut, and join the wire for each of the parts that require wire. Then wire the entire crown, three sides of the sideband, and the outer edge of the trim. If the bonnet is to be large, ribbon wire can be used to reinforce the width of the brim. Sew the wire on the separate pieces with an overcast stitch, using a waxed thread. Place the wire joining on the crown in the least conspicuous location (Illus. 127).

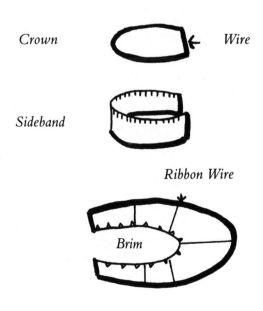

Illus. 127. Wiring, slashing, and notching the foundation.

Assembling the Buckram Foundation

In order to assemble the three parts, they must be slashed and notched so that they will fit together. Slash the sideband to fit to the crown. Notch the brim to fit to the sideband. Fold the slashes on the sideband down and fold the notches on the brim up so that you can assemble the pieces. Fit the outer side of the foundation so it is smooth. Sew the pieces together and check the buckram foundation for fit (Illus. 128).

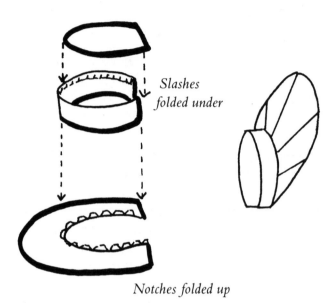

Slashes folded under

Notches folded up

Illus. 128. Fitting the parts of the foundation together.

Binding the Wire

Cover the wired edges of the crown, the sideband, and the outer edge of the brim with a bias strip of muslin. This is done to conceal the contour of the wire. Cut a bias strip 1 inch wide and, without turning under raw edges, stretch and sew the binding over the wire to the buckram, using a loose running stitch.

Interlining

Cover the entire bonnet frame with a muslin interlining to cushion the buckram texture and provide a padding for the outer fabric. The pattern pieces for the interlining and the outer cover are identical. Both are larger than the buckram so you can turn part of it under. Make two crown pieces, two sidebands, and two brims because both the inside and the outside of the bonnet must be interlined.

To make an interlining, follow these steps in the order they are given:

Brim
- Cover the underside of the brim, basting the interlining to the buckram brim. Don't turn the raw edges under.
- Cover the outer surface of the brim. Bring the interlining over the wired edge, trim it, turn it under and neatly slip-stitch it to the front of the underbrim. Don't turn under the back raw edge of the brim interlining but baste it to the buckram sideband.

Crown
- Cover the inside of the crown. Turn the neck edge only, and baste it to the buckram. Lay the opposite side flat and baste it to the buckram sideband. Cover the outside of the crown. Fold under the neck edge and slip-stitch it to the inner neck edge. Lay the opposite raw edge flat and baste to the buckram sideband.

Sideband
- Fold under all of the raw edges on the sideband.
- Sew the inside sideband in place through the buckram.
- Place the outer sideband so that it covers all of the raw edges and the basting stitches. Slip-stitch neatly to hold securely.

Covering the Supported Bonnet

Attach the bonnet cover in much the same way as you did the interlining. Cover the crown, sideband, and the outside of the brim with the outer material. Line the inside. The lining material can either be identical to that of the cover or a thinner material.

Brim
- Cover the outside of the brim. Turn under the seam allowance at the front and side edges; clip the excess fabric and slip-stitch the cover to the underside of the interlining. Lay the back of the brim cover flat without turning under and baste it flat to the interlining of the sideband.

Crown
- Cover the crown. Turn under the raw edge at the neck and slip-stitch it to the interlining. Lay the crown cover flat and baste to the interlining of the sideband.

Sideband
- Fold all of the edges of the sideband. Lay it on the bonnet so that all of the construction details of the crown and the brim are hidden. Tack the

joinings to hold the sideband in place. Slip-stitch the sides in place.

Lining the Supported Bonnet

It is easier when working on a small bonnet to construct the crown and sideband lining and then fit them into the interior of the hat. A few tacks in the seam line will hold the lining securely. Cover the underbrim of the hat with the outer fabric or fit with a finer shirred or pleated lining.

For an optional brim lining, cut a bias strip a little longer than the brim and about 1 inch wider. Turn the outer edge under and neatly sew to the outer wired edge of the brim. Then draw the lining inside and tack it. A large bonnet might require shirring of the lining in several parallel rows to hold it. This is done by stitching a casing in the lining and pulling a fine wire through it to hold the gathers. The sideband can be used to cover the construction detail.

Trimming the Supported Bonnet

The bonnet can be trimmed in a grand variety of ruffles, bows, lace, feathers, ribbon, and flowers or in a combination of all of them. The outer edge of the brim does require braid or lace to hide the stitching. A neck ruffle is often added to conceal the neckline stitching. A double ruffle inside the brim makes an attractive frame for the face.

Options

The supported hat is most effective when made in larger sizes. It is a detailed procedure and some options can be elected. It is not essential to bind the wire; a heavy outer fabric will permit the omission of an interlining. The pattern for the supported bonnet can be used in a different way by employing iron-on or woven and non-woven stiffenings to simplify the construction. Many changes in the shape of the brim and the crown can be elected, but the procedure is the same for constructing the true supported bonnet.

MAKING AN UNSUPPORTED HAT

Be sure to employ good dressmaking techniques in making an unsupported hat. Interfacing, stiffening, and wire are used at your option

to achieve desired effects. The patterns given in this chapter for constructing supported bonnets can also be used without foundations. Use the buckram pattern for the supported hat to make an unsupported bonnet.

Felt

Felt is available in a wide range of weights, from industrial to dressmaker weight. Fur felts are best for hatmaking, but the only sources for small pieces of fur felt are hats salvaged from thrift shops. The second choice is 100 percent wool felt available in industrial weights in grey and off-white only. Dressmaker or display felt, which is made in a variety of colors and in 50 percent to 70 percent wool with a balance of rayon fibre, can be bought by the yard. Felt that is less than 60 percent wool will not steam and shape well but can be seamed instead.

Shape felt by blocking it on a suitable object and steaming over a tea kettle. For doll hats improvise a block by using any object that yields the desired shape—a jar lid, pepper mill, or, in fact, any wooden object. Pull the felt over the block and steam, pull, pat, ease, and shape it while moist. Be sure to avoid wetting the felt too much and burning your fingers from the steam. Now let this shaped felt dry. There is some limit to the amount of shaping that can be accomplished with ordinary felt. A shallow-crown sailor hat with a wide brim can be blocked in one piece, but a deep-crown cloche with a brim should probably be constructed in two parts. Block and trim the exaggerated crown. Then attach the brim, which has been shaped separately. Notch the inner edge of the brim so that it will fit the crown; conceal the joining with a ribbon hatband. A flat brim can be wired to create a rigid shape. For stiffness glue together two layers of felt. Sizing, spray starch, or acrylic craft spray can also be used on the inside of the hat to provide stiffness. It is important to check before spraying for any adverse effects on the felt. Felt can be used in the same way as other fabric in hatmaking.

Straw

Straw braid is available from craft shops, millinery supply houses, and miniature shops. Imitation straw can be made by braiding 1-inch- or

1½-inch-wide strips of crepe paper. (Clamping one end of the braid under a sewing machine foot frees one of your hands.) Coil the straw braid and sew with tiny invisible stitches into the desired shape. It is helpful to draw the shape of the crown and use it as a pattern for coiling. After forming the crown into a flat shape, sew the straw perpendicularly to form a sideband and sew flat to form a brim (Illus. 129). To add shape, lace a thin wire through the edge of the brim. To form a rounded crown, use a block on which to coil the straw.

Shape real straw more readily by wetting. Stiffen and protect crepe-paper "straw" with an acrylic spray.

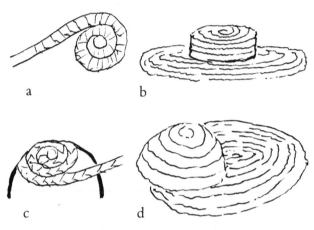

Illus. 129. Constructing a straw braid hat; (a) flat coil, (b) straw sailor hat, (c) curved coil, (d) straw bonnet.

PATTERNS

Here are several full-size patterns for you to use as a doll milliner. Measure the doll's head loosely over its wig and at the widest part of its head, just above the ears. The patterns will fit heads from 6 to 12 inches (sizes 6 to 12). See Illus. 130 for each of the seven sizes. Every pattern should be checked before using.

In keeping with the theme of this book, the patterns are meant to provide the basis for innovation and redesign. Minimal instructions are given for making the hats unless the procedure varies from a dressmaking technique. Seam allowances are already included in the patterns. The allowances are the narrowest feasible—usually not more than ⅛ inch. However, there is enough latitude in the pattern so the critical measurement is not important. Some of the patterns require large circles. In order to draw the appropriate sizes, follow the given compass settings. Make the setting by measuring against a ruler.

Infant's Cap

An infant's cap is easy to make. To avoid visible stitching, make it in two layers and line it edge to edge. Cut the two layers identically and seam them together at the face and neck edge. Turn, press, and close the bonnet at the back seam. Fit the circle into the gathered side. The bonnet is most attractive if you place a sheer white fabric, like lace or eyelet, over a solid pastel (Illus. 131). The pattern can also be varied to produce a 19th-century style bonnet.

Front-Gathered Bonnet

For a front-gathered bonnet, choose a stiff fabric like organdy. You will need two layers of fabric to provide sufficient stiffness, and they should both be transparent. Pinking the edges of the ruffles, if the fabric permits, is an historically accurate finish for this turn-of-the-century bonnet. Measurements for the hat, band, and ruffle are given in Illus. 132. Elaborately trim the bonnet with lace, flowers, and bows. The ruffles can be of the same material, lace, or eyelet. Two rows of ruffles are most effective. Place the maximum gathering over the front of the bonnet so that the crown rises in a high peak over the forehead.

Cut appropriate size hat, band, and ruffle according to the measurements given in Illus. 132. Gather the hat around the sides and the top between the indicated dots. Double the band and sew completely around the hat from dot to dot. Pull the gathers to the top of the bonnet. Attach the ruffles to the band. Hem and trim the neck edge with lace if desired.

Banded Mob Cap

A banded mob cap (Illus. 133) also requires a stiff fabric, like organdy or taffeta. It consists of a large gathered circle onto which a band is sewn. A single or double ruffle forms the brim. Appropriate trims include rosettes, flowers, and lace. The crown can be exaggerated by increasing the size of the circle. Use an underlayer of organdy to accentuate the stiffness.

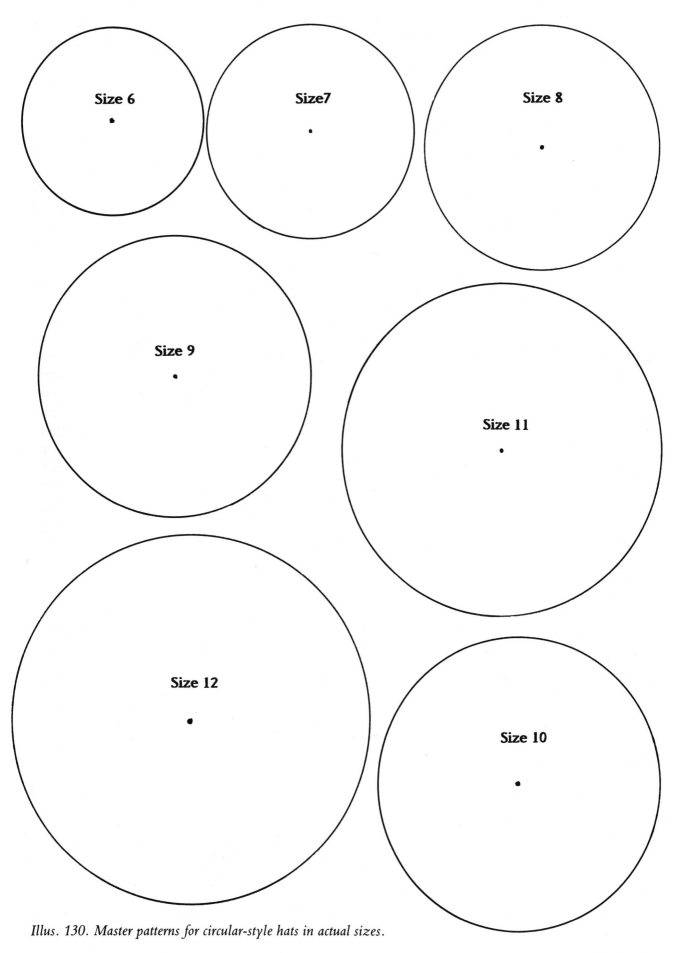

Illus. 130. Master patterns for circular-style hats in actual sizes.

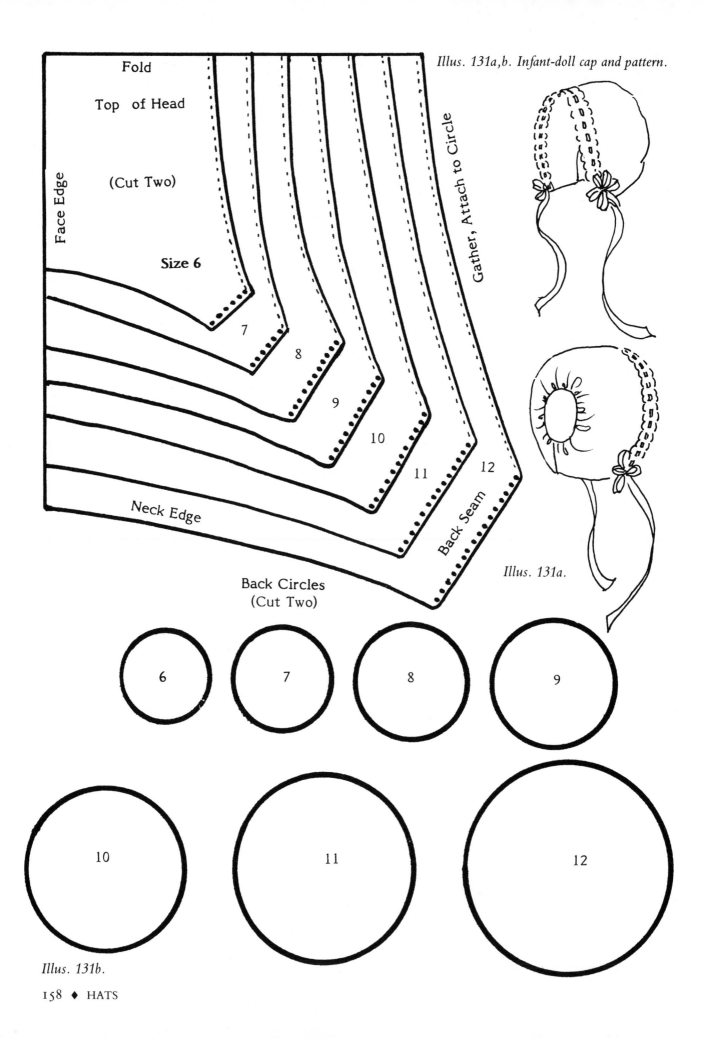

Fold

Top of Head

(Cut Two)

Face Edge

Size 6

7

8

9

10

11

12

Gather, Attach to Circle

Back Seam

Neck Edge

Back Circles
(Cut Two)

Illus. 131a,b. Infant-doll cap and pattern.

Illus. 131a.

6

7

8

9

10

11

12

Illus. 131b.

Illus. 132a,b. Front-gathered bonnet and pattern.

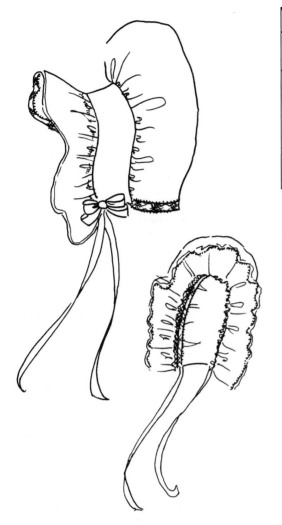

Head Size	Cut Hat		Cut Band		Cut Ruffle	
	Width Inches	Length Inches	Width Inches	Length Inches	Width Inches	Length Inches
6	2½	3¾	1	5½	1	11
7	3	4½	1	6	1	12
8	3½	5¼	1¼	6½	1¼	13
9	4	6	1¼	7	1¼	14
10	4½	6¾	1½	7½	1½	15
11	5	7½	1½	8	1½	16
12	5½	8¼	2	8½	2	17

Illus. 132a.

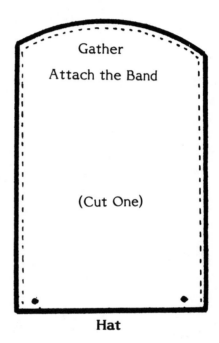

Gather

Attach the Band

(Cut One)

Hat

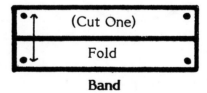

(Cut One)

Fold

Band

Illus. 132b.

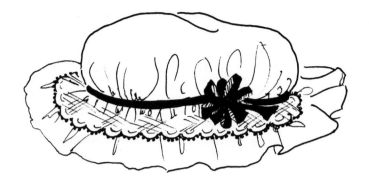

Head Size	Cut Circle	Cut Band		Cut Ruffle			
	Compass Setting★ Inches	Length Inches	Width Inches	Length Inches	Width Inches	Length Inches	Width Inches
6	1 15/16	7	¾	15	1	15	¾
7	2 3/16	8	¾	18	1	18	¾
8	2 9/16	9	1	20	1½	20	1
9	2 14/16	10	1	23	1½	23	1
10	3 3/16	11	1¼	25	2	25	1½
11	3 8/16	12	1¼	28	2½	28	2
12	3 14/16	13	1¼	30	2½	30	2
★The distance between the point of the compass and the pencil point							

Illus. 133b.

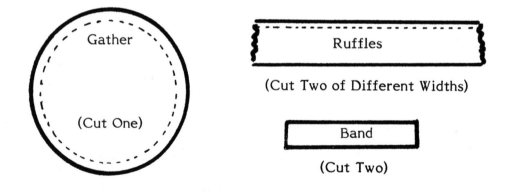

Illus. 133a,b. Banded mob cap and pattern.

It is easier to assemble the cap if you attach the ruffles to one piece of the band first, and then sew this band to the gathered circle. Sew the second part of the band invisibly on the inside so that the construction details are covered.

Driving Bonnet

A driving bonnet (Illus. 134) is similar to a banded mob cap in that a large circle defines the crown of the hat. A driving bonnet has a brim that attaches directly to the circle crown, which is gathered to fit it. The brim is made with two layers of the fabric interfaced for stiffness. For a more exaggerated crown, enlarge the compass setting. If you choose a soft fabric, stiffen the crown with an underlayer of organdy.

Head Size	Cut Crown	Cut Brim
Inches	Compass Setting★ Inches	Use size indicated
6	1^{15}/$_{16}$	
7	2^{3}/$_{16}$	
8	2^{9}/$_{16}$	
9	2^{14}/$_{16}$	
10	3^{3}/$_{16}$	
11	3^{8}/$_{16}$	
12	3^{14}/$_{16}$	

★The distance between the pencil point and the point of the compass

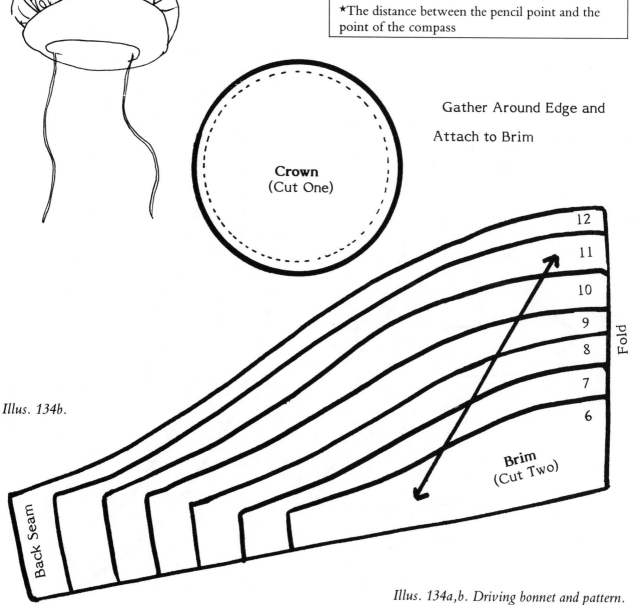

Illus. 134a.

Crown
(Cut One)

Gather Around Edge and

Attach to Brim

Brim
(Cut Two)

Fold

Back Seam

Illus. 134b.

Illus. 134a,b. Driving bonnet and pattern.

Five-Gore Hat

A five-gore hat (Illus. 135) can be made with either of two brims. The cloche brim, folded upwards, fits closely to the doll's head in the style of the 1920s. The alternative brim is used for dolls of any period; it turns slightly downwards. Allow ⅛-inch seam for the gores; any variation will result in a variation in the finished size. Vary the brim width according to your taste. Felt requires only a single thickness for the brim. A cloth hat, however, is best if you make it with a two-layer brim. Add an interlining if the fabric is not stiff. The brim can be trimmed with parallel rows of stitching.

Illus. 135a.

Illus. 135b.

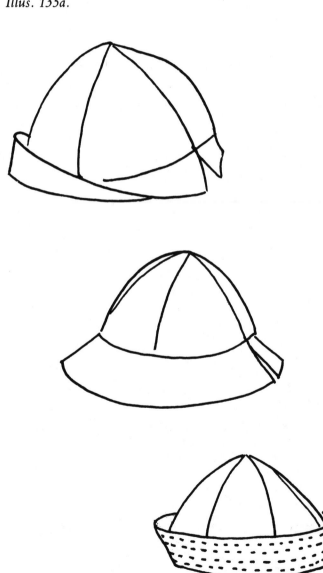

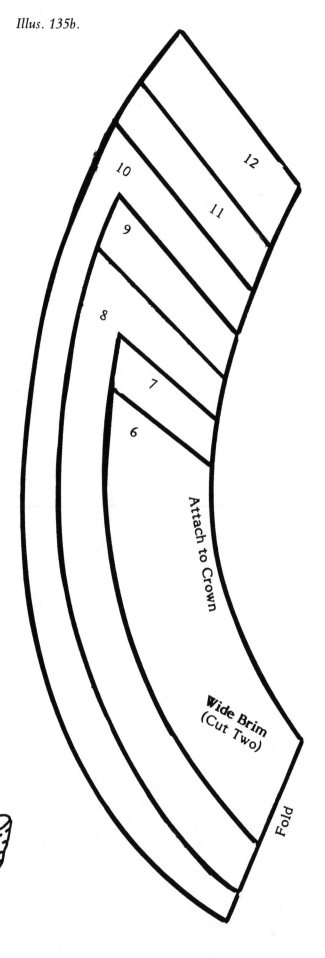

Illus. 135a,b. Five-gore hat and pattern.

Illus. 135b.

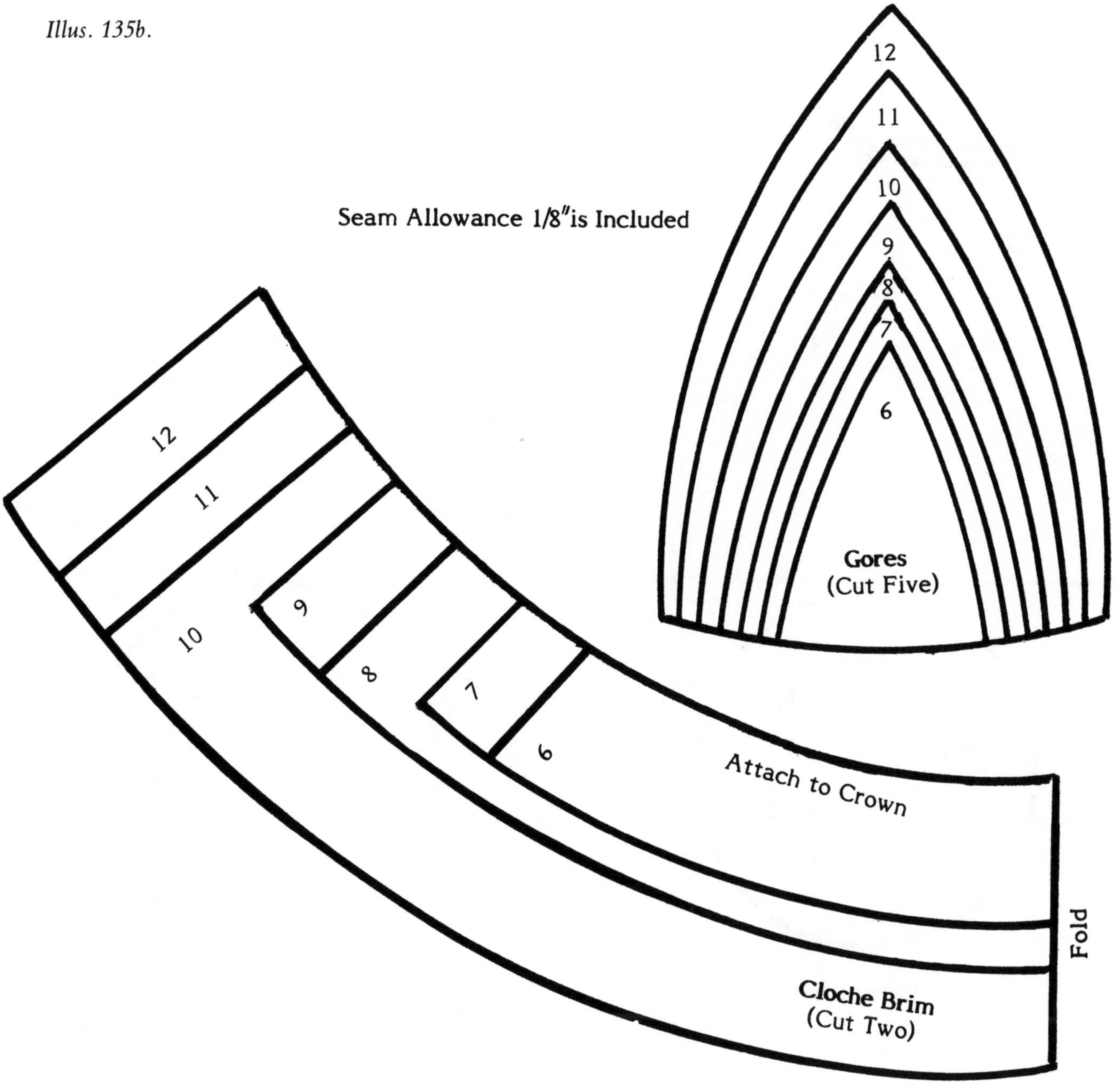

Seam Allowance 1/8" is Included

12

11

10

9

8

7

6

Gores
(Cut Five)

12

11

10

9

8

7

6

Attach to Crown

Fold

Cloche Brim
(Cut Two)

Sailor Hat and Beret

A sailor hat (Illus. 136) and a beret are both made of two identical circles seamed together. The sailor hat is constructed with an attached band; the beret, with a bound opening. See Illus. 136b for compass settings and band measurements for each size. To determine the size, refer to the master pattern in Illus. 130.

Suggested procedure:

• Select from the master pattern (Illus. 130) the correct head size.
• Trace the circle on paper and mark the center point.

• Set the compass to the appropriate brim size.
• Place the compass point in the center of the traced circle and draw the brim. This is the pattern for the underbrim. The upperbrim is the same size as the larger circle.
• Cut two brims of the hat fabric.
• Cut from the underbrim the head-size circle, narrowing the cut edge about ¼ inch to allow for the seam attachment of the band or binding.
• Seam the band and sew to the lower brim, slashing to ease joining.
• Join the two circles. Turn, press, and trim.

Head Size	Cut Brim	Cut Band	
	Compass Setting★ Inches	Width Inches	Length Inches
6	1¹²⁄₁₆	1¼	7½
7	1¹⁴⁄₁₆	1¼	8½
8	2⁴⁄₁₆	1½	9½
9	2⁷⁄₁₆	1½	10½
10	2¹⁰⁄₁₆	2	11½
11	3	2	12½
12	3⁷⁄₁₆	2	13½

★The distance between the point of the compass and the pencil point

Illus. 136a.

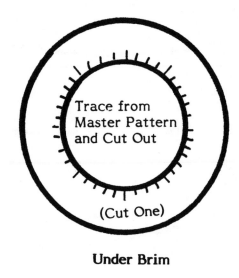

Under Brim

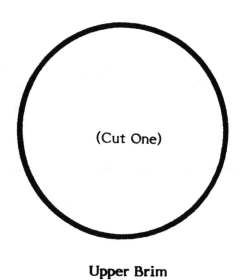

Upper Brim

Illus. 136b.

Band

Illus. 136a,b. Sailor hat and beret and pattern.

Gathered Poke Bonnet with Neck Ruffle

A gathered poke, or pioneer's, bonnet (Illus. 137) with a neck ruffle is simple to make. It can also be made in white with ruffles on the brim for a "sunbonnet baby." Line the crown edge to edge and make the brim with interfacing for additional stiffness. To make the bonnet adjustable, stitch a casing at the neck edge and insert a ribbon. Exaggerate fullness by lengthening and widening the crown. The style of the bonnet can be changed by adding a sideband.

Three-Piece Bonnet

There are three parts to this supported bonnet (Illus. 138): the crown, sideband, and brim. See Illus. 138b,c for the sideband pattern and the larger pattern. The interlining and the cover are shown in Illus. 138d–f. Sizes are for head circumferences of 6 to 12 inches, although it is difficult to use the supported method for making hats smaller than size 9. The same pattern can be used to make an unsupported bonnet of felt or interfaced fabrics. To do so, use the buckram pattern in Illus. 138b,c. The directions for making a supported bonnet appear on page 153.

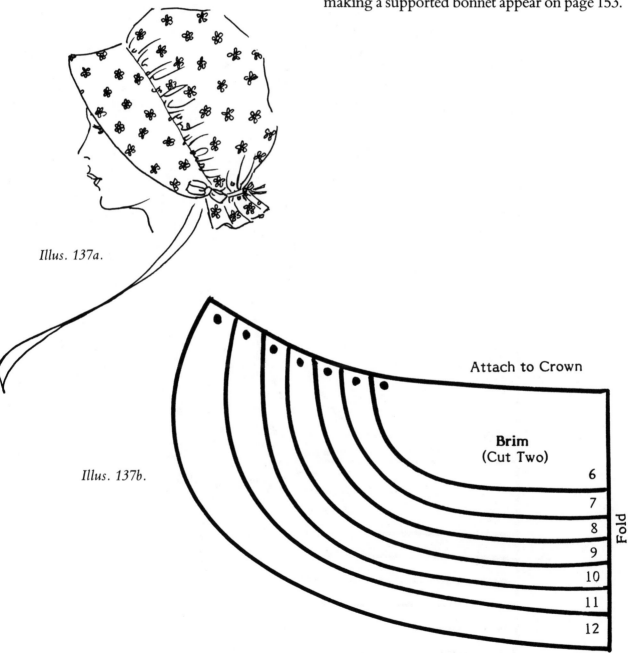

Illus. 137a.

Illus. 137b.

Attach to Crown

Brim
(Cut Two)

6
7
8
9
10
11
12

Fold

Illus. 137a–c. Gathered poke bonnet with neck ruffle and pattern.

(Continued)

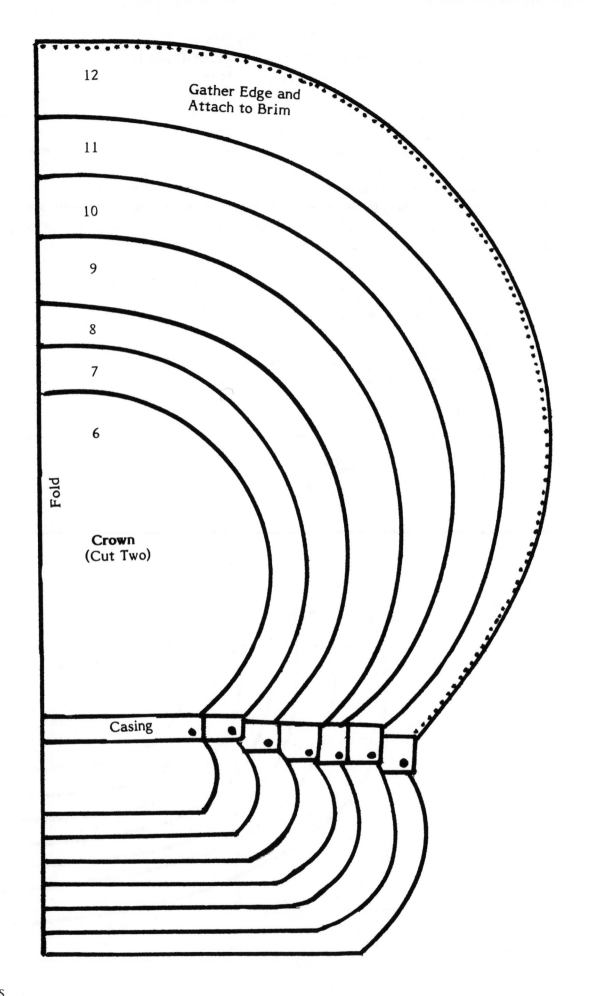

12

Gather Edge and
Attach to Brim

11

10

9

8

7

6

Fold

Crown
(Cut Two)

Casing

Illus. 137c.

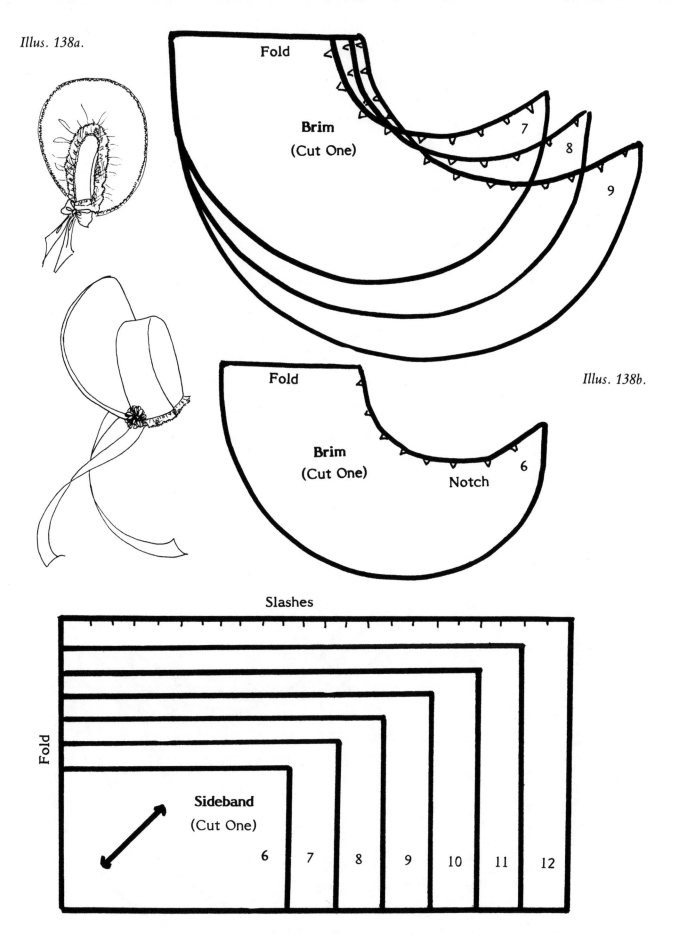

Fold

Brim
(Cut One)

7

8

9

Illus. 138b.

Fold

Brim
(Cut One)

Notch

6

Slashes

Fold

Sideband
(Cut One)

6 7 8 9 10 11 12

Illus. 138a–f. Three-piece bonnet and pattern.

(Continued)

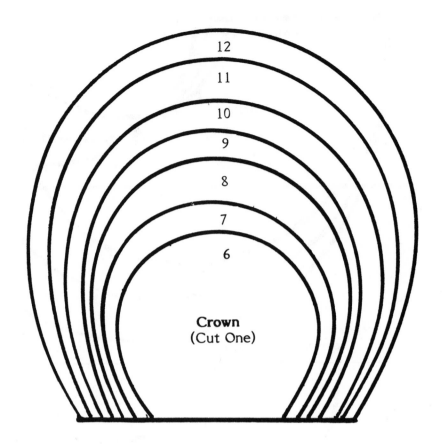

12
11
10
9
8
7
6

Crown
(Cut One)

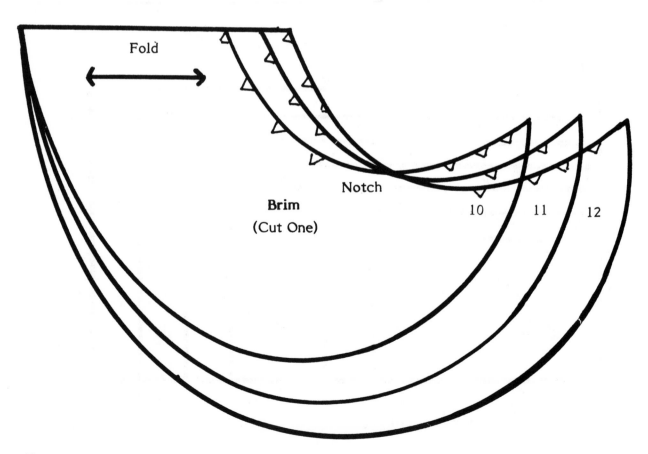

Fold

Notch

Brim

(Cut One)

10   11   12

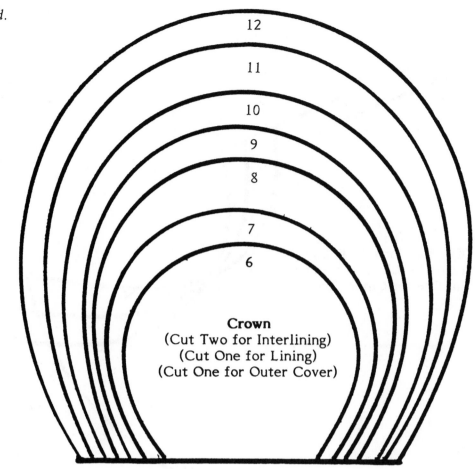

12
11
10
9
8
7
6

Crown
(Cut Two for Interlining)
(Cut One for Lining)
(Cut One for Outer Cover)

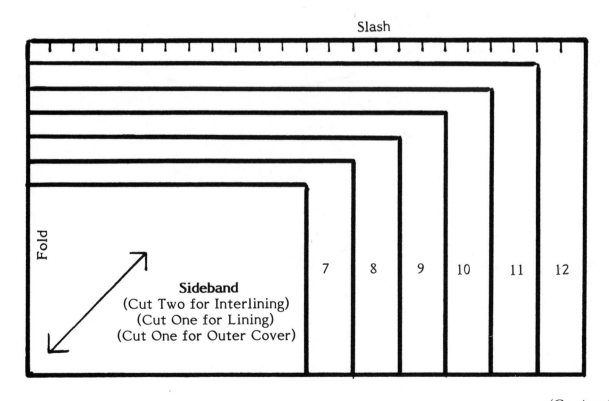

Slash

Fold

7 8 9 10 11 12

Sideband
(Cut Two for Interlining)
(Cut One for Lining)
(Cut One for Outer Cover)

(Continued)

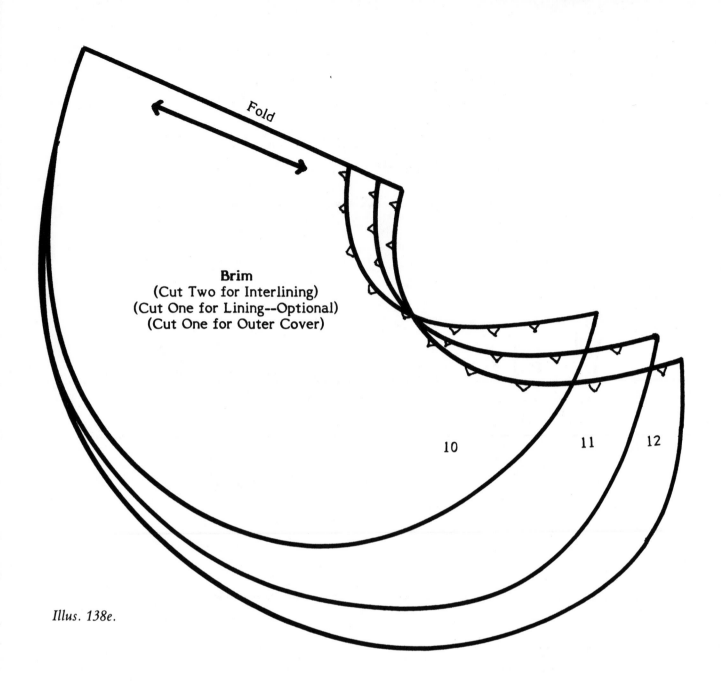

Fold

Brim
(Cut Two for Interlining)
(Cut One for Lining--Optional)
(Cut One for Outer Cover)

10   11   12

Illus. 138e.

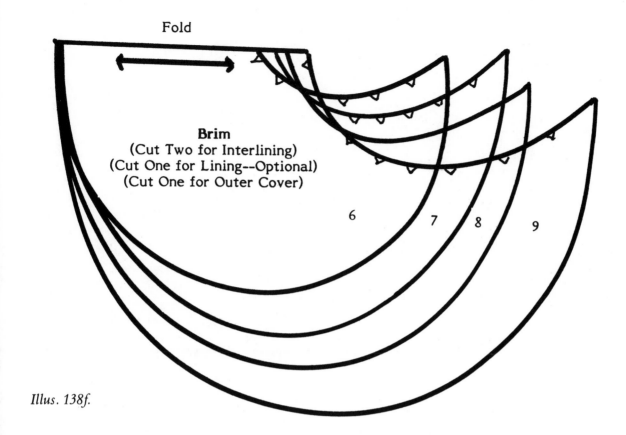

Fold

Brim
(Cut Two for Interlining)
(Cut One for Lining--Optional)
(Cut One for Outer Cover)

6   7   8   9

Illus. 138f.

Part III
THE EVOLUTION OF IDEAS

12   Other Dolls

Most doll artists borrow ideas from the work of other doll artists. This is not meant to imply that the dollmaker is a copier of others' work or a thief of ideas. That is not only unfair but counterproductive to creativity. Very little is new, however, and most ideas are evolutionary rather than revolutionary. Fine artists often painted the same subject, but each—rendering the subject in his or her own technique and interpretation—created entirely different masterpieces. The same is true of doll artists. There are many "children of the nostalgic past"—Alice in Wonderland dolls, animal "people," and clothespin dolls—but each expresses the individual artist's skill and viewpoint. Themes overlap, ideas repeat, but each builds new expressions.

In this short chapter are a few of my adaptations; they are new expressions developed from old ideas. For example, my version of clothespin "people" (Color Illus. 1F) is an extension of the four-pin clothespin dolls with macramé-ball heads, which appeared on the craft scene a few years ago. I have added a sculptured nose, joints, and in some instances padded bodies.

The second example is an adaptation of block "people." They were developed from a well-known clown pattern whose wooden block body is encased in a loose garment to suggest arms and legs. He has comic mobility. Santa and Hilda (Color Illus. 2F) are made the same way. Instead of a sock or a Styrofoam ball, the head is a needle-sculpture. The basic garment is made exactly like the clown suit but modified and supplemented. Hilda wears petticoats, a bodice, and a skirt over her "clown suit" construction. The characterizations are infinite.

The third example is a glamourized and detailed version of the homely little sock doll (Color Illus. 1H). It represents no change in construction but simply more careful detail. The fourth example demonstrates an adaptation of the Oval Body Pattern (Illus. 143)—a large baby in motion, called Crissy Creeper (Color Illus. 1H).

I hope that these simple adaptations will provide food for thought; they were inspired by an historical theme and by a famous masterpiece. The group of two porcelain dolls (Color Illus. 4D) was taken from a United States Bicentennial theme, while the porcelain doll (see Girl with Hoop on cover) is a duplicate of the child in Renoir's painting "The Umbrellas." There are no limits to the imagination in doll artistry.

JOINTED CLOTHESPIN DOLLS

A popular variation on the old-fashioned peg doll appeared on the craft scene a few years ago. A favorite in gift shops is the beguiling character made of four wooden clothespins. The body and legs are each composed of a whole clothespin, and the arms are made from a single pin that has been split lengthwise. The doll is assembled by drilling through the pins and fastening with wire. The face, hands, and shoes are painted with acrylics. The doll is most often clothed in a ruffled dress over which a white pinafore has been attached to give the illusion of a wider body. A sunbonnet adorns the head and is worn over curls or braids.

My variation includes augmenting the doll by adding moveable joints to the arms and legs, a sculptured nose to the face, and a stuffing to the body (optional). The costuming can be as varied as you wish.

The joints were developed by simply wiring together leg and arm segments out of the clothespin as shown in Illus. 139. A small cotter pin may be substituted for wire. The nose is made of Sculpey modelling compound and glued in place. Two small wooden beads (or other objects could be substituted) were added to give width to the shoulders. More dimension could be achieved by adding a body and some shoes. (See Illus. 128, 131–32 for patterns.) Clothing is made by simple adaptations of the T-shape patterns discussed on page 122. In Color Illus. 1F are just a few of the many dolls, including Santa Claus and a carefree clown, that can be made by using this technique.

BLOCK DOLLS

A clown whose body is a block of wood and whose limbs are formed only by his suit is an old favorite. A stuffed sock forms the head onto which felt features are glued. Only his feet and hands, which are fastened to the sleeves and trousers, are stuffed. The loose sleeves and trousers give him maximum mobility. See Color Illus. 2F for examples of block people—Santa, Hilda, and the clown.

Here are some of the variations that I employ:
- A needle-sculptured head built on an armature of a Styrofoam ball
- Glass eyes
- A body rounded by stuffing
- Hands made of felt; fingers articulated by inserting pipe cleaners
- Feet altered to suit each character
- Santa's suit is made from the same pattern as the clown suit but it has been trimmed with fur (Illus. 140).

- Hilda's blouse and pantaloons are made from the same pattern as the clown suit. A petticoat, skirt, and bodice have been placed over the suit, which serves as the body.

The patterns are full size with the exception of the foundation or body, which must be double in size. The characterizations are endless and limited only by the artist's imagination.

Suggestions for Assembly
- You will need a 7-inch-long 2 × 4 block of fir. Any heavy-weight wood is suitable.
- Cover the block of wood with a sock or stretchy cover in order to provide a means for attaching the head. Stuff the cover to shape an appropriate body.
- Needle-sculpt and sew the head securely to the body.
- Fashion the hands of felt and articulate the fingers with pipe cleaners. Stuff the hands and insert the head of a clothespin. Sew the hands securely to the clothespin.
- Sew the ankle to the shoe. (Although it requires a width of about 6 inches to attach to the shoe, the ankle length is variable. Five inches is suggested.) Close the back of the shoe and attach the sole.
- Stuff the foot and leg and insert a wooden clothespin. Sew the leg securely to the clothespin.
- Fasten the hands and legs into the foundation as discussed on page 120. It is called short-cut costuming.

Then dress the doll in any manner you wish by applying garments over the foundation. See Illus. 141 of a disassembled Santa, which will explain visually how this doll is made.

SOCK DOLLS

The sock doll (Color Illus. 1H) is an elaboration on a very old theme. One child's sock is used to make the body, and the second sock forms the arms (Illus. 142). The head is formed by tying the toe of the sock; the seat of the doll is formed from the heel of the sock. Any degree of elaboration is possible. The sock is a beginning for a wide variety of interesting projects. (*How to Make Sock Toys*, by Edna N. Clapper, is an excellent source of patterns and ideas.)

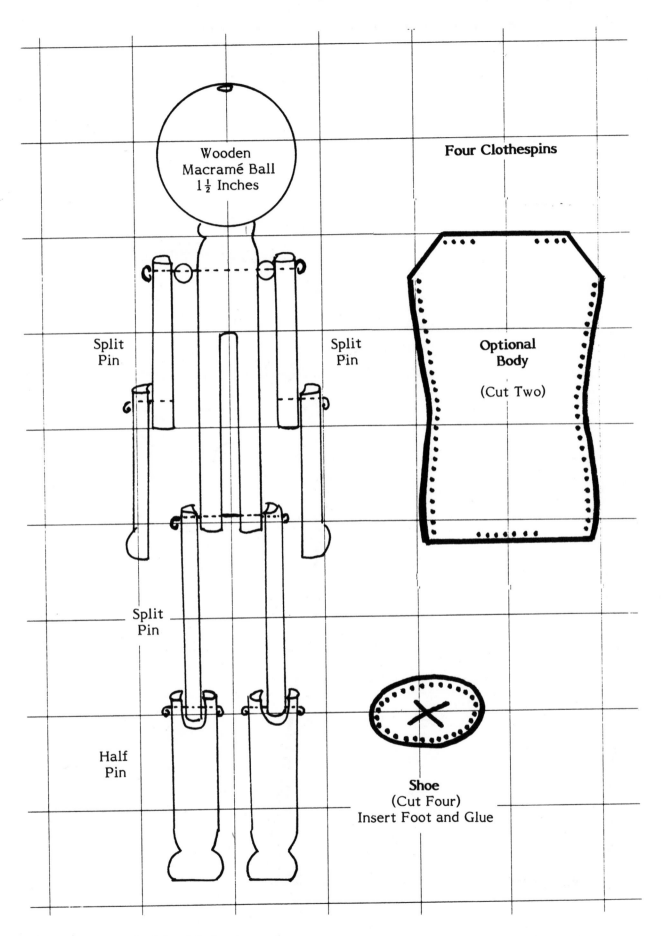

Wooden
Macramé Ball
1 ½ Inches

Four Clothespins

Split
Pin

Split
Pin

**Optional
Body**

(Cut Two)

Split
Pin

Half
Pin

Shoe
(Cut Four)
Insert Foot and Glue

Illus. 139. Pattern for jointed clothespin people.

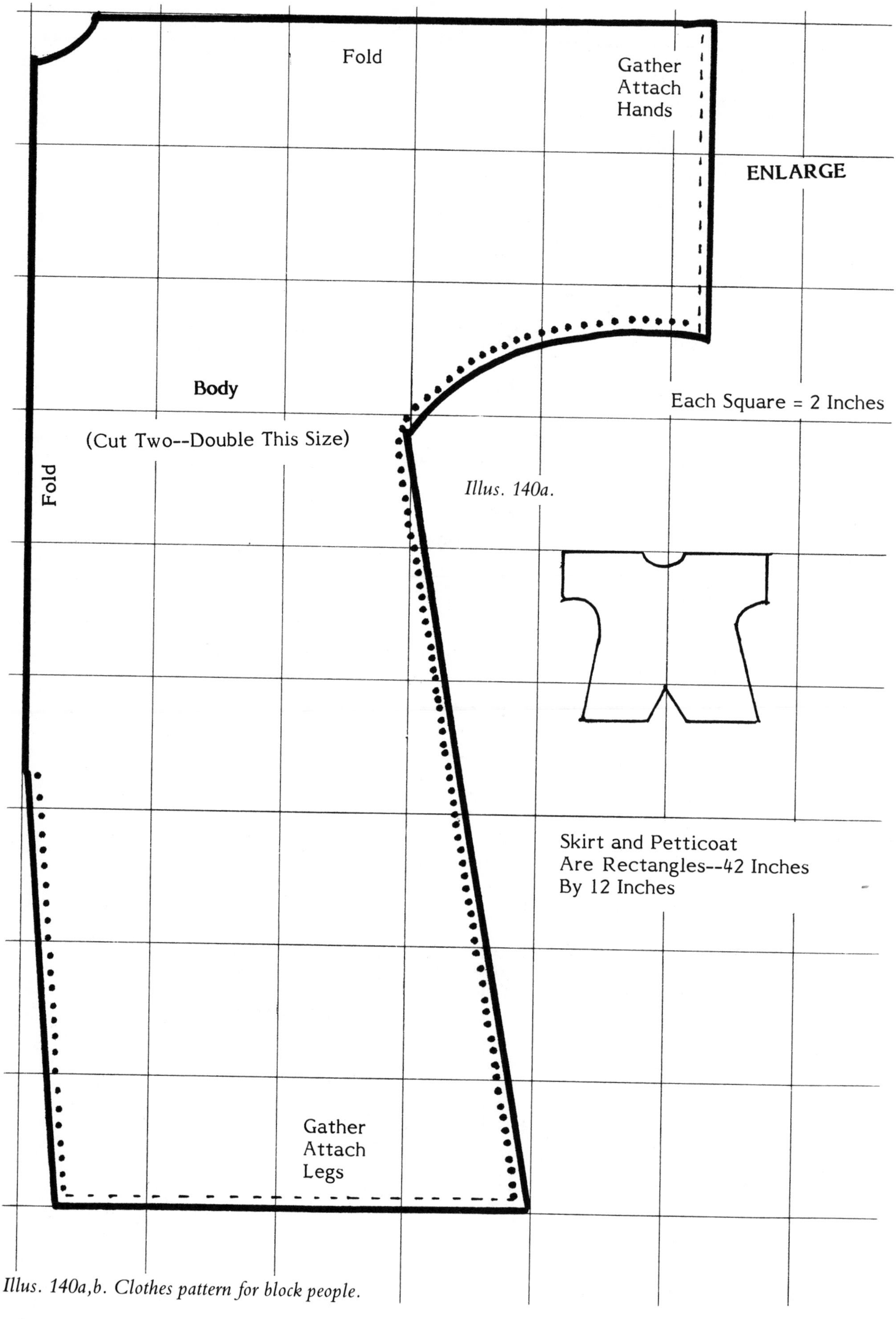

Fold

Gather
Attach
Hands

ENLARGE

Body

Each Square = 2 Inches

Fold

(Cut Two--Double This Size)

Illus. 140a.

Skirt and Petticoat
Are Rectangles--42 Inches
By 12 Inches

Gather
Attach
Legs

Illus. 140a,b. Clothes pattern for block people.

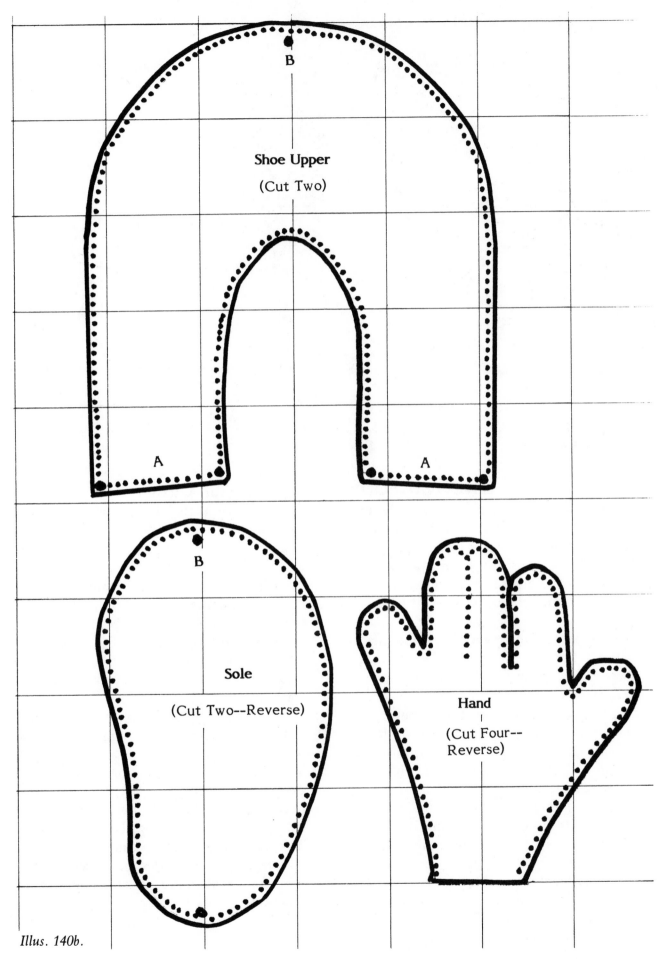

Shoe Upper
(Cut Two)

B

A   A

B

Sole
(Cut Two--Reverse)

Hand
(Cut Four--Reverse)

Illus. 140b.

Illus. 141. A block person—Santa—who has been disassembled to show his various parts.

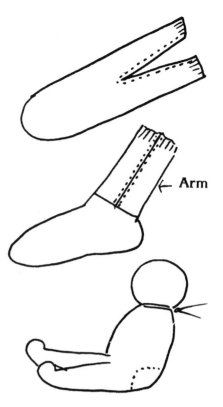

Illus. 142. Assembling sock people.

ADAPTATION OF THE OVAL BODY

Crissy Creeper is an adaptation of the infant with an oval body (page 38). Refer to the pattern for details (Illus. 143). The pattern has been enlarged so that Crissy is the size of a six-month-old baby. In addition to enlarging the pattern, I have redesigned the body so that the doll will maintain a curved back. The head is turned when sewn to the body to simulate animation. The doll has been needle shaped to indent dimples and emphasize contour. The nose is a stuffed and appliquéd triangle. The toes and fingers are shaped by stitching. The body is reinforced by inserting a piece of properly bent coat hanger and a dowel. The arms are reinforced with 14-gauge copper wire. The eyes are layers of felt glued together. The hair is embroidered by sewing loops of yarn to the head. Made in velour, as shown in Color Illus. 1H, Crissy is lined to preserve the contours. Several lead fishing weights (one ounce) have been inserted into the lower torso to give her balance. (In order to fit within the confines of this book, the pattern has been reduced by 25%. See page 30 for instructions on enlarging patterns.)

Suggestions for Assembly

- Sew the darts at the wrist only on the outer portion of the arm.
- Reinforce the body and arms with wire. Insert a dowel in the neck to preserve the rigidity.
- To form the nose, fold the seam allowances under, stuff lightly, and curl the outer corners to the center to form nostrils. If this does not produce a satisfactory nose, substitute a stuffed circle. It is best to sew the nose in place before closing the head so that the stitches can be concealed.
- Sew arms and legs to the torso where indicated and turn in such a way to suggest a creeping position.
- Sew head to the body in a turned position to suggest movement.
- Accentuate the buttocks by gathering and sculpturing while stuffing. Bring the doll to life by generous needle shaping.
- To construct the eyes, glue the felt sections one on top of the other. Form perfect pupils with a paper-hole puncher.

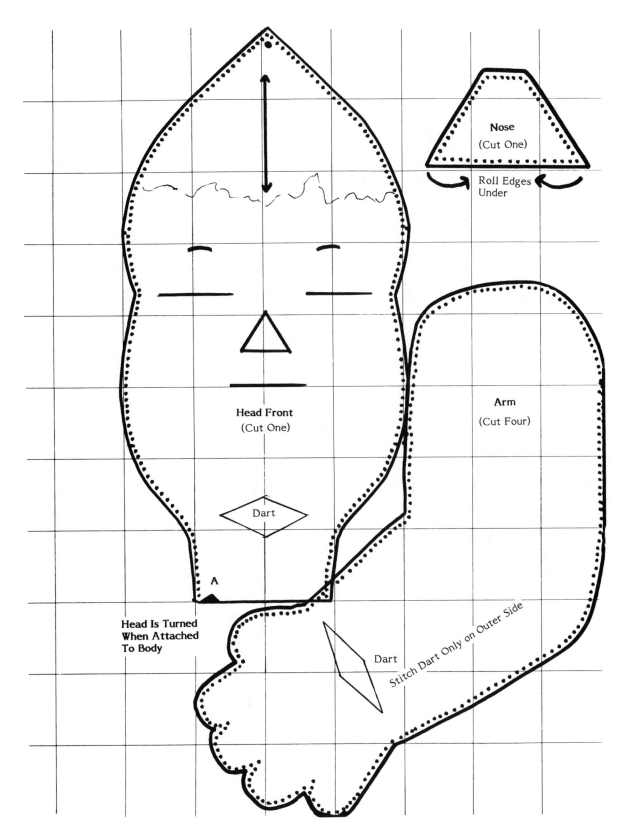

Nose
(Cut One)

Roll Edges
Under

Head Front
(Cut One)

Arm
(Cut Four)

Dart

A

**Head Is Turned
When Attached
To Body**

Dart

Stitch Dart Only on Outer Side

Illus. 143a.

Note: Illus. 143a–f have been reduced by 25%.

Illus. 143a–f. Pattern for Crissy Creeper.

(Continued)

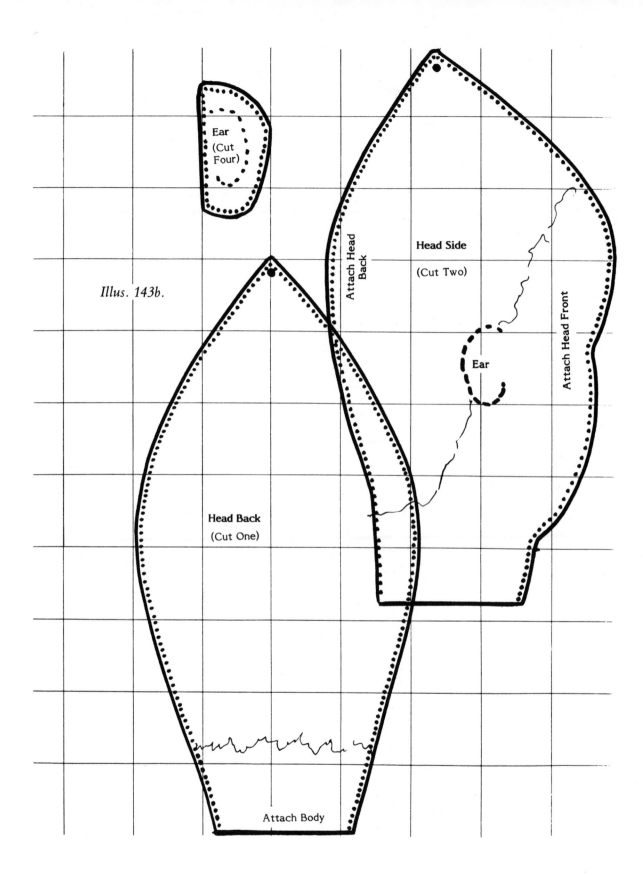

Ear
(Cut
Four)

Illus. 143b.

Attach Head Back

Head Side

(Cut Two)

Attach Head Front

Ear

Head Back

(Cut One)

Attach Body

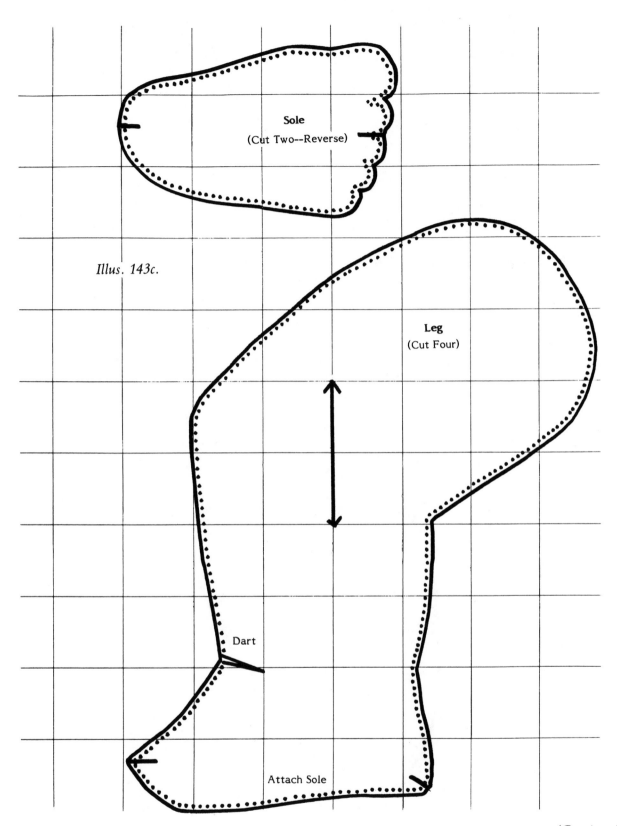

Sole
(Cut Two--Reverse)

Illus. 143c.

Leg
(Cut Four)

Dart

Attach Sole

(Continued)

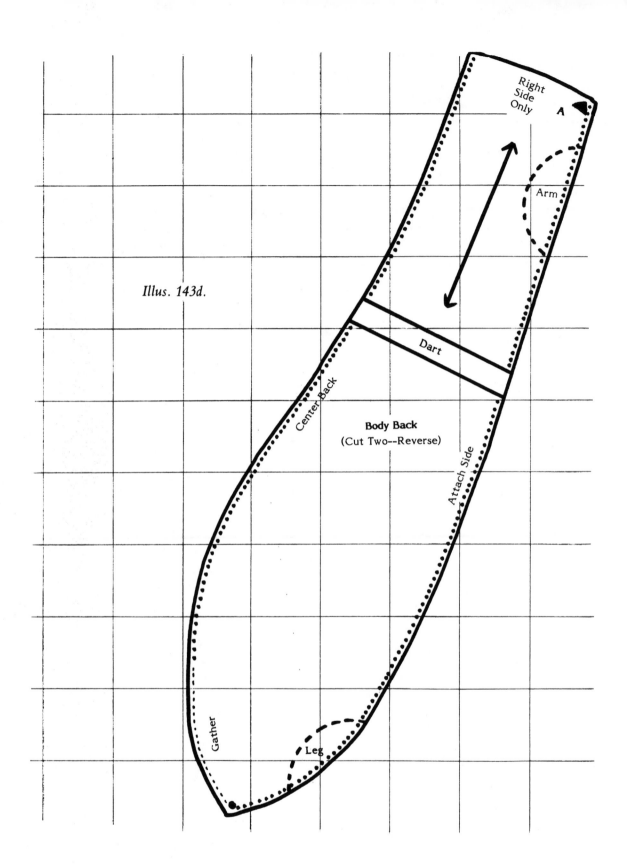

Illus. 143d.

Right Side Only

A

Arm

Dart

Center Back

Body Back
(Cut Two--Reverse)

Attach Side

Gather

Leg

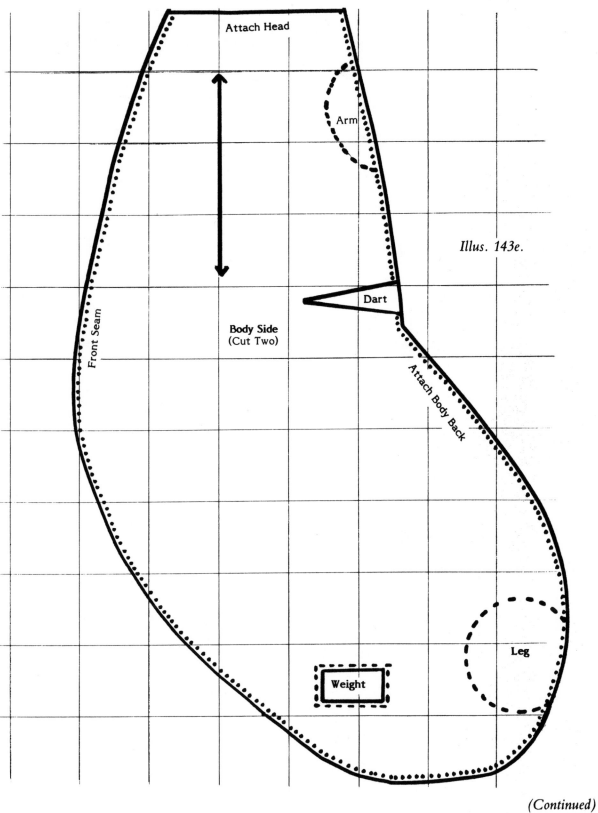

Attach Head

Arm

Illus. 143e.

Dart

Body Side
(Cut Two)

Front Seam

Attach Body Back

Leg

Weight

(Continued)

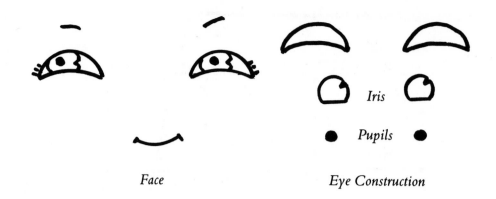

Face   *Iris*

Pupils

Eye Construction

Illus. 143f.

Bibliography

New books on the subject of dolls seem to appear daily. A comprehensive book list is published by Paul A. Ruddell, Division of Hobby House Press, Inc., 900 Frederick Street, Cumberland, Maryland 21502, and is available upon request. That book list supplements the card catalogue in every public library as well as *Books in Print*.

The list of books presented here is not intended to be definitive. It contains only those books that have been especially useful to me.

The Artist
Anatomy
Farris, Edmond J. *Art Student's Anatomy.* New York: Dover Publications, 1953.
French, Viola. *How to Draw and Paint Children.* Tustin, Calif.: Walter Foster Art Books.
Hamm, Jack. *Drawing the Head and Figure.* New York: Grosset & Dunlap, 1963.
Rimmer, William. *Art Anatomy.* New York: Dover Publications, 1962.
Vanderpoel, John. *The Human Figure: Life Drawing for Artists.* New York: Dover Publications, 1935.

Sculpture
Di Valentin, Maria and Louis. *Sculpture for Beginners.* New York: Sterling Publishing Co., 1969.
Grubbs, Daisy. *Modeling a Likeness in Clay.* New York: Watson-Guptill Publications, 1982.
Lucchesi, Bruno, and Malstrom, Margit. *Modeling the Head in Clay.* New York: Watson-Guptill Publications, 1979.

Ceramics
Kenny, John B. *Ceramic Sculpture: Methods & Processes.* Radnor, Pa.: Chilton Book Co., 1953.
Newell, Mardi. *Porcelain for the Hobbyist.* Los Angeles: Potluck Publications, 1976.
Rothenberg, Polly. *Complete Book of Ceramic Art.* New York: Crown Publishers, 1972.

Dollmaking—General
Baldwin, Ed and Stevie. *The WeePeeple: A Unique Adventure in Crafts in Americana.* New York: G.P. Putnam, 1983.
Benbow, Mary; Dunlop, Edith; and Luckin, Joyce. *Dolls and Dollmaking.* Boston: Plays Inc., 1968.
Bullard, Helen. *The American Doll Artist,* Vol. 1. Falls Church, Va.: Summit Press Ltd., 1977; also Charles T. Branford, Newton, Mass. , 1965.
———. *The American Doll Artist,* Vol 2. North Kansas City, Mo.: Athena Publishing Co., 1975.
Coyne, John, and Miller, Jerry. *How to Make Upside-Down Dolls.* New York: Bobbs-Merrill, 1977.
Gray, Ilse. *Designing and Making Dolls.* New York: Watson-Guptill Publications, 1972.
Hartman, Grietje, and Lens, Ellen. *Popmooi: European Dolls to Make Yourself.* San Francisco: Chronicle Books, 1979.
Holmes, Anita. *Making Dolls for Pleasure and Profit.* New York: Arco Publishing Co., 1978.
Holz, Loretta. *The How-To-Do Book of International Dolls: A Comprehensive Guide to Making, Costuming and Collecting Dolls.* New York: Crown Publishers, 1980.
Houston, Julie, ed. *Book of Best-Loved Toys and Dolls.* New York: Sedgewood Press, 1982.

Hutchings, Margaret. *Dolls and How to Make Them.* London: Mills and Boon.

———. *Toys from Alice in Wonderland.* London: Mills and Boon, 1979.

Ives, Suzy. *Making and Dressing a Rag Doll.* New York: Drake Publishers, 1972.

Janitch, Valerie. *Dolls in Miniature.* Radnor, Pa.: Chilton Book Co., 1976.

Lasky, Kathryn. *Dollmaker: The Eyelight and the Shadow.* New York: Charles Scribner's Sons, 1981.

Laury, Jean Ray. *Dollmaking: A Creative Approach.* New York: Van Nostrand Reinhold, 1970.

Leisure Time Publishing, Inc. *Puffy People.* Tempe, Arizona: Leisure Time Publishing, Inc., 1982.

Lockwood, Gillian. *Making Soft Toys.* New York: Watson-Guptill Publications, 1967.

McCracken, Joann. *Dollhouse Dolls: Making, Detailing and Costuming Dolls 1-Inch to 1-Foot Scale.* Radnor, Pa.: Chilton Book Co., 1980.

Ondori Publishing Co. *Stuffed Toys.* 1975.

Rogowski, Gini, and De Weese, Gene. *Making Folk Art Dolls.* Radnor, Pa.: Chilton Book Co., 1975.

Roth, Charlene Davis. *Making Original Dolls of Composition, Bisque and Porcelain.* New York: Crown Publishers, 1980.

Russell, Joan. *The Woman's Day Book of Soft Toys and Dolls.* New York: Simon and Schuster, 1975.

Sinnett, Doreen. *Classic Clothespin Dolls.* Newport Beach, Calif.: Doreen Sinnett Designs (P.O. Box 2055, 92663), 1980.

Soft Toys and Dolls. Menlo Park, Calif.: Lane Publishing Co., 1977.

Tyler, Mabs. *The Big Book of Dolls.* New York: Dial Press, 1976.

Westfall, Marty. *The Handbook of Doll Repair and Restoration.* New York: Crown Publishers, 1979.

Witzig, H., and Kuhn, G.E. *Making Dolls.* New York: Sterling Publishing Co., New York: 1969.

Worrell, Estelle Ansley. *Dolls, Puppedolls and Teddy Bears.* New York: Van Nostrand Reinhold, 1977.

Yoneyama, Kyoko. *The Collection of Stuffed Dolls from a Fancy World.* Tokyo: Ondorisha Publishers, 1976.

Young, Helen. *Dollmaking for Everyone.* New York: A.S. Barnes and Co., 1977.

Costuming

Anderton, Johana Gast. *Sewing for Twentieth-Century Dolls.* North Kansas City, Mo.: Trojan Press, 1972.

Carter, Eleanor-Jean. *Doll Modes: Doll Fashions with Patterns.* Hyattsville, Md.: Carter Craft Doll House, 1972.

★★Coleman, Dorothy S.; Elizabeth A.; and Evelyn J. *The Collector's Book of Doll Clothes: Costumes in Miniature 1700–1929.* New York: Crown Publishers, 1975.

★★———. *The Collector's Encyclopedia of Dolls.* New York: Crown Publishers, 1968.

Dreher, Denise. *From the Neck Up: An Illustrated Guide to Hat Making.* Minneapolis: Madhatter Press, 1981.

Greenhowe, Jean. *Making Costume Dolls.* New York: Watson-Guptill Publications, 1972.

Johnson, Audrey. *How to Repair and Dress Old Dolls.* Newton, Mass.: Charles T. Branford Co., 1967.

———. *Dressing Dolls.* Newton, Mass.: Charles T. Branford, 1969.

Jones, G.P. *An Easy-To-Make Godey Doll.* New York: Dover Publications, 1976.

———. *Easy-To-Make Dolls with Nineteenth-Century Costumes.* New York: Dover Publications, 1977.

Morgan, Mary H. *How to Dress an Old-Fashioned Doll.* New York: Dover Publications, 1973.

★★Sirkis, Susan. *The Wish Booklets:* Vol. 1, *1861–1865;* Vol. 2, *1831–1835;* Vol. 3, *1871–1875;* Vol. 4, *First Ladies 1789–1865;* Vol. 5, *First Ladies 1865–present;* Vol. 6, *Turn-of-the-Century Costumes;* Vol. 7, *Miniature Fashions 1750–1770;* Vol. 8, *Miniature Fashions 1848–1896;* Vol. 9, *19th-Century Fashions;* Vol. 10, *Wardrobe for a Little Girl 1900–1910;* Vol. 11, *La Petite Bébé 1833–1887;* Vol. 13, *Fashions 1885;* Vol. 14, *1776;* Vol. 15, *Empire Fashions 1806–1810;* Vol. 16, *Fashions 1820–1825;* Vol. 17, *Fashions, 1840–1845;* Vol. 18, *Fashions 1853–1858;* Vol. 19, *Fashions 1895–1896;* Vol. 20, *Men's Fashions 1776–1850;* Vol. 21, *Men's Fashions 1860–1970.* Reston, Va.: Susan Sirkis (11009 Blue Spruce Rd., 22091). (Patterns for Period Costuming.)

Warwick, Edward; Pitz, Henry C.; and Wyckoff, Alexander. *Early American Dress*. New York: Benjamin Blom, 1976.
★★Worrell, Estelle Ansley. *The Doll Book*. New York: Van Nostrand Reinhold, 1966.

Dollmaking—Porcelain

Seeley's Ceramics (Oneonta, N.Y.) is a manufacturer and distributor of ceramic and composition materials, moulds for reproduction and artist dolls, and all related supplies. The company has also published a series of books explaining the process of porcelain dollmaking. A book list is available.

Seeley, Mildred D. *Porcelain and Low-Fire Dollmaking*. Oneonta, N.Y.: Seeley's Ceramic Service, 1973.
———. *Making Original Dolls and Molds*. Oneonta, N.Y.: Seeley's Ceramic Service, 1977.

Dollmaking—Wax

Carlton, Carol. *Modern Wax Doll Art*. Altaville, Calif.: Carol Carlton (P.O. Box 159, 95221).
Newman, Thelma R. *Wax as Art Form*. New York: A.S. Barnes & Co.; London: Thomas Yoseloff, Ltd., 1966.
Nussle, William. *Candle Crafting: From an Art to a Science*. New York: A.S. Barnes & Co.; London: Thomas Yoseloff, Ltd., 1971.
Webster, William E., with McMullen, Claire. *Complete Book of Candlemaking*. New York: Doubleday, 1973.

Painting—China

Taylor, Doris W., with Button, Anne. *China Painting*. New York: Van Nostrand Reinhold Co., 1962.

Plaster Mould Making

Chaney, Charles, and Skee, Stanley. *Plaster Model and Mold Making*. New York: Van Nostrand Reinhold, 1981.

Stuffed Animals

Many of the techniques used in making stuffed animals are also integral to dollmaking.

Chappel, Phyllis. *Make Your Own Soft Toys*. London: Thomas Nelson and Sons, Ltd., 1961.
Clapper, Edna N. *How to Make Sock Toys*. Park Ridge, Ill.: Clapper Publishing Co., 1967.
Dyer, Anne. *Design Your Own Stuffed Toys*. Newton, Mass.: Charles T. Branford Co., 1969.
Friedrichsen, Carol S. *The Pooh Craft Book*. New York: E.P. Dutton & Co., 1976.
Hutchings, Margaret. *Modern Soft Toy Making*. Newton, Mass.: Charles T. Branford Co., 1959.
———. *Teddy Bears and How to Make Them*. New York: Dover Publications, 1964.
———. *Toys from the Tales of Beatrix Potter*. New York: Hawthorn Books, 1973.
McLaren, Esme. *The Craft of Stuffed Toys*. London: G. Bell and Sons, Ltd., 1961.
Roth, Charlene Davis. *The Art of Making Cloth Toys*. Radnor, Pa.: Chilton, 1974.

Periodicals

The Doll Artisan, Doll Artisan Guild, Oneonta, N.Y.
Doll Castle News, Castle Press Publications, Inc., Washington, N.J.
Doll Crafter, Daisy Publishing Inc., Seattle, Wash.
Doll Reader, Hobby House Press, Cumberland, Md.
Doll World, Tower Publications, Seabrook, N.H.

★★Invaluable for the doll costumer.

Index

Page numbers in italics refer to illustrations.